Digital Publishing with Adobe® InDesign® CC

Sandee Cohen

Diane Burns

Adobe

Digital Publishing with Adobe® InDesign® CC

Sandee Cohen and Diane Burns

Copyright © 2015 by Sandee Cohen and Diane Burns

Adobe Press books are published by: Peachpit, a division of Pearson Education
For the latest on Adobe Press books, go to www.adobepress.com.

To report errors, please send a note to errata@peachpit.com

Proofreader: Patricia Pane
Indexer: Valerie Haynes Perry
Cover design: Mimi Heft
Interior design: Sandee Cohen and Diane Burns

Notice of Rights

Notice of Liability

The information in this book is distributed on an "As Is" basis, without warranty. While every precaution has been taken in the preparation of the book, neither the authors, Adobe Systems, Incorporated., nor the publisher shall have any liability to any person or entity with respect to any loss or damage caused or alleged to be caused directly or indirectly by the instructions contained in this book or by the computer software and hardware products described in it.

Trademarks

Adobe, Adobe Digital Publishing Suite, Illustrator, InDesign, and Photoshop are either registered trademarks or trademarks of Adobe Systems Incorporated in the United States and/or other countries.
All other trademarks are the property of their respective owners.

Many of the designations used by manufacturers and sellers to distinguish their products are claimed as trademarks. Where those designations appear in this book, and Peachpit was aware of a trademark claim, the designations appear as requested by the owner of the trademark. All other product names and services identified throughout this book are used in editorial fashion only and for the benefit of such companies with no intention of infringement of the trademark. No such use, or the use of any trade name, is intended to convey endorsement or other affiliation with this book.

Printed and bound in the United States of America

ISBN-13: 978-0-133-93016-0
ISBN-10: 0-133-93016-5

9 8 7 6 5 4 3 2 1

Our Thanks To

Victor Gavenda, our Adobe Press editor who helped guide the initial development of the book; **Dennis Fitzgerald**, our production editor; **Patricia Pane**, our proofreader, **Valerie Haynes Perry,** our indexer; **Mimi Heft**, the cover designer, and **Nancy Ruenzel**, the publisher of Peachpit Press.

Douglas Waterfall of Adobe Systems for answering our questions about the intricacies and fast-moving developments of digital publishing from InDesign.

Chris Kitchener of Adobe Systems for his support and quote for the back cover.

Gabe Harbs of In-Tools for his support in allowing us to use of the Side-Heads plug-in. http://www.in-tools.com/

Steve Werner for his contribution to the ePub and HTML chapter.

Bob Levine for his guidance on working with ePub, HTML, and DPS.

Anne-Marie Concepcion for her emergency answers to ePub questions.

Robert Shaw of Weldon Owen for use of images.

Denise Lever of TransPacific Digital for design support.

From Sandee

Terry DuPrât for her support during the deadlines. **Cini**, my Russian Blue cat. And once again, my co-author, **Diane Burns**, without whom I could not have done this book.

From Diane:

Ditto on the co-author thing, **Sandee Cohen**.

Colophon

This book was created on Macintosh computers.

Layout was created in Adobe InDesign CC. Illustrations were created using Adobe Photoshop CC and Adobe Illustrator CC. Fonts used were Chaparral Pro and Gill Sans Std.

Screen shots were taken using SnapzPro (Mac).

The automatic positioning of anchored side heads was created using the Side Heads plug-in from in-tools (in-tools.com).

The word cloud illustrations at the front of each chapter were created using the Wordalizer script from indiscripts (indiscripts.com).

Files were shared using Dropbox Pro.

Liquid Layout Rules

Digital Publishing Tablets

Digital Publishing InDesign HTML

Suite PDF

Producer Interactive ePub Apps

Video Digital Overlays ePubs

Movies Tablet TOC

Elements Buttons Folios

Digital Overlays Publishing Digital Hyperlinks

Folio Builder Export Options

Alternate Layouts DPS Audio Animations

Applications

Table of Contents

Introduction

In This Chapter

THREE YEARS AGO, WHEN WE WROTE THE FIRST VERSION OF THIS BOOK, we called the changes that were happening to the field of graphic design and publishing "disruptive." Programs that had been developed to create printed books and magazines were being adapted to create books for digital readers. A new type of document called an "app" was generating great excitement for all types of companies that wanted to get their message on tablet devices. Designers who had mastered print skills suddenly had to get up to speed on the new digital technologies.

It was for that reason that we wrote this book. We had many students and clients who had no idea what the right choices were for digital devices. They needed direction and education on the new digital formats.

Three years later that is still the case—in fact, the need to publish digital documents is even more vital. But instead of publishers and electronic stores settling one into one or two major formats, there are even more choices and workflows to learn. As we said three years ago, "It's a whole new world of digital publishing. Exciting times, yes, but the print designer has to rethink and relearn a whole new world."

Who Are We?

We both have backgrounds in traditional publishing, including advertising and design. But individually we have worked with clients to help them create interactive PDF presentations, ePubs, and tablet apps. We've added movies and interactive elements to educational materials that were originally created for print output, and posted them online. Both of us have taught hundreds of hours of classes on the new digital output formats. We've written articles and books on how to create interactive PDF documents. And the two of us have seen our own print books sold as ePubs on Amazon and iTunes.

It hasn't been easy   That's not to say we haven't struggled. Both of us had to learn how to format media files so they work on multiple output devices. We had to learn how to read basic HTML and CSS code and learn the proper formats in which to hand over our projects to web designers. Both of us had to learn how to apply and modify animation controls. And most of all, we had to learn how to think differently about the presentation of information that's in a digital format, free from the printed page.

So we feel much empathy with you. That's why we wrote this book. This is the book that we wish we'd had years ago to take us through learning the intricacies of digital publishing.

Who Are You?

You are the students we've taught for the past few years who are struggling to keep up with the new technologies. You might be a designer who suddenly realizes that you need to master new workflows. You could be a department head who is looking to expand from print into digital production and needs to know the right format for each job. You're a freelancer who needs to improve your skills to keep up with the latest trends.

Most likely you're confused and overwhelmed. This book was written with you in mind.

Don't feel alone. This sea change affects every designer, publisher, and creative professional in every field. The following sections outline the impact on those in many different roles.

Advertising designers
Advertising has been at the forefront of creating ads and marketing information for digital publications. For instance, interactive 360° images can be used to show a car interior, and panoramas can show the beautiful vistas seen from the newest resort hotel. Videos can show any product in a way that print never could.

Today's advertising art directors and creative directors need to understand the possibilities for converting the layouts for print ads and brochures into digital publications. They need to know how to convert television commercials into videos that can be incorporated into digital delivery. They will want to change an ad's orientation from horizontal to vertical — while perhaps changing its content as well.

This ad for MasterCard takes advantage of the dual orientation for tablets. It shows certain information in the vertical orientation (left) and different information in the horizontal view (right).

Book designers
It's hard to find a major (or minor) publishing house that is not creating ePubs. Their challenge is to choose between the reflowable ePub format with their limited layout controls or the newer fixed layout ePubs that

maintain the design of all the pages in a document. And they need to evaluate what new workflow and staff are necessary to manage both print and digital publishing.

The broad distribution of ePubs has added new life to old books.

Magazine designers

Many major magazine publishers have enthusiastically embraced converting their magazines into digital publications. Their designers have been leaders in using InDesign's Digital Publishing Suite (DPS) for designing interactive apps to achieve exciting results.

Wired was the very first magazine to use InDesign and DPS tools to create an app for the iPad. With help from Adobe, that first issue became a landmark publication, with almost every interactive technique featured in the magazine. Since then, *Wired* has continued to make their digital publication as cutting-edge as possible.

Wired magazine has used videos in its digital version. In this example, an article on spies features a video of the opening of the James Bond movies.

Magazines have even created content for their digital versions that doesn't appear in the print version. For instance, *People* magazine's digital version has a final page feature that shows different covers from the past 35 years.

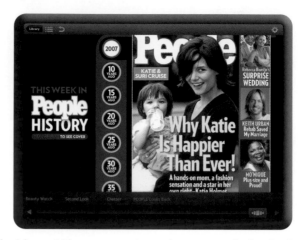

An example of the special feature on cover images that appears in the digital — but not the print — edition of *People* magazine.

In addition, magazine publishers have created new subscription options. Many print subscriptions now also include access to the digital version. Condé Nast, Hearst, Meredith, News Corp., and Time Inc. have created a new subscription model called Next Issue. Sometimes referred to as "Netflix for magazines," it allows, for a monthly fee, unlimited access to the publishers' entire catalog of magazines.

In-house marketing designers

We've worked with many marketing departments that long ago embraced digital publications. Even if it was just a simple PDF of a print brochure, they were already using digital delivery for their sales message. They also were pleased with the relatively small cost of digital distribution compared to that of print runs with shipping and mailing costs.

Then they discovered how the features of interactive displays, video, and form fields could further enhance their PDFs. Today these designers are looking to interactive PDFs as well as adding new digital formats to their marketing programs.

Instead of having a printed brochure mailed to them, Cunard customers can instantly download a PDF brochure.

Clients   Many clients are asking their design firms or ad agencies to "put something on the iPad." That sort of vague direction doesn't target the right audience for their product. In fact, there are many different types of files that can be delivered via tablet devices, including those we discuss in this book: interactive PDF, ePub, tablet app, and HTML. So a vague direction is no good at all.

The best clients are those who understand the possibilities (and limitations) of digital publications. They understand which format does what. And they understand that a certain format may be better for their needs. More than ever, today's designers need to educate their clients about what options make sense for them.

The reflowable ePub format is suitable for an instructional guide such as *Understanding the Golf Swing* (left). But a catalog or magazine, like *Martha Stewart Living* (right), is more effective as a tablet app, where the user can tap each item for more information.

What you need to know before you use this book

While you may be a beginner in digital publishing, you shouldn't be a beginner when it comes to creating InDesign documents. We're assuming you have a pretty good knowledge of how to import graphics, format text, and use paragraph styles, object styles, and layers. If you need basic training, we recommend the *InDesign CC Visual QuickStart Guide (2014 release)* by Sandee Cohen.

However, we don't expect you to have extensive knowledge of interactive features such as buttons, form fields, hyperlinks, electronic tables of contents, and media. We'll take you through those features completely.

Print isn't dead!

The rise of digital publishing doesn't mean that there won't still be print books, magazines, and so on. *LensWork* magazine is a good example of how print and digital can work together. The print magazine is a 96-page bimonthly that focuses on photography and the creative process. It uses duotones and high-quality printing to present photographers' portfolios.

LensWork Extended is a PDF-based bimonthly multimedia publication containing lots of additional content that simply won't fit in the 96 pages of *LensWork*. It also features color portfolios not seen in the print publication. The magazine has editions formatted specifically for the iPad and for Android tablet devices.

All the formats work together for the benefit of *LensWork* subscribers.

Digital Publishing Formats

There are many different formats for digital output from InDesign. The following are the digital formats you're most likely to use as you explore the possibilities of digital publishing.

Format	Description	Benefits/Disadvantages	Chapter
Reflowable ePub	Documents, often long, that can be read on eReaders such as iBooks, Kindle, and Nook. ePubs can also be read on computer screens using eReader software.	Can be sold through Amazon, iBooks, and other online marketplaces. Requires a certain degree of skill to export successfully. Limited layout choices.	5
Fixed layout ePub	Highly designed documents where layout is critical. Often used for children's books. Often includes animation and interactive elements.	Can be sold through iBooks and some other online stores. Fixed layout format for Amazon not easily created from InDesign. Can be difficult to find a reader on certain computers or devices.	6
DPS	Interactive applications that can be uploaded onto devices such as the Apple iPad and Android tablets.	Can be sold through the Apple App Store and Google Play. Requires a high degree of skill to create. Requires an expensive license from Adobe to publish multiple editions.	7
PDF	Page-based documents that can be downloaded from websites or distributed via email or disks. Can be viewed on computers or tablets, but not all features are supported by all readers and devices.	Easily exported with interactive features. Interactive features are limited on tablet devices with certain PDF readers. No online sales stores.	8
HTML	Code-based text and images that are posted to web pages and viewed on computers or tablets.	Can be passed on to developers to include in websites. InDesign does not create a finished website automatically.	5
SWF	Based on Adobe Flash technology, these formats can be used as interactive presentations containing motion graphics and videos.	Easy to create sophisticated motion graphics. Not available on any tablet devices. Requires special downloads to play on desktop computers.	8

The takeway from this table is there is not one single format that fulfills *all* the needs of publishers and businesses. We hope that eventually some of the more complex workflows can be made simpler.

Fad formats

We've had students come in who want to learn how to "make an app." They're not sure why they want to create one, but it's what all their friends are talking about. When they investigate the pros and cons, they often decide that a PDF or fixed layout ePub is a better choice.

We've seen interactivity used just because it can be done, with no real purpose. For instance, one of the DPS magazine apps we've looked at has photos that require you to click a button to view the photo caption. There is plenty of room on the page for the caption. And clicking the button is actually more work for the reader. But the designer of the app wanted to have the reader play with a button rather than just see the image and read the caption. That's when your digital publication becomes a fad, not communication.

InDesign Workflows

InDesign has been, and is, at the center of the print design and production workflow, bringing together text, illustrations, and photographs from other programs. For digital publications, it becomes even more central in the workflow. It assembles information and assets, and its powerful export features and integration with Adobe's Digital Publishing Suite make it more essential than ever — the "hub" of your publishing workflow.

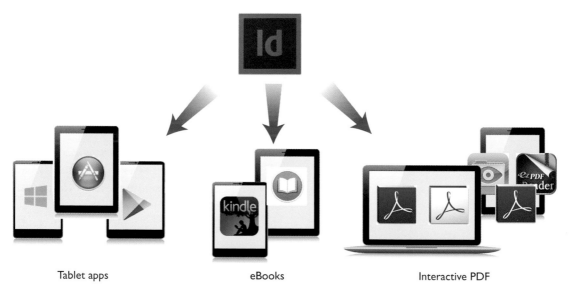

| Tablet apps | eBooks | Interactive PDF |

InDesign is one of the only tools that can create content for multiple digital formats.

InDesign as the "hub" This book is very "InDesign-centric," focusing on InDesign documents as the center of your workflow. Once you have created an InDesign file, it can be exported to a print PDF, an interactive PDF, two types of ePubs, a tablet app, and so on. Corrections, updates, and changes are made to the original InDesign file and then re-exported to the various output formats.

Focus on InDesign features

We've had to narrow the scope of the book to cover InDesign's interactive features. For instance, InDesign lets you add interactive buttons and forms to documents for PDF export. However, many people add annotations in Acrobat as part of an editorial workflow. You could call these comments interactive, but since they don't start in InDesign, we've chosen not to cover them.

Similarly, the workflows to create DPS apps and ePubs for the iPad rely on working with Apple to get approval for those products. We mention the process only briefly, as we can't fully cover the requirements of third-party companies, especially those for creating apps.

And we don't focus on some of the very important overall strategies. For example, building responsive websites using HTML5 may turn out to be one of the best and most flexible ways to produce digital content. But InDesign's role in that strategy is quite limited, so we don't cover building websites.

What is expected of a print designer?

It's likely that when you started as a print designer, you had a basic understanding of the print process. You may have interacted directly with a printing company, making sure your files were set up to print correctly. But you never had to print the job yourself. And you usually were not responsible for the distribution of the printed piece, because that was up to your client or your client's marketing department.

But with digital publishing, there are many different things you may need to know. When a client says, "I want my document on Kindle and iPad," there's a lot more involved in setting up your files correctly. You need to understand much more about how files are distributed and the limitations of each digital format. We'll cover what jobs you need to know how to do and what you can safely ask others to finish.

For instance, many design firms have separate departments for print and web. You may not need to know Cascading Style Sheets (CSS) or Hypertext Markup Language (HTML), but you should know the proper ways to create the InDesign file that you'll hand off to the next team.

One of the most important things you'll need to know is how to create styles. Styles are essential; not only paragraph and character styles, but also object styles and table and cell styles have become essential in creating digital content. If you aren't up to speed on using styles for print documents, few would know the difference (though you may spend extra hours producing the work), but you can't live without them in the new digital world.

Thinking Digitally

There are other new skills that you need to use to work with digital publications. Most of all, you need to think differently.

Planning ahead It does no good to be halfway through a project only to find out that the videos you were relying on won't play in all formats, or that there's no software to play your document on a certain type of tablet.

These chapters contain many tables that compare which features can be used in each type of digital publication. This can help you choose the right type of format. You'll also find a few "war stories" that illustrate how a lack of planning can cause problems when the product is published.

Thinking non-linearly As a print designer, you're used to linear documents. Books start at the front page and work their way to the end. Ads start at the top of the page and read down. But digital publishing allows you to move off in many different directions.

Consider the story "Little Red Riding Hood." While a book may flow from one page to another, a tablet app of the story can have tangents that send the reader to recipes for the goodies in the basket, an article on the wolves of North America, and the medical options for senior citizens.

Digital publications also provide opportunities for non-text features. For "Little Red Riding Hood," this could include interactive maps for the route to Grandma's house, videos of the latest movie about the story, or puzzles and games for children reading the story.

The depth of a page In print documents, a page has no depth. Images don't hide under each other. There are no layers to turn on to see things underneath others. But in digital publications, a page can be as deep as you want. Images can be stacked one on top of another and be revealed by clicking buttons. The digital publishing designer should learn how to think in this new dimension.

Better Homes and Gardens magazine uses a scrolling area to display more copy than would ordinarily fit on the page.

The size of the objects on a page is flexible. One of the exciting techniques in DPS apps is to have text scroll into view within a small opening on the page. This makes it possible to present long recipes and other instructional text without taking up a lot of page real estate or reducing the type size. It's a new way to present material on each page.

Adding multimedia to magazines and books

Creating digital publications means that you can use video and audio files to enhance the reader's experience. This means you have to own or acquire the rights to use these files. Files also have to be in the proper format.

All of this requires a little extra work, but media files add tremendously to publications. We worked with an author who wrote an ePub guidebook based on his years of taking tourists around Rome. Instead of just describing a certain market or attraction, he inserted videos that show what to look for. The ePub guidebook is selling well — especially considering it was self-published, with little outside marketing.

Special features

Some features are automatically added to digital publications. Those who have read ePubs know that there is a built-in dictionary in iBooks and Kindle devices. Readers can look up the definition of any word they don't know, and the definition is displayed right on the eBook page.

Readers can also highlight text, add notes, and search within text. This definitely enhances the process of reading. And the designer doesn't have to do a thing to make it happen.

The size of the objects on a page is flexible. One of the exciting techniques in DPS apps is to have text scroll into view within a small opening on the page. This makes it possible to present long recipes and other instructional text without taking up a lot of page real estate or reducing the type size. It's a new way to present material on each page.

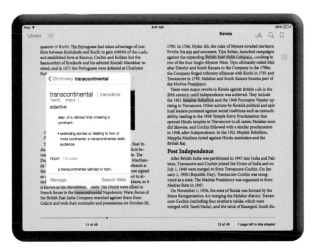

A reflowable eBook page in iBooks with a highlight, a note, and the definition of a selected word.

DPS apps, when published through Adobe's Enterprise service, can even provide analytics on how the readers interacted with the pages. This includes how long someone stayed don the page, which images were important, and if they clicked to go to hyperlinked web pages. This is very important for understanding the effectiveness of the content.

Engaging the reader

One important thing about advertising, especially direct mail, is that the longer someone engages with your material, the more likely they are to buy the product. Adding interactivity and multimedia to digital content, including advertising, helps keep the reader engaged. The longer someone plays with the buttons, watches movies, and works with elements on the page, the more positive feelings they will have toward the content or product.

Educating the reader

While it's not necessary to show readers of print books how to turn a page, you do need to educate your audience on how to use the interactive and media features in your document. This may include an opening screen with instructions for the icons and features in your document. It may also include text and icons on the pages that alert the reader to an interactive feature.

A page of instructions appears at the top of the digital version of *Better Homes and Gardens*.

As readers become more familiar with the conventions used in digital publications, these types of instructions will become less necessary. Of course, as the next generation of readers comes of age, they will be far more comfortable using screens for digital publications. We're reminded of a YouTube video that shows a 1-year-old expertly using an iPad — pinching and swiping — and then trying the same moves on a paper magazine without results.

Keeping Up With It All

Unlike print production technology, the digital publishing standards that are in effect when you start a project may change by the time you're done. Apple may change the process to upload apps or ePubs. Adobe may release new versions of the DPS tools or change the services it provides to post DPS apps to the App store. New PDF readers may become available for the iPad and other tablets. Amazon or Apple may change the features in their Kindle or iBooks publications.

You also may need to buy and maintain different hardware devices and software so you can test to make sure your digital publications run properly on each device. This includes computers running different operating systems; various versions of the iPad or iPhone; and different versions of Android tablets, Amazon Kindles, and Barnes & Noble Nooks. In fact, you will most likely be designing for devices that haven't been invented yet.

If it seems confusing, part of the reason is that digital publishing is in its very early stages and it's a bit like the wild, wild West out there.

Herding cats | When we started writing this book, we tried to diagram which InDesign interactive features could be output in each format. We soon ended up splitting the diagram into different devices, different manufacturers, and different reader apps to the point that it became more confusing than helpful.

As of this writing, for example, video in an ePub doesn't play on a branded Kindle reader, but it will play when viewed by Kindle reader software on a laptop or iPad. Or take buttons in PDFs: They work great when viewed on a computer, but when it comes to the iPad, different reader apps have different capabilities — buttons work in PDF Expert on the iPad but not in other readers. And on it goes.

Digital publishing is as disruptive a technology to designers and publishers as desktop publishing was back in the 1980s. Standards are yet to be set; temporary players in the market have yet to be winnowed out. But still, you have to start somewhere. We hope that you'll find this book an ideal starting point.

Why "digital publishing" isn't quite right

We went round and round trying to come up with the right title to describe the techniques and digital formats we cover in this book. "Digital delivery" and "electronic publishing" were just two of the other choices. Our problem was that there really isn't any uniform label that covers the broad range of digital publishing. And if you think about it, any document, even one destined for print output, is "digital" when it's created in InDesign. When asked by our friends and family what our book was about, we'd give them the title. But then we'd expand on it by saying, "It's about creating the non-print export formats from InDesign."

So despite a title that isn't perfect, if you've read this far, you must have recognized what this book covers and why it's the right book for you.

Interactive Tools

In This Chapter:

IMAGINE THAT HENRY LUCE, THE MAN WHO CREATED *TIME*, *LIFE*, AND *SPORTS ILLUSTRATED* MAGAZINES, were to come from the past to visit you today. What would you show him to get him excited about the power of digital publications?

Well, you'd start by showing him how each digital publication could have hyperlinks and buttons that allow the reader to click one page and instantly jump to another. You'd definitely want to play movies and sounds that enhance the printed text. You might even have him fill out an electronic subscription application that could be instantly transmitted back to Time/Life magazines.

This chapter is all about creating the interactive tools that give digital publications the figurative—and literal—bells and whistles that make them so exciting to view.

Types of Interactive Elements

There are nine types of interactive elements you can add to InDesign documents from the Window > Interactive menu: hyperlinks, cross-references, bookmarks, audio/video files, multi-state objects, buttons, forms, animations, and page transitions. Each has its own particular uses, but some of the features may overlap. Before you start work, you need to decide which type of interactive element is right for your job or you could be stuck with an effect that can't be exported for your finished project.

You also need to know what kind of device(s) will be used to view your project. For instance, it used to be that PDFs were read only on computers, but now many people open PDF files on iPads (iOS devices) or Android tablets. A PDF that works fine on a computer may have elements that don't work on an iPad. Or a PDF that works fine when viewed using one app on an iPad may not be visible at all when viewed using another.

There aren't simple answers for these problems. If you try to get all features to work on all devices, you may find you can't use any interactivity at all.

Feature	What It Does	How Used	Limitations	Available for
Hyperlinks	Adds a hotspot area to text or objects where you can click to move to other parts of the document, other documents, or web pages. Can also be used to send email documents.	Can be applied directly to the text inside a story. Hyperlinks can also be automatically applied to the entries in a table of contents or index using those InDesign features.	Provides only very primitive visual indications of the linked area.	DPS apps ePubs PDF (Not all Link To options are supported in ePubs and DPS apps.)
Cross-References	Adds a hotspot area to text that is linked to other parts of the document.	Adds dynamic text that indicates the position of the cross-reference.	Provides only primitive visual indications of the linked area.	ePubs PDF
Table of Contents	Creates a list of all the text in paragraphs that have specified paragraph styles applied, along with the page numbers. The list for each paragraph is a type of hyperlink to the referenced page.	Used to create navigational elements in ePubs and PDFs.	Requires the use of paragraph styles and TOC styles for text.	ePubs PDF
Bookmarks	Adds a navigational element that is visible in the Bookmarks pane of Adobe Reader or Adobe Acrobat.	The Bookmark pane can be set to be visible at all times in the PDF document. Can be created automatically using the Table of Contents feature.	Requires some education to teach the reader how to use the Bookmarks pane in the Reader. Is not directly on the document page. No special visual indication in the document.	PDF
Audio or Video Files	Adds sounds or video files to documents.	Adds sound and motion to the finished file. Can be prompted by buttons.	Adds to the size of the exported file.	ePubs (Not supported by all eReaders.) DPS apps PDF

Feature	What It Does	How Used	Limitations	Available for
Object States (aka Multi-State Objects or MSOs)	Creates a single element that can display different text and or graphic objects.	Can create slideshows or other displays of elements on a page. Interactive elements such as buttons and movies can also be made part of an MSO.	Can be exported only for DPS applications.	DPS apps Fixed layout ePub
Buttons	Adds a hotspot area that can contain text or graphics. This hotspot can be set to invoke a wide variety of behaviors, including navigation as well as movie or audio playback.	Offers the most navigational and design choices.	Buttons can't be created automatically from text or styles. Requires the most work to create.	DPS apps PDF Fixed layout ePub
Forms	Adds an area that can be used in Acrobat to enter information or to mark check boxes or radio buttons.	These forms can be filled out in the PDF and the information then sent back to the creator for tabulation.	Forms can't be created automatically. Requires the most work to create.	PDF
Animations (*covered in Chapter 3, "Animations"*)	Applies motions and special effects to page elements.	Can be displayed as part of a fixed layout ePub or SWF video. (*See Chapter 5, "Reflowable ePubs & HTML Export".*)	Problems using SWF in tablets and most desktop versions of Reader or Acrobat.	Fixed layout ePub
Page Transitions (*covered in Chapter 8, "Interactive PDFs"*)	Creates an effect, such as a dissolve, when you move from one page to another.	Easy to apply.	Works only in PDFs.	PDF

Defining Hyperlinks

A hyperlink is an area of a page that can be clicked to send the reader to a new page, open a new document, move to a web page, or send an email message. There are two parts to a hyperlink: The *source* is the object or text that is clicked to trigger the hyperlink; the *destination* is the page, web URL, or action that you go to. Any object or text can be made into a hyperlink.

Hyperlinks applied to selected text are automatically styled with a character style called Hyperlink. Hyperlinks applied to objects display a dashed line around the bounding box. However, this dashed line does not show when exported. It is there as a convenience to easily find object hyperlinks. If you need a visible indication of hyperlinks on objects, it's best to apply a dashed stroke or other graphic format to the object.

THE WALRUS AND THE CARPENTER
BY LEWIS CARROLL
"THE SUN WAS SHINING ON THE SEA,
SHINING WITH ALL HIS MIGHT:
HE DID HIS VERY BEST TO MAKE
THE BILLOWS SMOOTH AND BRIGHT
AND THIS WAS ODD, BECAUSE IT WAS
THE MIDDLE OF THE NIGHT.

THE MOON WAS SHINING SULKILY,

The appearance of text and object hyperlinks in the InDesign document.

TIP if you make an entire text frame into a hyperlink, you can still make any of the text within that frame into a separate link.

Creating a hyperlink

If the Hyperlinks panel is not visible, choose Window > Interactive > Hyperlinks to open the panel. In addition to the panel menu, there are buttons at the bottom of the panel that control many of the hyperlink functions.

The Hyperlinks panel is where you apply new hyperlinks to text or objects.

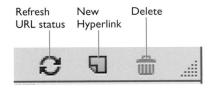

The three buttons at the bottom of the Hyperlinks panel.

The easy way to create a hyperlink

There are two ways to create hyperlinks. The easy way creates a hyperlink using the URL field in the Hyperlinks panel. It creates a link without setting some of the more detailed features for the hyperlink.

Start by selecting the text or object that you want to make the hyperlink source. (The New Hyperlink button isn't available unless text or an object is selected.) Enter the code in the URL field. This can be any of the protocols such as http://, file://, ftp://, or mailto://. Press the Return/Enter key or click the **New Hyperlink** button in the panel. The URL is applied to the text or object.

The selected text or the name of the object appears in the panel and the URL is applied as the hyperlink. If you want to change the name of any hyperlink that appears in the Hyperlink panel list, choose **Rename Hyperlink** from the panel menu.

TIP The selected text does not have to be the same as the code entered in the destination field. So the selected text could say "Visit Our Website" while the hyperlink uses the http:// protocol.

The Hyperlinks panel lists all hyperlinks you've applied. The panel also shows the page that the link appears on as well as a status icon indicating if the hyperlink is working or not.

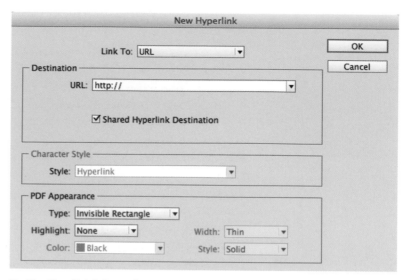

The New Hyperlink dialog is where you set all the attributes for a hyperlink including the link type, destination, character style, and appearance.

An even simpler way to create hyperlinks is to automatically convert URL hyperlinks. This is somewhat like a Find/Change for URLs. Choose the Convert URLs to Hyperlinks from the panel menu. This opens a dialog where you can set the options.

- **Scope** lets you search through the entire document, a selected story, or the text selection.
- The **Character Style** options lets you choose the character style to format the text.
- The **Find**, **Convert**, **Convert All**, and **Done** buttons let you work through all the URLs or convert them all in one fell swoop.

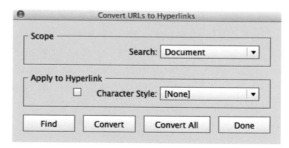

The Convert URLs to Hyperlinks dialog lets you search for URLs and convert them into hyperlinks.

We're pretty impressed with this command because it knows that URLs without the "http://www" code are still URLs. But you can't rely on it being perfect. So don't skip proofreading your file.

The detailed way to create a hyperlink

The more detailed way to create a hyperlink uses the New Hyperlink dialog. There are extra features you can apply to hyperlinks using this feature. Start by selecting the text or object that you want to be a hyperlink.

Choose **New Hyperlink** from the panel menu. This opens the New Hyperlink dialog. Set the options for **Link To**, **Destination**, **Character Style**, and **Appearance** as described in the following sections.

Setting the Link To and Destination options

There are five types of Link To settings for hyperlinks. You can specify a URL to go to a web page in a browser, open a file, send an email, or jump to a specific page or location in the document. The type of hyperlink you choose in the Link To: menu determines the options that appear in the Destination area of the New Hyperlink dialog.

As you create hyperlinks, be aware that some of the destinations or attributes do not work in all media, but you can rely on all these features to work in PDF viewed on a computer. For instance, a PDF file on a computer using the free Adobe Reader will support opening another type of file or going to another page in the document. But the same hyperlink may not be functional when viewed on any other of the various PDF readers for iOS or Android devices. At the moment, we can't tell you any PDF reader for tablets that works for all PDF hyperlink features.

Some hyperlink destinations may not work when you export to a DPS app or an ePub. And even then there may not be any consistency among the various eBook readers.

An email destination works just fine in iBooks on an iPad, or on a Kindle Fire, because there is a built-in email program on these devices. But the email destination may be ignored entirely on a basic Kindle or Kindle Paperwhite. So a destination that works for iBooks may not work for a Kindle or other readers. We know it's expensive to keep up with all the new tablets and eReaders, but in order to truly rely on certain links, you must test them on the physical devices your readers are going to be using.

Here are the types of hyperlink destinations found in the Link To menu:

URL: Choose this to enter a universal resource locator (URL) as the destination. It's best to use a complete URL, such as http://www.adobe.com. Once again you can enter any of the protocols such as http://, file://, ftp://, or mailto://. However, instead of using the codes for file and email, you can instead use their separate Link To controls.

TIP If you have an extremely long URL, it may not work correctly. In that case you can use one of the URL shortening services, such as bit.ly, tinyURL.com, or goo.gl.

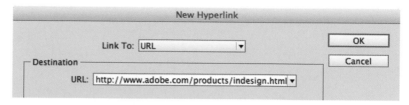

When you choose URL as the Link To option, the Destination area gives you a URL field where you can enter the address for the web page you want the hyperlink to go to.

File: This creates a link that opens a file in another application. This is used for PDF documents, which can then open a file such as another PDF, a word-processing file, or a spreadsheet document. This is very helpful when sending a price list along with the PDF of a catalog, for example. File links are not used in ePubs or DPS applications.

When you create a destination to open a file, you need to enter the absolute path for the file, either from a hard drive or a URL domain. If the file is on a hard drive, you can do this by clicking the folder next to the Path field or by typing in the path manually.

The path needs to be the complete route from the hard drive or URL domain down to the directory that contains the file. This is so that Acrobat knows where the file is located. A relative path, with just the name of the file, won't work, even if the file is located in the same folder as the PDF document. In addition, the person who clicks the link must have the appropriate software to open the linked file.

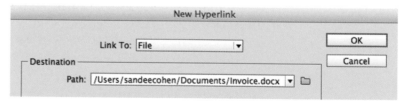

When you choose the File Link To option, the Destination area gives you a Path field where you can enter the path where the file is located. You can also click the folder icon to navigate to the file.

Email: This option creates a link that opens the default email application on the user's device. Use the **Address field** to enter the email address, such as user@domain.com. Use the **Subject Line field** to enter a subject for the message. An email destination requires the proper software on the reading device. A Kindle Paperwhite, for example, doesn't have any email software, so a link to open an email application doesn't do anything on that device. But iPads and other tablets do have mail programs, so clicking the email link will prompt a new email.

New Hyperlink

Link To: Email

Destination

Address: user@domain.com

Subject Line: Hello

☑ Shared Hyperlink Destination

OK

Cancel

When you choose Email as the Link To option, the Destination area gives you an Address field where you can enter the email address. The Subject Line field lets you enter a subject for the message.

Page: This creates a link that goes to a new page in your current document, any open documents, or any other documents on your computer. Open documents are listed in the Document menu or you can choose Browse to navigate to an unopened file. Once you have chosen the document, you can enter the page number. This type of hyperlink is not used in ePub or DPS applications.

You might hesitate to apply a page link if you expect to add or delete pages to the document, figuring that the page you designated as the destination would move to a different position. That's actually not a problem. The hyperlink is tied to the text on that page, not the page number. So if you have a link from page 1 to the text on page 3, and you insert two new pages not connected to the story between the pages, the link will then take you to the same text—the text that is now on page 5.

However, the opposite situation happens if you add two pages of text within the same story so that the text that was on page 3 reflows to page 5. In that case, the hyperlink continues to take you to page 3, which no longer contains the same text.

If all this is a bit confusing, you should link to a text anchor to ensure that the link always goes to a specific point in the text.

New Hyperlink

Link To: Page

Destination

Document: Old Man and the Sea.indd

Page: 3

Zoom Setting: Fixed

OK

Cancel

When you choose Page as the Link To option, the Destination area displays the options for document, pages, and zoom setting.

Text Anchor: This creates a link to a point in the text that has previously been defined as a text anchor. The text anchor can be in the same document or a different document. This is the only type of destination that needs to be created before you define the source link. (*See the section on page* 36 *to learn how to create text anchors.*) We have gotten excellent results using text anchor links in ePubs.

TIP The difference between a Page link and a Text Anchor link is that the Page link uses the entire page as the destination. The Text Anchor link allows you to focus on a specific position on the page.

The Zoom setting for both Page and Text Anchor links lets you choose the view magnification for the page that you jump to. Your choices are Fixed, Fit View, Fit in Window, Fit Width, Fit Height, or Fit Visible.

When you choose Text Anchor as the Link To option, the Destination area lets you choose a document as well as a previously created text anchor.

Shared Destination: If you will want to use the same hyperlink destination in many locations of a document, choose Shared Destination from the Link To menu. This shows you a menu of the shared destinations that were created using the other settings in the New Hyperlink dialog.

When you choose Shared Destination as the Link To option, the Destination area gives you a Document menu where you can choose from the open document that contains the shared link. The Name menu contains all the shared destinations for that document.

When you choose Shared Destination as the Link To option, you can choose the destination document as well as the name of the destination.

Viewing the icons in the Hyperlinks panel

As you define hyperlinks, they appear in the Hyperlinks panel. Each type of hyperlink displays a different icon.

Name		
Bishop Museum	6	●
Hawaii arts	4	●	URL
Page 6	1	▯	Page
Hole in the water	5	⊡	Page link to different document
email sandee	1	✉	Email
Warranty	1	▭	File
Goa	1	⚓	Text Anchor
looking	6	▨	Missing text anchor
asdfjkl; text	1	●	Non-working URL
Hawaii	6	●
Whirlpool	6	✉
<He was a wonderful man,...	6	●

The icon next to each hyperlink tells you the type of destination for that link.

TIP A selected URL hyperlink displays the full URL at the top of the the Hyper-links panel.

To rename a hyperlink click the name of the link in the panel and retype it. You can also choose Rename Hyperlink from the Hyperlinks panel.

Using the Hyperlinks panel controls

Once you have hyperlinks in the panel, you can use the information to the right of each hyperlink in the list to navigate and check the settings for the links.

Each hyperlink displays a blue number in the Page column that indicates where the hyperlink appears in the document. Click one of these numbers to go to that source of the hyperlink. Each link also has an icon in the Status column. In addition to telling you the type of link, these icons act as navigation controls for the hyperlink.

- If it is a web page URL, it opens the default browser for the device.
- If it is an email link, it opens the default email application with a new email available.
- If it is a page or text anchor link, it takes you to that page or text anchor.
- If it is a file link, it opens that file using the appropriate software for the file.

There are also two alert icons in the Status column. A red ball indicates that the URL is broken or not active. A red flag indicates that the page or text anchor is missing.

Setting the style and appearance of hyperlinks

In addition to setting the destinations for hyperlinks, you can control how a hyperlink appears in the exported document. These settings are almost always ignored by the software in ePub readers. Each eReader software has its own display for hyperlinks. However, these options translate perfectly to PDF files or DPS apps.

Setting a character style for hyperlinks

When you create the first hyperlink for a document, a character style named "Hyperlink" is automatically created and applied to the link. The style uses a swatch defined as C=86, M=57, Y=0, K=16. This is close to the blue seen in most browsers. The style also adds an underline to the text. Make any changes you want to this style for any of your hyperlinks.

You can also use the **Character Style** menu to apply other styles to hyperlinks.

The Character Style menu lets you apply a character style to the text of a hyperlink. The character style "Hyperlink" is automatically created and applied to each text hyperlink.

> **TIP** Character styles are not available when an object is selected as a hyperlink.

Setting the appearance of a hyperlink

You can also create visual indicators around text hyperlinks. This is controlled using the Appearance settings.

The Appearance controls let you apply formatting to the hyperlink in the exported document.

Use the **Type** menu in the Appearance area to choose a setting for the visibility of the rectangle around the hotspot. **Invisible Rectangle** hides the rectangle around the link; **Visible Rectangle** displays a rectangle around the link.

Use the **Width, Style**, and **Color** menus to format the rectangle around the link. We recommend either using a Thin width or, better yet, simply using Invisible Rectangle, as any rectangle style tends to look rather clunky.

Use the **Highlight** menu to choose the appearance of the hotspot area when clicked. **None** applies no change to the look of the area when clicked. **Invert** changes the colors in the area to their inverted RGB colors—black becomes white, white becomes black, red becomes green, and so on. **Outline** draws a rectangle around the area. **Inset** creates the appearance of the area being pushed into the page. These effects are not very sophisticated, and we recommend using them sparingly.

To use the Style menu: Choose a solid or dashed line for the visible rectangle. Solid is fine. Dashed is clunky and ugly—we never use it!

To use the Color menu: You can choose one of the colors for a visible rectangle. These colors are not from the Swatches panel.

Editing the source settings

As you work, you can edit the settings for the text area or object that has the hyperlink applied. Double-click the hyperlink entry in the Hyperlinks panel, or select the hyperlink in the Hyperlinks panel and choose Hyperlink Options in the Hyperlinks panel menu. This opens the Hyperlink Options dialog, which contains all the options of the New Hyperlink dialog. Make whatever changes you want.

To delete a hyperlink

Select the hyperlink you wish to delete. Click the **Trash** icon in the Hyperlinks panel, or choose **Delete Hyperlink** from the Hyperlinks panel menu.

TIP Deleting a hyperlink does not delete any character style that was applied to the text. You need to highlight the text and remove the character style using the Character Styles panel.

Creating destinations without sources

The easiest way to create a hyperlink destination is to create it as you define the hyperlink. However, it's also possible to define destinations without defining the hyperlink source at the same time. This is helpful if you have a lot of destinations that you want to define but don't know where you will apply them. For instance, it may be helpful to create a destination for a company's website before actually applying it within the text. It is also the only way to create a text anchor destination in the document.

TIP Destinations don't appear in the Hyperlinks panel. You can see the destinations for a document when you define a new hyperlink. They are listed in the Destinations pull-down menu.

Choose New Hyperlink Destination in the Hyperlinks panel menu. The New Hyperlink Destination dialog appears. Choose **Text Anchor**, **Page**, or **URL** from the Type menu. You must have an insertion point in the text location for Text Anchor to be available. The File and Email options are available only by typing in the full path or typing the address using the mailto: syntax.

The New Hyperlink Destination dialog lets you define hyperlink destinations without first selecting a source object or text.

Creating a text anchor destination: This is the only type of destination that *must* be defined here before you create the source hyperlink. Select the text, or place your insertion point at the position where you want the text anchor to be located. Then open the New Hyperlink Destination dialog and choose Text Anchor from the Type menu.

Use the Name field to name the destination. The text anchor indicator appears in front of the selected text as two dots stacked in a vertical line, when Show Invisibles are on.

The options for a Text Anchor hyperlink destination.

Creating a URL destination: This is the same as creating a URL destination in the New Hyperlink dialog, which is covered on page 25.

Creating a Page destination: This is the same as creating a Page destination in the New Hyperlink dialog, as covered on page 25.

Editing hyperlink destination options

To edit destinations, choose Hyperlink Destination Options from the Hyperlinks panel menu. This is the only place in the document where you can see a list of all the destinations. Select a destination, and click **Edit** to change the name, the link, or other features. These are the same options you had when you first created the destination.

TIP Editing the hyperlink destination doesn't change the appearance of the link. That needs to be modified using the Edit Hyperlink dialog.

Choose Hyperlink Destination Options to edit existing destinations.

Viewing hyperlinks in the Story Editor

If you don't apply any appearance settings or character styles to text hyperlinks, you may not be aware of where they are in the text. One of the best ways to view the location of a hyperlink source is to view your text in the Story Editor. The Story Editor displays a special character for hyperlinks and makes them easy to find in the text.

To access the Story Editor, choose Edit > Story Editor or use the keyboard shortcut Cmd/Ctrl-Y. The Story Editor opens in a separate window. The text in the Story Editor is dynamic, and any changes made in the Story Editor will be reflected immediately in your layout.

TIP Type Cmd/Ctrl-Y again to jump back to the layout at the same position that you were in the Story Editor.

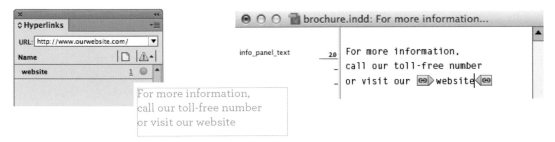

The Story Editor displays special markers for hyperlink sources that make them easy to spot.

It's easy to spot hyperlinks that have been applied to objects. A dashed line in the color of the layer appears around the object. This line does not appear in the final output.

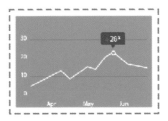

Hyperlinks applied to objects have a dashed line around them.

Creating Cross-References

Cross-references are a cousin of hyperlinks; but instead of taking you to a website or external file , they show you the text that is being referenced as well a providing the page number. So you can create a cross-reference that says "for more information, see page ###." The page number then updates if the document is modified. Even better, when the document is exported, the cross-references become hyperlinks that take you to the referenced text.

TIP In addition to using cross-references to create links in digital publications, you can use cross-references when creating long print documents. We used them everywhere you see a reference to another page in this book. Without cross-references, we would have had to manually enter the correct page numbers.

Cross-References in ePubs

Because ePubs have no concept of pages, there's no need to use cross-references to insert dynamic page numbers in text. But that doesn't mean you won't want to use cross-references in ePubs.

A cross-reference can insert text from the destination paragraph or text anchor. This allows you to refer to text elsewhere in the book. For instance, you could have a cross-reference that says *for more information, see the chapter "Looking at Birds."* Then, if the chapter title changes to "Bird Watching," the cross-reference changes accordingly.

Also, using the cross-reference feature creates an electronic link within the ePub document. This allows your readers to click to go from one place to another.

Setting a cross-reference

Place your insertion point in the text where you want the cross-reference to appear. Unlike hyperlinks, cross-references can be inserted only into text. You can't use an object as the source for a cross-reference.

Open the Cross References panel (Window > Type & Tables > Cross-References.) Click the **New Cross-Reference** icon in the panel. This opens the New Cross-Reference dialog. Set the options as described in the following sections.

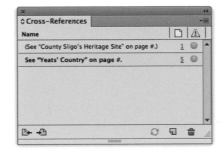

The Cross-References panel with two cross-references already defined.

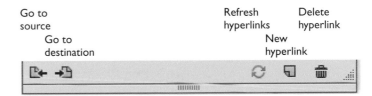

The icon controls in the Cross-References panel.

Setting the cross-reference Link To options

Like hyperlinks, cross-references let you point to a destination that you want to link to. However, the links for cross-references are to a specific position in the text. They can also pick up the page number or paragraph content in the linked text. Use the **Link To** menu to choose which type of cross-reference you want. The options are to a text anchor or to a paragraph with a specific paragraph style applied.

TIP As with the Text Anchor option for hyperlinks, you need to create a text anchor before you open the New Cross-Reference dialog.

The New Cross-Reference dialog lets you set the destination, format, and appearance of a cross-reference.

Setting a text anchor cross-reference

When you choose a text anchor for a cross-reference, the dialog displays the options for the document and all the text anchors in that document. You need to have previously defined the text anchor for it to appear in that list. You create text anchors for cross-references the same way that they are created for hyperlinks as covered on page 32.

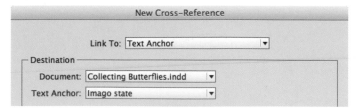

When you link to a text anchor, you get the options to choose a document destination and a text anchor in that document.

To create a text anchor, place your insertion point where you want the anchor to be. You can also select the text. This automatically names the text anchor with the selected text.

Choose New Hyperlink Destination from the Cross-References panel. (This shows how cross-references are a distant relative of hyperlinks.) The New Hyperlink Destination dialog appears.

Setting a paragraph cross-reference

Paragraph cross-references are incredibly versatile. As long as you have previously applied paragraph styles to text, you can easily create cross-references to those paragraphs. (They are of no use, however, if you don't use paragraph styles.) After you choose Paragraph for the Link To option, you can then choose the document for the cross-reference. Underneath, on the left, you see all the paragraph styles in the document. Choose the style that governs the text that you want to link to. For instance, if you want to refer to a chapter title, you would choose the paragraph style applied to all chapter titles.

Once you choose a paragraph style, all the text with that paragraph style appears on the right. Scroll through the list to find the paragraph that you want to link to. (If your paragraphs are long, you will see only a short section of the text.) Click the text. This sets the link to that paragraph.

When you link to a paragraph, you get the options to choose a document destination and the paragraph styles for the text in the document. You can then choose the specific paragraph you want to link to.

Formatting the text inside the cross-reference

Once you have chosen the Link To and Destination options for the cross-reference, you need to choose exactly what text will be used as the cross-reference. Use the Cross-Reference Format menu to control what text is placed inside the cross-reference.

InDesign ships with seven pre-made cross-reference formats. These formats provide most of the typical text for cross-references. For example, the Page Number format will insert the cross-reference text page <#> into the text. The code <#> is replaced by the actual page number in the document. Here are the pre-made cross-references and the text they insert. The quotation marks are part of the text that is inserted.

TIP There is a setting in the Preflight panel that will alert you if you have missing or unresolved cross-references.

Format Name	Text Inserted
Full Paragraph & Page Number	"<all the text in the paragraph (including bullets or numbered lists)>" on page <#>
Full Paragraph	"<all the text in the paragraph (including bullets or numbered lists)>"
Paragraph Text & Page Number	"<all the text in the paragraph (excluding bullets or numbered lists)>" on page <#>
Paragraph Text	"<all the text in the paragraph (excluding bullets or numbered lists)>"
Paragraph Number & Page Number	<number from a numbered list> on page <#>
Paragraph Number	<number from a numbered list>
Text Anchor Name & Page Number	"<name of the text anchor>" on page <#>

Format Name	Text Inserted
Text Anchor Name	"<name of the text anchor>"
Page Number	page <#>

Just as you can style hyperlinks, you can also format the appearances of cross-references. These are the same as the options covered in "Setting the style and appearance of hyperlinks" on page 29.

TIP Since reflowable ePubs don't have page numbers, use the cross-references that don't insert a number for those documents.

Creating a Table of Contents (TOC)

Creating a table of contents (TOC) in an InDesign document is like creating a massive set of cross-references. The TOC not only keeps track of the location of a specific paragraph in a document (along with the page number on which it appears), but it also automatically creates electronic links from the text in the TOC to the text in the document. Creating a TOC also creates bookmarks for PDF documents, which is covered in the section "Working with Bookmarks" on page 44.

Setting the table of contents paragraphs

A TOC is simply a list of all the paragraphs in the document that have a certain paragraph style applied. You must, however, create and apply paragraph styles to the text in your document in order to generate a TOC.

Once you have the paragraph styles applied to the text in your document, choose Layout > Table of Contents. This opens the Table of Contents dialog.

TIP The entire TOC generated by the dialog is placed in one text frame linked to the paragraphs in the document. The TOC text can be edited and formatted once it is created, but those changes will be discarded if you update the TOC. That's why it is important to do as much of your work as possible using the features in the Table of Contents dialog.

Setting the Title listing

At the top of the Table of Contents dialog, you'll see the **Title** field. This is simply the text that will be inserted to label the table of contents. The default is "Contents," but you can substitute any text you want. For instance, we used the title "In This Chapter" for the TOC we put at the front of each chapter of this book.

The Style menu to the right of the Title field allows you to set the paragraph style for the title text. Once again, this paragraph style needs to be defined ahead of time.

TIP An often-requested feature is the ability to select character styles for TOC listings. Unfortunately, this is not currently available in InDesign.

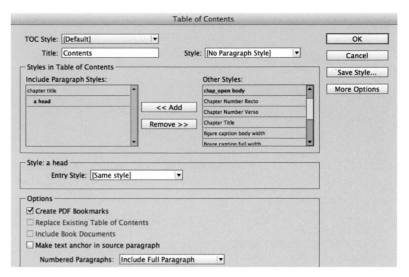

The Table of Contents dialog is where you choose the paragraph styles and settings for the TOC. In this case, the chapter titles and a head styles are used to create the TOC.

Choosing the listings for the TOC

The **Styles in Table of Contents** area is the main area where you choose which text will be included in the TOC. The right side of this area has a list of styles called **Other Styles**. This is a list of all paragraph styles in your document.

Click the name of a style that you want listed in the TOC, and then click the **Add** button. This moves the style name from Other Styles to the **Include Paragraph Styles** area. For instance, if you want the chapter titles to appear in the TOC, you would choose the paragraph style applied to the chapter titles. (This is why using descriptive names for your paragraph styles is important.) Continue with the rest of the styles that you want to add to the TOC.

Styling the TOC listings

The paragraph styles now need to be styled. Click the name of one of the paragraph styles in the **Include Paragraph Styles** area. Under the section Style: [name of style], you'll see the **Entry Style** menu. Once again, this is a list of all the styles in your document. Unlike the styles that you selected to be the listings in the TOC, this menu is used to format those listings. If you want the TOC list to use the same formatting that appears in the document, leave the setting as [Same Style]. If not, select a paragraph style from the list. We like to style the TOC with its own paragraph styles since most of our chapter titles are far too big to use in a TOC. Continue by selecting the next paragraph style and setting the Entry Style for that listing.

Opening the rest of the options

Just when you think you're finished choosing and formatting the styles for the TOC, there are still other formatting options. Click the **More Options** button. This opens up the rest of the Table of Contents dialog.

The additional options for styling the listings in a TOC.

Controlling the page numbers

With the additional options available, you can control the position and style of the page number for the entry listing. Use the Page Number menu to choose one of the following:

- **After Entry** positions the number after the end of the text for the listing.
- **Before Entry** positions the number before the start of the text for the listing. We used this setting for the TOC at the beginning of this chapter.
- **No Page Number** deletes the page number from the listing. This option can be used for ePubs, which don't have page numbers.

Use the Style menu to the right of the Page Number menu to apply a character style to the numbers in the list. Or you can leave this setting as [None], which leaves the numbers styled with the paragraph style for the entry.

TIP We like to create two different character styles for the numbers: plain black text for documents that will be printed, and blue text for interactive links in PDF documents.

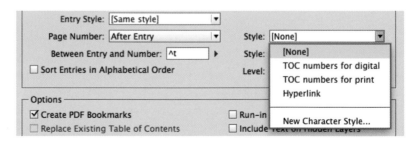

The Style menu that applies character styles to the page numbers in a TOC.

The Between Entry and Number field allows you to enter the characters that separate the entry and the page number. The default setting is the code for a tab character (^t), but you can enter any character you want. Click the triangle to the right of the field to open the menu of characters.

These include the various space characters, em and en dashes, bullets, tabs, forced line breaks, and the end nested style character.

But you aren't limited to inserting just the items in the menu. You can type your own characters in the field. For instance, if you want the word "Page" to appear before the page number, just type the word and a space after the code for the tab character.

Use the Style menu to the right of the Between Entry and Number field to style those characters with a character style sheet. This can be very helpful if you have a tab leader character, such as a period, filling in the space between the entry and the page number. In that case, you might want to apply a character style that reduces the size and increases the tracking between the periods, or applies a color.

Setting the TOC levels

You may wonder what the Level setting in the TOC dialog does. Although each level gets indented in the Paragraph Styles list, they aren't indented in the TOC. If you want the sections of your TOC indented, you have to apply paragraph styles to the entries. The level listing does indent entries in table of contents that are sorted alphabetically. And it also nests entries in Bookmarks if you select that option.

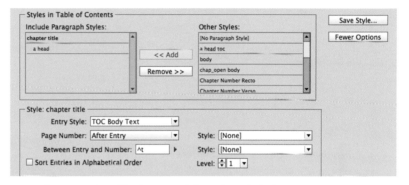

The Level setting in the Table of Contents dialog indents the listings for the paragraphs to be included in the TOC. Here, the listing for the chapter title has a level 1 setting, while the listing for the a head has a level 2 setting.

But all that is different with the output to ePubs. When you set the levels for each listing in a TOC, you also control the indents and nesting for the items in the electronic TOC in an exported ePub. When you set the levels in the TOC, those levels can then be used in the electronic TOC that is created for the ePub. This is handled when you create a table of Contents style. (*See page 43 to learn how to create a Table of Contents style.*)

Entries in an ePub nested in the electronic TOC generated from the TOC in InDesign.

Sorting the TOC entries   A TOC doesn't have to be in the order that the items appear in the document. You could, for example, have a TOC list of all the names of the photographers in your book. In that case you might want to alphabetize the list to make it easier to find a specific person. Just select **Sort Entries in Alphabetical Order**.

Setting the TOC options   Additional controls for creating a TOC are found under the Options area.

The Options area for the Table of Contents dialog.

Create PDF Bookmarks

Bookmarks are navigational controls that appear on the side of a PDF document in Reader or Acrobat. Select the option Create PDF Bookmarks to automatically add these to the InDesign Bookmarks panel. The bookmarks can then be exported as part of the PDF. (*See the next section, "Working with Bookmarks," for more information.*)

Replace Existing Table of Contents

Choose this option if you already have created a TOC in the document and now want to replace it with a new one after altering any of the settings in the TOC dialog, including formatting and styles. This is used a little differently from the Update Table of Contents command in the Layout menu. That command doesn't change any settings in the TOC dialog, but simply updates the text and page numbers.

Include Book Documents

This command is available only if a Book file is open. Then the TOC that you create will list all the entries in all the documents in the book.

Adding Text Anchors

The option to "Make text anchor in source paragraph" adds a text anchor before the paragraph that the TOC is linking to. When unchecked the source paragraphs are treated correctly for PDF documents, but not necessarily for ePubs.

Setting a TOC to run as a single paragraph

Select the Run-in option to set all the entries in the TOC to run in a single paragraph. The entries are separated by a semicolon (;) and a space.

Including non-printing text

The entries for a TOC don't have to be visible in the finished document. Select the option Include Text on Hidden Layers to create a list of items such as the copyright information for photographs or illustrations.

Working with numbered paragraphs

If you have TOC entries that come from numbered paragraphs, that is, paragraphs that are part of a numbered list, you can control how those numbers are handled. Choose one of the following from the Numbered Paragraphs menu.

- **Include Full Paragraph** includes the text and its number.
- **Include Numbers Only** includes just the numbers for the paragraph.
- **Exclude Numbers** includes the text but not the numbers.

Flowing the table of contents text

Once you have set the paragraph styles for the TOC, click the OK button to close the dialog. You should now have a cursor loaded with the TOC text.

Click to place the TOC text on a page. Once you place the text, there are no indicators on the layout that the text is linked to other pages, but as with hyperlinks, you can see the link markers in the Story Editor. Of course, if you export as a PDF or ePub, the hyperlinks do work.

Creating a Table of Contents style

There is a special feature of the TOC that makes it easy to apply all the settings in the Table of Contents dialog to other documents. But more importantly for digital publications, it is used for creating the built-in, navigational TOC for an ePub. In an ePub, you can create a list for all the chapters or headers in your document. The reader then clicks the entry in the list to jump to a new section of the book. This navigational list comes from creating and saving a TOC style for the document.

It's very simple to create a TOC style. Just set up the Table of Contents dialog with the paragraphs that you want in the navigation list. Click the Save Style button and name the TOC style. You don't have to actually create a TOC. You only need the style settings captured under a style name. Then, when you create an ePub for the document, you can choose the TOC style to create the navigational list. (*See Chapter 5, "Reflowable ePubs & HTML Export," to learn how to create ePub documents.*)

Working with Bookmarks

Bookmarks are used in PDF documents. They provide a different way to navigate within a document. Instead of being elements on the page, bookmarks are displayed in the Acrobat or Reader Bookmarks pane. The reader clicks each bookmark to move to that position in the document. One of the advantages to using bookmarks is that the Bookmarks pane can always be visible next to the area being read, and it is particularly useful for long documents.

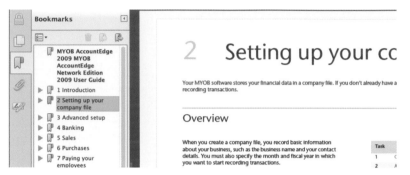

Bookmarks in Adobe Reader and Adobe Acrobat let the user easily navigate to pages in the document.

TIP Bookmarks from InDesign can be converted into a navigational table of contents for fixed layout ePubs. (*See Chapter #, "Name of Chapter."*)

Creating individual bookmarks

To create individual bookmarks, choose Window > Interactive > Bookmarks to open the Bookmarks panel.

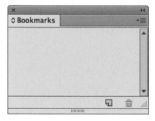

The Bookmarks panel as it first appears.

You can create various types of bookmarks, depending on what you select first:

- Place the insertion point within the text and click the New Bookmark icon. This creates a generically named text bookmark.
- Select the text and click the New Bookmark icon. This creates a text bookmark named with the selected text.

- Select a frame or graphic and click the New Bookmark icon. This creates a page bookmark.
- Click a page in the Pages panel and click the New Bookmark icon. This creates a page bookmark.

Nesting bookmarks

You may have a lot of bookmarks in a document. Instead of scrolling through a long list of those bookmarks, you can *nest* them, or move bookmarks so they are contained within others. The top bookmark is called the *parent*; the nested bookmark is called the *child*. This not only shortens the list of bookmarks, it shows the structure of how some items are subheads of the others in the list.

Drag the bookmark you want to nest onto the name of the parent bookmark. When the name is highlighted, release the mouse button. The child bookmark is indented under the parent. A triangle controller appears that lets you open or close the parent bookmark.

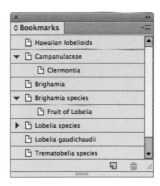

The Bookmarks panel with nested bookmarks. These bookmarks were created automatically by creating a table of contents in the document.

Creating bookmarks from a table of contents

You don't have to manually create bookmarks. You can automatically generate bookmarks by creating a table of contents for the document. When you create the table of contents, select the option **Create PDF Bookmarks** in the Table of Contents dialog. The bookmarks are automatically added to the Bookmarks panel.

As soon as you create the loaded cursor for the table of contents, the bookmarks appear in the panel. Click to place the table of contents text on a page. You must keep the table of contents in the document. If you delete it, the bookmarks are deleted from the panel.

TIP If you don't want the table of contents in your document, you can put its text on a non-printing, hidden layer. This keeps the bookmarks in the panel without showing the table of contents.

If you use Levels in a generated TOC, the different levels will be nested in the bookmark panel. They'll also be nested in the exported PDF.

Working with Object States

Another type of interactive element is created with the Object States panel and is sometimes called a multi-state object, or MSO. Multi-state objects are one of the most important features in creating interactive DPS app files. If you are going to create DPS apps, you *must* learn to work with MSOs. We can't stress this enough.

Choose Window > Interactive > Object States to open the Object States panel. Select the objects for the MSO. You can have a variety of objects in each state. The simplest use for an MSO is to create a slideshow where one object seems to change into another. In that case, each image is shown in its own state in the Object States panel. When the slideshow is played as part of a DPS app, each state can dissolve into another.

But MSOs can do much more than just slideshows. In fact, you can trigger an MSO with buttons. That means you can have each button trigger different states, with each state containing multiple objects, such as an image with explanatory text to the side.

Left: A stack of objects ready to be converted. Right: The same objects converted into a multi-state object.

TIP You can create the effect of one object changing into another. Before you add the objects to the Object States panel, make all the objects the same size. Then use the Align Centers command in the Align panel so that all the states are in the same position. This is much more precise than trying to line them up with guides.

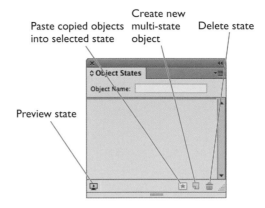

The Object States panel without any states.

If you want mulitple objects in one state, you must first group them. Once all of your objects or grouped objects are positioned correctly, click the **Create new multi-state object** button. This puts each object into its own state, which appears in the Object States panel.

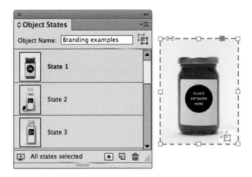

The Object States panel with a multi-state object selected.

Editing a multi-state object

Once you have created a multi-state object, you can make changes to each state, make changes to the object as a whole, edit the content of a state, or add states.

To edit the multi-state object as a whole, use the Selection tool to select the multi-state object on the page—not in the Object States panel. The icon in the Object States panel indicates that the entire multi-state object has been selected. Then make whatever edits you want to the object. All the states will be modified. For instance, if you change the size of the object, the size of all the states will change.

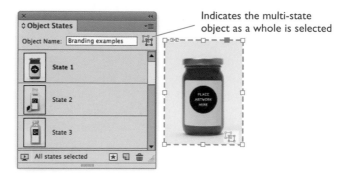

Indicates the multi-state object as a whole is selected

The Object States panel with three states visible. The multi-state object is selected.

To edit a single state, select the state in the Object States panel. The indicator icon in the panel indicates that just that specific state has been selected. Make whatever changes you want to the object. Only that specific state will be modified.

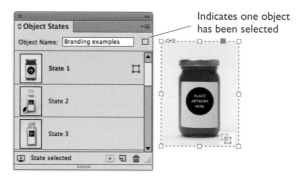

Indicates one object has been selected

The Object States panel with an individual state selected.

To edit the content of a state—change an image or retype text—select the state in the Object States panel. Double-click the content grabber to select an image or double-click to place an insertion point in text. The indicator icon in the panel changes to show that the content of the state is selected. Make the changes you want.

Indicates the content of the multi-state object is selected

The Object States panel with the content of a state selected.

Adding elements to a multi-state object

It isn't hard to create an MSO, but you need to learn some special techniques to add new states or add new elements to existing states. This is important because once you have created an MSO, you don't want to have to convert its states back to ordinary objects to make changes.

To paste new elements into a state

You may want to add new images or text into an existing state of an MSO. Select the MSO and then use the Object States panel to display that state. Next, select the object or objects that you want to add to that state. Copy or cut them to the clipboard. Then, click the Paste copied objects into the selected state button or choose **Paste Into State** from the Object States panel menu. (This button won't be available unless you've got something copied to the clipboard.) This adds the objects to that state. However, they won't be pasted in the same position they were on the page. They will always be pasted directly on top of the original objects in the state.

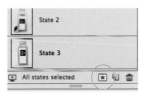

Click the Paste copied objects into selected state button (circled) to add items from the clipboard into a selected state.

To add a new state to an existing multi-state object

This is probably the most common technique needed. You've created an intricate MSO and suddenly realize you need a new object, or several new objects as an additional state or states. This command is tricky because the necessary icon isn't visible in the Object States panel, unless you have the MSO and additional objects selected.

Select the original multi-state object *and* the objects that need to be added. The Object States panel changes from displaying the multiple states to instructions with two new icons at the bottom. Click the **New** icon. This adds the objects as new states in the multi-state object. Each object selected will be in its own state in the MSO.

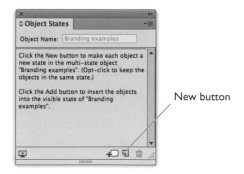

New button

The New button lets you create additional states for a selected Multi-state object.

To add objects to an existing state

This technique is similar to pasting copied objects into an existing state, but in this case the objects are added to the state in the same position where they were on the page. Start by selecting the MSO. Make sure the correct state is selected in the Object States panel to make it visible. Select the object(s) you want to add to the state. Click the Add objects to visible state button. The objects are added to the state. If necessary the area of the MSO expands to fit the position of the new objects.

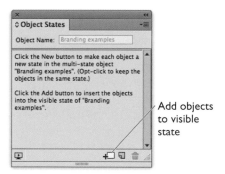

Add objects to visible state

The Add objects to visible state button adds the selected objects to whatever state is visible on the page.

- To duplicate a state, select a state and then choose **New State** from the Object States panel menu.
- To convert a single state back to an object on the page, select the state in the Object States panel and choose **Release State to Object** from the panel menu.
- To convert all states in the multi-state object to objects, choose **Release All States to Objects** from the panel menu.
- To delete a state and remove its contents, select the state and click the **Delete State** button, or choose **Delete State** from the panel menu.

■ To change the order that the states appear, drag the state(s) up or down within the Object States panel.

Using buttons to display object states

Once you have created a multi-state object, you can use the actions in buttons to cycle forward and back through the object states or jump to specific object states. (*See the section later in this chapter "Our Favorite Button Effects" for an exercise on how to create these buttons.*)

Hiding multi-state objects until triggered

You can use buttons to cycle through the states of a multi-state object. However, there may be times when you don't want the object to be seen until the button to show the states is activated. To hide the multi-state object until it's triggered by a button, choose Hidden Until Triggered from the panel menu.

TIP The state that will first be visible is the state that is selected when the file is saved.

Previewing and testing multi-state objects

To quickly see how buttons can display the states of an MSO, use the HTML Preview panel or the SWF Preview panel. For more information on using the preview panels, see Chapter 3, "Animations."

TIP You can use interactive buttons to trigger each of the object states. See "Creating Buttons" on page 60.

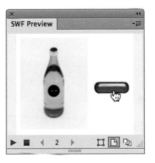

The SWF Preview panel or HTML Preview panel can be used to preview the buttons that trigger the display of MSOs.

Audio and Video Formats

For many of us coming from the print world, it's surprising how enjoyable it is to work with sounds and movies in documents. It's thrilling to add click sounds to buttons or to look and listen to our own instructional movies in interactive files. If you are publishing for digital documents such as PDF, ePub, and DPS, you can easily add sounds and movies to those formats.

But not all audio and video formats work in all types of digital publications. Here are some of the most common audio and video file formats and where they can be used.

File Format	PDF	ePub and Fixed Layout ePub	DPS Apps
FLV	Yes	No	No
F4V	Yes	No	No
MP4	Yes	Yes	Yes (video)
MP3	Yes	Yes	Yes (audio)
MOV	Yes	No	No
AVI	Yes	No	No
MPEG	Yes	No	No

As you can see, the most versatile formats are MP4 (for video) and MP3 (for audio). However, you may have files in other formats that you need to convert. In that case, you can use the Adobe Media Encoder. The application will automatically be installed when you install Premiere, After Effects, or Prelude. You can also download the Media Encoder from http://helpx.adobe.com/media-encoder/archive.html.

Converting files using the Adobe Media Encoder

Open the Media Encoder. Don't let the size of the window overwhelm you. All you need to focus on is the **Queue pane** in the upper-left corner.

Click the plus (+) sign to add files for conversion. For best results, use the Format control to choose the new format for the file. Choose H.264 (Legacy) to create MP4 video files; choose MP3 to create audio files.

When you have added all the files you want to convert, click the **Start Queue button** (green triangle). The new files appear in the location specified in the Output File area.

The Queue pane of the Adobe Media Encoder is where you can convert video and audio files to the correct format for digital publications.

The Future of Flash Videos

In 2009, the future of Flash videos, animations, and games was exciting. Many companies had converted their websites to Flash-based interactive displays. But in 2010, Apple unveiled the first iPad. At the same time, Steve Jobs reaffirmed his statement that Apple would never allow a Flash Player to be added to the iPod, iPhone, or iPad devices. The future for animations would be HTML5.

It didn't take long for companies to abandon SWF formats for their websites. It just didn't make sense to rely on technology that couldn't be seen on any iOS devices. Not too long after, Adobe stopped making a Flash Player for Android devices. It didn't take long for SWF to be an endangered species on its way to extinction.

All this is to say that the only formats for audio and videos that are well supported for both computers and portable devices are MP3 (sound) and MP4 (video). Fortunately Flash formats are easy to convert into those formats. But Adobe doesn't ship the Flash player along with Adobe Reader and Acrobat. So PDF files, which can play Flash formats, require a separate download of the player.

We wish we could be more positive about using Flash formats, but the handwriting is on the wall.

Working with Audio Files

Despite the mind-bending concept (to a print person) of adding sound to a page layout, it's actually very simple to work with audio files, or sounds. Our favorite use for a sound is as a click effect that plays when a button is clicked or tapped. We might also add short bits of music that play when a document is first opened. If you know how to place an image into InDesign, you already know how to place a sound in a document.

However, not all features for sounds work for all export options. Use the following table as a guide for what you can expect to do with sounds in digital publications.

Feature	PDF	ePub	Fixed Layout ePub	DPS
Poster	Yes	No	Yes	Yes
Controller	Yes	Yes	Yes	No
Button prompts	Yes	No	Yes	Yes

Choose File > Place, and then choose the sound file you want to import. The cursor changes into the Sound Clip cursor. Click or drag the Sound Clip cursor to add the sound clip to the document. The sound clip appears inside a frame with diagonal lines and a small sound identification icon.

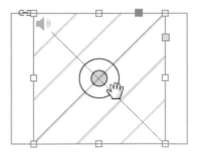

A sound clip, indicated by the diagonal lines, inside its container frame.

Unlike placing images, there is no size or resolution or proper ratio for the sound clip inside the frame. If you click the sound clip cursor, the sound imports as 5 pixels wide by 5 pixels high. However, if you drag the cursor, the clip can be made taller, wider, or inside any shaped frame. The diagonal lines indicate the area on the page that the sound clip takes up. The width of this area is the width of the controller that can be used in PDF and ePubs to play and stop the sound.

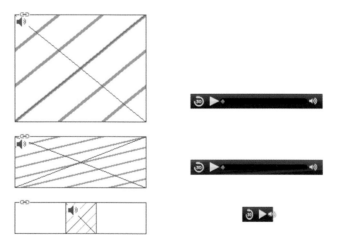

Different sound clips inside different-sized frames. Only the width of the clip governs the size of the controller.

But you can't "clip" or mask the sound clip inside the frame for PDF output. The mask will be adjusted to display the entire size of the sound clip rectangle, even though there is no visual for the sound.

Using the Media panel to set sound options Once you have the sound clip on the page, choose Window > Interactive > Media. The Media panel appears. Use the Media panel to preview the sound as well as set the options for the sound in PDFs and ePubs. Use the Audio panel of the Folio Overlays panel to set the option for audio files in DPS apps, as discussed in Chapter 7, "Tablet Apps."

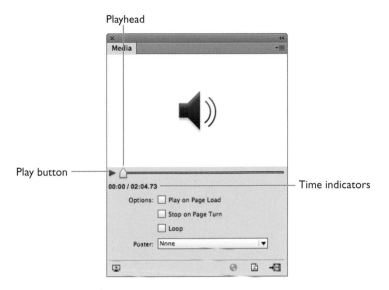

Playhead

Play button

00:00 / 02:04.73

Time indicators

Options: ☐ Play on Page Load
☐ Stop on Page Turn
☐ Loop

Poster: None

The Media panel with the sound controls visible.

Setting the sound options

The Media panel also lets you apply various sound options for how the sound plays in the document.

- **Play on Page Load** sets the sound to automatically play when the page is visible. This makes sense for PDF and fixed layout documents that display individual pages. However, there are no pages in reflowable ePubs. So if you do set a sound to play when the page loads, it will play as soon as the ePub opens—even if the sound itself is placed much further along in the document. This may confuse your readers, so use it with caution.

- **Stop on Page Turn** sets the sound to automatically stop when the page is no longer visible. Again, reflowable ePubs don't honor this command as there is no concept of a page turn.

- **Loop** repeats the sound until it is manually stopped. Most designers don't set sounds to look as it is considered "evil." DPS apps do not support looping at this time.

Previewing sounds with the Media panel

The Media panel also lets you play the sound from start to finish or select specific portions of the sound.

TIP In the exported document, a sound file can be prompted to play by clicking the element, or you can set a button to play the sound. See "Creating Buttons" on page 60 for more information on using buttons to play media.

Select the sound on the page. The Media panel shows the controls and the poster image for the sound.

Click the **Play** button to hear the sound. The playhead moves along the sound play line to indicate the current playback position within the clip. As the sound plays, the Play button is replaced by a Pause button. Click the **Pause** button to stop the playback.

TIP The two time indicators show how far along the playback is and the total length of time of the sound clip.

TIP You can also use the SWF Preview panel or HTML Preview panel to hear sounds.

Setting the poster for sounds

When a sound is included on a page, it acts like a button that can play the sound when clicked. So you might want to include a *poster,* or visual indicator, that lets people know there is a sound in that location.

Use the Poster menu in the Media panel to choose an image that will be used to show where the sound is in the document. These poster controls aren't visible in either reflowable or fixed layout ePubs exported directly out of InDesign.

- **None** leaves the sound clip frame empty. The sound is still there, but there is no visual.
- **Standard** uses the standard sound poster image—sound waves coming out of a stylized audio speaker. It's not a bad identifier, but it's not your own.
- **From File/Choose Image** lets you import a custom image to use as the sound poster. Click the Choose button to choose the custom image. This image can contain text or graphics or both.

TIP Not all graphic file formats can be used as a sound poster. We have found that the best choices are pixel-based files, such as JPEGs or PSDs.

The standard sound poster (left) and an image used as a sound poster (right).

Hiding the audio rectangle in PDFs

When a sound file plays in a PDF, you see the sound's audio controller as well as a gray rectangle that covers the size of the sound file within the frame. The controller lets your viewers play, stop, or change the volume of the sound. Usually this is a good thing. Unfortunately most designers don't want the ugly, gray rectangle popping up. They create their own buttons to control the sound and don't want any distractions on the page.

We used to hide the rectangle and controller by making the sound and frame that holds it only a pixel in size. But it was hard to work with a sound frame that was microscopic. Fortunately we discovered a better way. The trick is to cover the sound file with a white button above the sound. This button can then be set to do nothing with no actions. Because it is above the sound, it stays above the sound in the finished PDF.

However, the Hand icon will still display when the cursor passes over this non-functional button. You can turn that off in Acrobat Pro by selecting the white button and changing it to Read Only in Acrobat's Button Properties dialog.

Controlling the controller in ePubs

ePubs always show the controller for a sound. This is helpful if you want readers to be able to start or stop the sound themselves. But if you want the sound to automatically play, you may not want the controller visible.

For a fixed layout ePub, just draw an opaque object over the sound clip. For a reflowable ePub, you'll need to group the opaque object with the sound clip.

Read Aloud ePubs

One of the exciting uses for sounds in fixed layout ePubs, is the Read Aloud feature that highlights each word of the text as a recorded voice reads along. (This is a recording created by an actual person. It is not Apple's Siri or the Kindle's automated voice reading along.)

It's a terrific feature; unfortunately there is no way to export the text with sound from InDesign. The read aloud sounds and word highlights have to be manually added after the ePub is created. This is why the feature is mostly found only in children's books that have limited amounts of text.

Working with Video Files

One of the more exciting interactive features is the ability to add movies or videos to InDesign for digital publications.

TIP Once again, as with other interactive elements, not all export formats support playing videos in documents. See "Audio and Video" formats on page 51 for more information on using and converting the formats.

Adding videos to documents

Choose File > Place, then choose the video file you want to import. The cursor changes into the Video Clip cursor. Click or drag to place the video on the document. This adds a video object to the document.

Once you have the video on the page, you can use the Media panel to modify and set the playback options for PDF and ePub files. Use the Video panel of the Folio Overlays panel to set the option for movies and videos in DPS apps, as discussed inChapter 7, "Tablet Apps."

Using the Media panel with videos

Choose Window > Interactive > Media. The Media panel appears. With the video selected, set each of the options.

- Select **Play on Page Load** to play the video automatically when the page is visible.

■ Select **Loop (SWF export only)** to repeat the video until manually stopped. This option doesn't apply if the file is exported as a PDF or ePub, nor does it work in DPS apps.

TIP In the exported document, a video file can be prompted to play by clicking the element, or you can set a button to play the sound. See "Creating Buttons" on page 60 for more information on using buttons to play media.

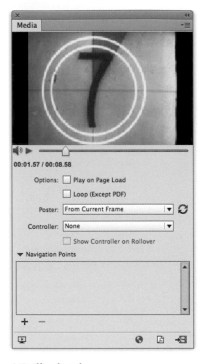

The Media panel with an MP4 file selected.

Setting the poster for movies

Like sound files, videos act as buttons that play the video when clicked. So you may want to set a poster that appears on the page to let the viewer know that there is a video at that position. Since they are movies, they have more poster options than sound files.

Use the Poster menu to choose an image that will be used to show where the movie is in the document:

■ **None** leaves the frame empty.

■ **Standard** uses the standard video file icon.

■ **From Current Frame** uses the frame currently displayed in the Media panel.

■ **Choose Image** lets you import a custom image to use as the movie poster.

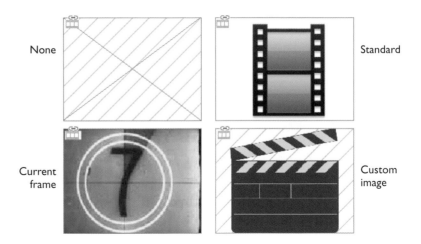

The four types of posters for movie files.

Setting a controller for the video

Use the Controller menu to apply one of the controllers that can be used to control the playback of the movie, play it in full screen, adjust the sound, and show captions. The name of each controller explains which features it has. For instance, **SkinOverAll** contains all the features for controlling videos. The controller **SkinOverPlay** contains only the Play button. These options have no effect in DPS apps.

Select **Show Controller on Rollover** to have the controller appear and disappear when the mouse moves inside and outside the area of the video. When Show Controller on Rollover is not selected, the controller is always visible.

The Media panel also lets you preview a movie from start to finish or move to specific portions of the movie. To preview a movie using the Media panel, click the **Play** button to play the movie within the Preview area of the Media panel. As the movie plays, the Play button is replaced by a **Pause** button. Click the Pause button to stop the playback.

TIP The two time indicators show the current playback location and the total length of time of the movie.

Streaming videos to documents

When you place a video onto an InDesign page, the video is embedded in the exported file. But video files take up a lot of space and may not be practical to include in a PDF that will be emailed to someone. That's when you can use the option to place a video from a URL. As handy as this technique is, it works only with videos that are exported as PDF files; it doesn't work for ePubs. And videos can be played from URLs in DPS apps, but this is set in the Folio Overlays panel; the setting here has no effect.

Create an empty frame on the page. It helps if the frame has the same aspect ratio as the video. With the frame selected, choose **Video from**

URL from the Media panel menu. This opens the Place Video from URL dialog, which allows you to set the URL path for the video. This needs to be a complete path to the video file, such as http://www.domain.com/videos/videofile.mp4. Once you have created the link to the URL, you can choose a poster for the file and set the other video options.

The video must be one of the formats that can be played by the Flash Player. However, the use of Flash videos is limited. (*See the sidebar on page 53.*) If you are working with files that will be viewed on an iPad or any other portable device, you are limited to the MP3 or MP4. formats.

Special options for PDF videos

You have additional options for videos in PDF document. Click the **Export Interactive PDF** icon on the Media panel or choose PDF Options from the Media panel menu. This opens the PDF Options dialog.

In the **Description** field, enter the text that will be used as a tool tip for the video clip. This text is also heard by visually impaired users who use screen readers to listen to the text in a document.

Click **Play Video in Floating Window** to display the video in a separate window above the PDF file. If you have the video play in a floating window, you can set a size for the display. Use the Size list to choose a size, such as 1/5 of the video or 2 times the size of the video. If you have chosen a QuickTime MOV file, you can also set the position of the video to the corners or center of the screen.

TIP The MOV file format can be used only in interactive PDF files, not SWF documents.

Creating Buttons

Like hyperlinks, buttons can send the user to destinations. But buttons are more powerful than simple hyperlinks. Buttons contain the code that can link you to destinations, flip pages in a document, open web pages, play movies, show and hide other buttons, and do other tricks.

Use the Buttons and Forms panel to create and apply actions to buttons. Choose Window > Interactive > Buttons and Forms to open the panel. There are two types of interactive elements that can be created in the Buttons and Forms panel: *Buttons* are objects that apply actions; *forms* are objects that allow the user to enter text or click to set the status of a field. We'll look at buttons first and look at forms in the next section.

Creating and naming a button

Select an object. Any object, except media files, can be used as a button. Choose Object > Interactive > Convert to Button, or click the **Convert Object to Button** icon in the Buttons and Forms panel. The object is converted into a button and displays the button icon.

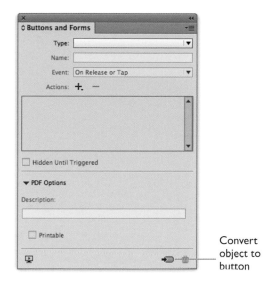

Convert object to button

The Buttons and Forms panel with no button selected.

Use the **Name** field in the Buttons and Forms panel to change the default name to something more descriptive. It's helpful to name buttons with their functions. For example, buttons that move the viewer to the previous page or next page would be labeled Previous Page and Next Page.

TIP You can remove the button properties from an object by selecting the button and either choosing Object > Interactive > Convert to Object or clicking the Convert Button to Object icon in the Buttons and Forms panel.

If you create a button for a PDF document, you should open the PDF Options area and fill in the **Description** field. Type a description or tool tip that explains to the viewer the function of the button. For example, if the button moves the reader to the next page, the description might say "Click to move to the next page." That tool tip is visible when the viewer moves their mouse cursor over the button. The tool tip is not visible when the button is viewed in tablet applications, as there is no cursor to place over the button.

The Description field is also the text that is read by electronic screen reader devices for visually impaired users. You may be required by law to add these descriptions to your documents. Buttons aren't the only elements that require descriptions to be read by screen reader devices. Images also need descriptions. (*See Chapter 8, "Interactive PDFs," for more information on adding descriptions to images in PDF documents.*

Section 508 Accessibility

The tool tip description for PDF documents is one of the accessibility settings for electronic documents that are required by many government agencies under Section 508 of an amendment signed in 1998 to the Workforce Rehabilitation Act of 1973. (Many countries outside the US require similar accessibility options for electronic documents.)

If you do work for a department of the US government — or any part of your company works with the US government — you need to make your electronic documents accessible. In addition, companies may require that documentation for human resources and other departments be accessible under the Americans with Disabilites Act.

And aside from the laws, it's only polite to create description tool tips in your PDF documents.

Adding events to buttons

A button without an action is like a light switch that's not connected to a lamp. You can click the switch all you want, but nothing's going to happen. There are two parts to setting actions. First you use the **Event** menu to choose what type of mouse, keyboard action or gesture will prompt the button to perform the action.

- **On Release or Tap** applies an action under two circumstances: when the mouse button is released after a click and when a tablet screen is tapped. This is the only action that can be used for tablet apps. This also includes PDF documents that normally can use the other actions, but don't when viewed on a tablet. Unless you know that your PDF will only be shown via a computer and mouse, stay with On Release or Tap.
- **On Click** applies an action as the mouse button is pressed down.
- **On Roll Over** applies an action when the mouse cursor is moved over the button's bounding box.
- **On Roll Off** applies an action when the mouse cursor is moved away from the button's bounding box.
- **On Focus** (**PDF**) applies an action when the Tab key is used to jump onto the button. Jumping onto the button is called putting the focus on the button. On Focus works only for buttons in PDF documents, where you can press the Tab key to navigate.
- **On Blur** (**PDF**) applies an action when the Tab key is used to jump off the button. In this case, the term blur is used as the opposite of focus, although the button's visibility doesn't actually change. On Blur works only for buttons in PDF documents, where you can press the Tab key to navigate.

TIP You can set multiple events for a button. For example, a button can play a sound when the mouse rolls over it but open a web page when it is clicked.

Choosing actions for buttons
Once you have chosen the mouse event, you then choose the *action* that follows the event. Not all actions can be used with all types of exported files.

Even if the action is listed for all media, some actions may work in some ePub readers but not in others. For example, videos can play in iBooks but not on Android readers.

Action	Description	Used for
Go To Destination	Goes to a previously defined text anchor.	All exported media, but with limitations in DPS apps
Go To First Page, Last Page, Next Page, Previous Page	Goes to the first page, last page, next page, or previous page.	All exported media.
Go To URL	Goes to a web page or the action specified in the URL.	All exported media
Show/Hide Buttons and Forms	Reveals or hides a previously defined button or form.	PDF, fixed layout ePub, and SWF
Sound	Adds the controls to play, pause, stop, or resume playing a sound placed in the document.	All exported media
Video	Adds the controls to play, pause, stop, go to navigation points, or resume playing a video placed in the document.	All exported media Navigation points not supported in DPS
Animation	Adds the controls to play, pause, stop, or resume playing an animation created in InDesign. *For more information on creating animations, see Chapter 3.*	Fixed layout ePub
Go To Page	Goes to a specific page.	DPS apps and SWF only
Go To State	Goes to a specific state in a multi-state object.	DPS apps and fixed layout ePub
Go To Next State, Previous State	Goes to the next state or previous state in a multi-state object.	DPS apps and fixed layout ePub

Action	Description	Used for
Clear Form	Resets form fields in the PDF page to their default values.	PDF only
Go To Next View, Previous View	Goes to the previous view or next view in the PDF.	PDF only
Open File	Opens an external file. You must specify an absolute pathname, such as C:\docs\sample.pdf.	PDF only
Print Form	Opens the Print dialog to print the contents of a PDF page with form data.	PDF only
Submit Form	Opens a dialog that lets the reader choose how to email a PDF page with form data. The URL field for this action needs to be an email link, such as mailto:person@domain.com.	PDF only
View Zoom	Displays the page according to one of the PDF zoom options.	PDF only

Applying actions to buttons

With the event selected, click the **Add Action** icon in the Actions area of the Buttons panel. This displays the Actions menu.

Choose the action that you want to apply. The action appears in the Actions area of the Buttons panel. Depending on the action, additional controls may appear in the Buttons panel. Set those controls as necessary. Repeat these steps to apply more actions to the form.

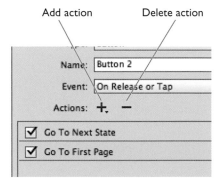

Click the Add Action or Delete Action icon to apply or delete the actions applied to events.

To delete the action for a button event, select the action in the Actions area and click the **Delete Action** icon.

TIP Instead of deleting an action, you can disable it by deselecting the check box next to its name. This keeps the action available, but the action does not export with the button.

If you have multiple actions for an event, the actions are applied in the order that they appear in the list. Drag the action up or down in the Actions list to change the order in which the actions are applied. This order can be important when playing sounds and movies. For instance, you might want the action for a click sound to play before the action to play a movie.

Button appearances

One of the benefits to working with buttons is the ability to change their appearance so that the button itself responds to the actions of the user. This means that the button can change its color when the mouse presses down, or the button can "wake up" with a glow when the cursor passes over the button boundary. However, the best appearance changes are subtle.

When you create a button, it has only one appearance, called the **Normal** state. There are two additional states: **Rollover** and **Click**. The Normal state is the appearance of the button when the mouse is not near it. The Rollover state is the appearance of the button when the mouse cursor enters the button area. The Click state is the appearance of the button when the mouse presses down on the button. Only the Normal and Click states are used in DPS apps.

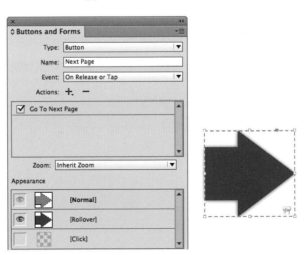

The Buttons and Forms panel with a button selected. The name is Next Page. The event is On Release or Tap. The action is Go To Next Page. The Normal and Rollover states have been created.

Creating button appearances

The following exercise shows how to create the appearance for a button that starts as a native InDesign object.

1. Use the Buttons and Forms panel to convert the object into a button. This automatically creates the Normal state. The selections for Rollover and Click are empty.

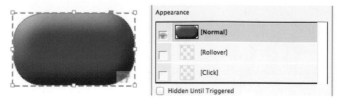

The Normal state of a button in the Appearance area of the Buttons and Forms panel.

2. To create the Rollover state, click its listing in the panel. This adds the Rollover state appearance that contains the same artwork as the Normal state.

The Normal state duplicated into the Rollover state of a button.

3. To modify the appearance of the Rollover state, keep it selected in the panel and change the size, shape, or effects applied to the object.

4. Click the listing for the Click state in the panel. This adds the Click state to the panel. It too contains the same artwork as the Normal state.

5. To modify the appearance of the Click state, keep it selected in the panel and change its size, shape, or effects.

The Click state modified from the Normal state.

One of the effects we like to create for the Rollover state is the look that the button is moving up, toward the viewer. We create a Normal state and then add the Rollover appearance. We then increase the size of the Rollover state, lighten the color, and add a slight drop shadow. We also modify the Click state so that it looks like it is moving down, away from the viewer. For that look we decrease the size of the button, darken the color, and remove the drop shadow.

Appearances versus actions

You may be confused about the difference between appearance and action for the Rollover and Click states. Both respond to the user moving into the area of the button or clicking the button. So what's the difference?

Button appearances are limited to displaying the look of the new state. The user moves into the area of the button, and the appearance of the Rollover state is displayed. Or the user clicks the button, and the appearance of the Click state is shown. But that's it. Applying a button appearance doesn't do anything except change the look of that button.

Button actions do things—change the page, play a movie, show a field. Actions can be applied to any of the button events. It just so happens that the names of those events—On Rollover and On Click—are the same as the events that show the button appearances.

This means you can have a Rollover appearance that displays a glow around the button. You can also have an action applied to the Rollover event that plays a sound. Two distinct things happen—one for the appearance and the other for the action.

Applying text to button states

You can also use text as a button. For instance, you can have buttons that are labeled "Stop," "Play," "Print," or whatever action has been assigned to the button. Select the text frame and convert it to a button. This creates the Normal state. Duplicate the Normal state and then change the text or appearance of the button as desired.

You can't, however, place text on top of a button in order to label a button. Buttons automatically jump to the top of the stacking order of a document when exported as a PDF. (This is the same as hiding the audio rectangle mentioned on page 56.)

Using imported images for button states

We like to use images created in Adobe Photoshop or Adobe Illustrator for buttons.

Start by selecting the images you want to use. Most of the time we use images that are all the same size. This creates the effect of one state of the button magically changing to another state when the button is rolled over, clicked, or tapped. You can resize the artwork after you create the button, but it is easier to do so before you create each state.

1. Select the image for the Normal appearance and convert the object to a button. This converts that image to the Normal state in the Buttons and Forms panel.

67

2. Add the Rollover or Click state to the button. This duplicates the image from the Normal state into the Rollover or Click state.

3. Select the image you want to use for the Rollover or Click appearance. Copy or Cut the image to the clipboard.

4. Select the Rollover or Click appearance in the Buttons and Forms panel.

5. From the Edit menu, choose the **Paste Into** command. The new image becomes the Rollover or Click appearance for the button.

TIP You can also use the Place command to import an image directly into the appearance state.

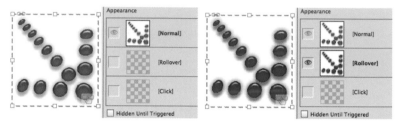

To use a different image in the Rollover or Click appearance, use the Paste Into command.

TIP Instead of using the Paste Into command to change the image in a button, you can create separate layers in a Photoshop or Illustrator file by putting each image on its own layer. Once you use the image in a new state, select the object and then choose Object > Object Layers to turn the layers on or off for the image you wish to use.

Deleting or hiding button states

Select the Rollover or Click state and click the **Delete State** icon. You can't delete the Normal state.

Instead of deleting states, which tosses out their content, it may be better to change whether or not the state is exported. To change the visibility of a state, click the eyeball icon next to the name of the state. If the eyeball is visible, it means the state is enabled and will export. If the eyeball is not visible, it means the state is disabled and will not export. The exception to this rule is the Normal state, which is always visible and can't be deleted.

Using buttons to play sounds or movies

Sound or movie files can be prompted to play by clicking the placed sound or movie file. But you can also set a button to play, stop, or pause the sound or video file. (Buttons don't work in reflowable ePub documents.)

Creating a button to play a sound or movie is fairly simple. Open the Buttons and Forms panel (Window > Interactive > Buttons and Forms). Create an object and then click the Convert to Button icon at the bottom of the panel. The object displays the button icon when Show Frames is turned on.

Next, you need to set the the event. This is the mouse or finger gesture that will prompt the action. If you are creating for PDF, you can choose any one of the events listed: On Release or Tap, On Click, On Roll Over, On Roll Off, On Focus, or On Blur. However, if you are creating a button for DPS or expect that your readers will read the PDF on a tablet, you should only use the event On Release or Tap; the other events won't work.

Click the plus sign (+) next to the Actions options. The button actions appear. Choose Sound or Video to display the options for playing these files.

The sounds or videos that have been placed on the page are listed in the Sound or Video menus. Choose the one you want to control. Then use the Options menu to choose what you want the button to do: Play, Stop, Pause, or Resume playing the sound or movie.

Working with navigation points

If you have placed a movie, there is an additional action for buttons for PDF files. This is to play the movie starting at a navigation point. Navigation points can be used for any reason. You can divide a tutorial into chapters that cover a certain topic. Or you can simply use a navigation point to skip the intro for a movie.

To create a navigation point, move the movie playhead in the Media panel to the point where you want the navigation point inserted. Click the triangle twistie to open the Navigation Points area. Click the plus (+) sign to create the navigation point. Name the point.

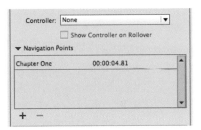

Navigation points for movies appear in the Media panel.

Once you have the navigation points defined, you can choose Play From Navigation Point in the Options menu for controlling videos. The button will play the video from that navigation point in PDF files, but not in DPS apps.

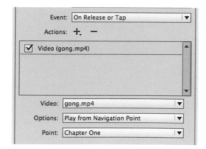

Navigation points for movies appear in the Media panel.

Our Favorite Button Effects

With the various events and actions, there are literally thousands of ways to work with buttons. Rather than try to cover them all, here are two step-by-step exercises for creating our favorite button effects.

Show/hide rollover effect

This exercise creates an effect wherein moving the mouse over a small image reveals a larger version of that image. Because it relies on a button rollover, it is available only for PDFs viewed on a computer.

Using the rollover on one button to show or hide a separate button. When the mouse is off the button, the large image is hidden. When the mouse is inside the area of the button, the large image is displayed.

1. Start by creating two buttons. Place both the small and large images on the page. Select each image and convert it to a button. We like to name the small image "Image Trigger" and the large image "Image Target."

2. With the Image Trigger button selected, set the event to On Roll Over. This sets the button to respond when the mouse enters the area of the button.

3. You now want to add an action to the Image Trigger button. With the Image Trigger button still selected, click the Add New Action icon. Then choose Show/Hide Buttons and Forms from the Actions menu. When you choose this action, the panel expands to show the added controls for the Show/Hide Buttons and Forms action.

4. Set the visibility of the Image Trigger button's On Roll Over event. The visibility controls for the Show/Hide action allow you to set

whether buttons are hidden or shown when the event happens. All the buttons and forms in the document are listed in the Visibility area. Click the Show icon at the bottom of the Visibility area. This means that when the mouse rolls over the Image Trigger button, the Image Target button will be displayed. Understand that you are working on the Image Trigger button but setting the visibility of the Image Target button.

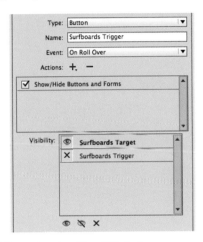

The On Roll Over visibility settings for a Show/Hide button

5. Now that you have set the On Roll Over event and action, you need to set the On Roll Off behaviors. This is necessary so that the Image Target disappears when the mouse leaves the area of the Image Trigger. With the Image Trigger button still selected, set the event to On Roll Off.

6. Choose Show/Hide Buttons and Forms from the Actions menu.

7. Click the Hide icon at the bottom of the visibility area. This means that when the mouse moves away from the button area, the Image Target button will be hidden.

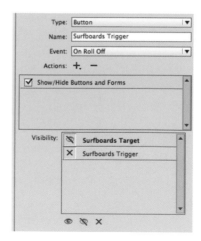

The On Roll Off visibility settings for a Show/Hide button.

8. There's one more setting that is necessary. At the moment, the Image Target will be seen when the page opens. You want it to be hidden until the mouse rolls over the Image Trigger. Select the Image Target button, and select the option **Hidden Until Triggered**. You only need to select this one option for the button.

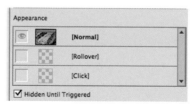

The Hidden Until Triggered setting keeps a button object hidden until it is triggered to be visible by another button.

Creating buttons to show object states

This exercise creates a button that cycles through all the states in a multi-state object, and creates other buttons that display a specific state in the multi-state object. The images displayed by the buttons are in different positions on the page. Because these buttons use actions for object states, they do not play in PDF files. (*See Chapter 8, "Interactive PDFs"*). They work beautifully, however, in DPS apps.

1. Start by placing the images where you want them on the page. In this example, we have a full map of the United States, as well as maps for the North, South, Midwest, and West of the country. We arrange the full map in the center of the page, with the sections offset slightly. This will cause the different sections to "jump" out from the map when displayed.

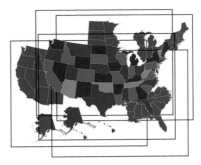

Stacking the images for a multi-state object. Here, the areas of a map of the United States are stacked into position.

2. With all the images selected, click the New Multi-state Object button in the Object States panel. This combines each image into its own object state. The states are positioned as they were before being converted into the multi-state object.

TIP The order of the object states comes from the stacking order of the original image. The top image becomes the first state, and so on down the list. Also, the top object state is, by default, the object displayed in the interactive file. You can re-arrange the order by moving them up and down in the panel.

3. For the sake of your sanity, click to change the object name of the multi-state object. We call ours "Map of the US." Also, change each object state's name from its default to the name of its area. This is especially important if you are working in a file with many multi-state objects with many object states.

TIP You can change the name of the object state with a "slow" double-click. Click once on the object state's name, pause a moment, and then click again. The name field will be available for you to type in a new name.

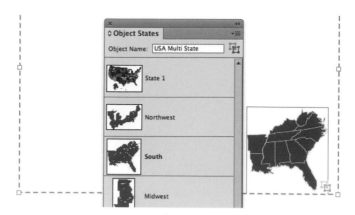

The Object States panel with one of the object states visible. Notice that the art for the object state is positioned in the lower-right corner of the multi-state object. This is the same position it was in when the multi-state object was created.

4. Next create five text frames. One has the label "USA" for the entire map. The others have the labels "North," "South," "Midwest," and "West" for the four sections of the map. Select each frame and convert it into a button by clicking the Convert to Button icon at the bottom of the Buttons and Forms panel.

5. If the page is going to be used in computer desktop applications such as Adobe Reader, you can set the appearance for the Rollover effect of the button. Click the Rollover state in the Buttons and Forms panel. This duplicates the text from the Normal state into the Rollover state. Highlight the text in the Rollover state and change it to red. If the page is only going to be used in a DPS application, there is no use for the Rollover effect for the button. You can use Click instead.

Five buttons created to show the states of a multi-state object. The South button displays the Rollover state. The other buttons show the Normal state.

6. You now need to create the actions for the buttons. Start by selecting the USA button, and set the event to On Release or Tap. This is the only event that is recognized by tablets.

7. Click the **Add Action** icon in the Buttons and Forms panel. Choose **Go To State** from the menu. If you have only one multi-state object in the document, the Object menu will automatically list that object. Choose the state that shows the map of the entire USA.

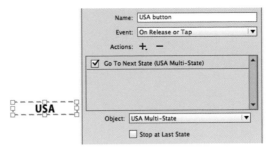

The setting for a button that will cycle through all the states in a multi-state object.

8. The other buttons display the specific states of the multi-state object. Select one of the area buttons (North, South, and so on), and set its event to On Release or Tap. Then click the Add Action icon and choose Go To State from the Actions menu. The Object menu displays the multi-state object.

9. Click the State menu to show the five object states. Choose the appropriate state for the button.

The setting for a button that will display a specific state in a multi-state object.

10. Repeat steps 8 and 9 for the rest of the buttons.

11. You can use the SWF Preview panel or HTML Preview panel to quickly preview if the buttons display the object states correctly.

Creating PDF Forms

Most likely you've gotten a PDF where you click inside areas of the form and fill them out with the information requested. InDesign lets you add form fields to your documents so you can create these types of interactive

PDF files without having to open Acrobat. Just as with buttons, you use the Buttons and Forms panel to create forms.

TIP While buttons can be used in PDF, fixed layout ePubs, and DPS documents, forms can be used only in interactive PDF documents.

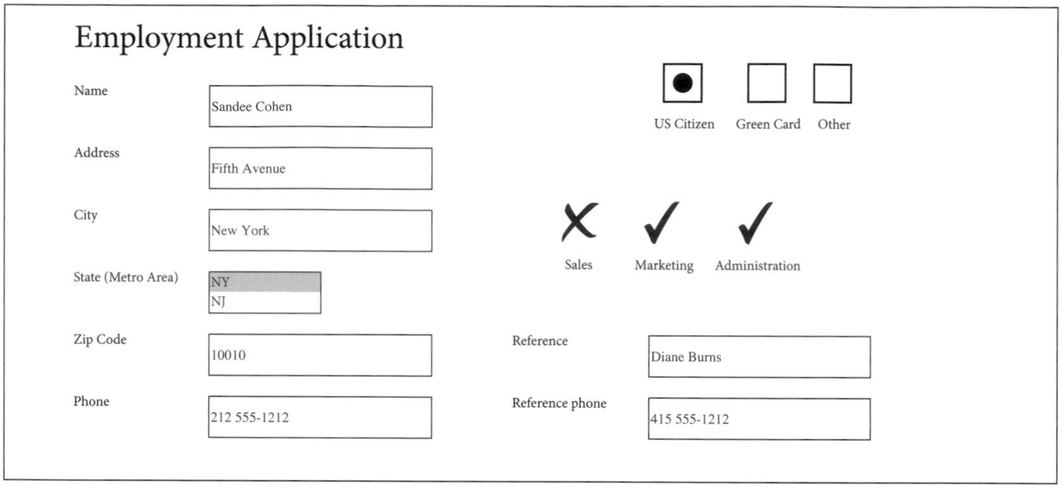

A PDF document with interactive form fields.

Creating and naming forms

Select an object. Any object, except media files, can be used as a form object. Choose Object > Interactive > Convert to [form name], or choose one of the types of forms from the Type menu in the Buttons and Forms panel. The following are the types of forms available:

- **A Check Box** creates a Normal On state and a Normal Off state that set on or off options for the form. Set the appearance for each state to create the display of the check box. If there are multiple check boxes, the viewer can select as many as desired.

- **A Combo Box** lets the user choose a value from a menu. This could be a favorite hobby or the way they commute to work. Use the List Items field to enter the items for the menu.

- **A List Box** lets the user choose a value from a list of terms. This could be something like countries the user has visited or classes the user wants to take. Use the List Items field to enter the items for the list.

- **A Signature Field** creates a field where the user can electronically sign a PDF document.

- **Radio buttons** come in groups of buttons. The user can select only one button in the group. If one is selected, the other buttons are deselected. All radio buttons with the same name work together as a group. Style the Normal On or Normal Off states for how the button looks when clicked on or off.

- **A Text field** lets the user enter their own custom text, such as name, address, or phone number.

Use the **Name** field in the Buttons and Forms panel to change the default name to something more descriptive. Leave the Event setting as **On Release or Tap**. Fill in the **Description** field with the text that will be used as a tool tip for the form field. This also lets visually impaired users hear a description of what the form field does.

Combo Mambo for forms

Combo boxes and list boxes require a list of terms to be entered to create the menu items for the form. Unfortunately, each item in the list needs to be entered one at a time. Sandee was presenting the features of forms in InDesign at an InDesign User Group with Chuck Weger, scripting genius, in the audience. She mentioned the limitation.

When she finished her 10-minute presentation, Chuck bounded up to the stage. He had created a script—in just five minutes—that allows the user to point to an external text file and add those items to both combo and list boxes. Incredible!

The script is free. You can download it at http://indesignsecrets.com/downloads/ComboMamboCC.zip. The script has been updated to work with CC, but it hasn't been tested exhaustedly. Chuck has moved on to other projects, and he won't be able to keep updating it. So we make no warranties on its future performance.

Setting the options for forms

There are different options that appear when you choose each type of form. Here are the options and the types of forms they are applied to.

Option	Function	Used in
Printable	Allows the field to be printed.	All forms
Required	Hides the field's content as a series of asterisks. The contents of the field is exported as real data. Note: At the time of this writing there is a bug in InDesign that allows forms to be submitted even though text fields are set as Required. The fix is to set the fields as Required in Acrobat.	All forms
Password	Hides the field's content as a series of asterisks.	Text fields
Read Only	Prevents the contents of the field from being modified.	All forms
Multiline	Allows text to wrap to multiple lines.	Text fields

Option	Function	Used in
Scrollable	Applies scroll bars if the contents exceed the depth of the field. Scroll bars are automatically applied to combo boxes and list boxes even if this option is unavailable or not selected.	Text fields, combo boxes, and list boxes
Selected by Default	Applies the selection when the PDF document is opened.	Check boxes and radio buttons
Sort Items	Arranges the list items alphabetically or numerically.	Combo boxes and list boxes
Multiple Items	Allows the user to select more than one item in the list by pressing the Shift or Cmd/Ctrl key and clicking the additional items.	List boxes

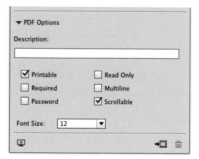

Form options displayed in the Buttons and Forms panel when the Text Field type is selected.

Applying actions to form events

This feature adds great flexibility to working with forms. You can add an action to what happens when a form field is clicked or rolled over. The action is added to the form using the same steps as you would use to apply an action to a button: Click the Add Action icon in the Actions area of the Buttons panel, and choose an action from the Actions menu. (*For more information on working with actions, see the section on choosing actions for buttons on page 63.*)

There are many ways to use actions with forms—too many to cover here. But one way we like to apply actions to forms is to create radio buttons that display other fields when clicked.

In our example, three radio buttons represent the state where the user lives and three list boxes represent the major areas in that state. The list boxes are stacked on top of each other, and the setting Hidden Until Triggered is chosen. The action Show/Hide Buttons and Forms is applied to the radio buttons so that when the radio button for one state is chosen, the list box for that state is shown and the other list boxes are hidden. Instead of scrolling through a long list of cities, the user is directed to choose from a smaller list.

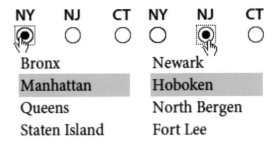

Actions applied to radio buttons can show or hide other form fields on a page. When the radio button for New York is chosen, the list box that displays the boroughs of New York appears. When the radio button for New Jersey is chosen, the list box for New Jersey cities appears and the other list boxes are hidden.

Form formatting

One of the advantages to creating form fields in InDesign is the ability to add fills, strokes, special effects, and imported graphics to the field. These options are not available when creating form fields in Acrobat Pro. Unfortunately, not all of these options are available for all form fields.

You can apply any effect or formatting to form fields, and they will display on the InDesign page. Note that only fills and strokes are maintained in text fields, signature fields, list boxes, and combo boxes when the PDF is exported and opened in Acrobat or Reader; only radio buttons and check boxes maintain all the formatting applied in InDesign.

Radio buttons and check boxes appearance states

Unlike ordinary buttons, which only have three appearance states (Normal, Rollover, and Click), radio buttons and check boxes have six states. This is because you may want different information in the field depending on whether or not the form field has been selected. The choices are as follows:

- **Normal On** is the state that is visible when the object has been selected.
- **Normal Off** is the state that is visible when the form field has been deselected.
- **Rollover On** is the state that is visible when the mouse cursor moves over the form field when the field has been selected (the Normal On state).
- **Rollover Off** is the state that is visible when the mouse cursor moves over the form field when the field has not been selected (the Normal Off state).
- **Click On** is the state that is visible when the mouse button is pressed when the field has been selected (the Normal On state).

- **Click Off** is the state that is visible when the mouse button is pressed when the field has been deselected (the Normal Off state).

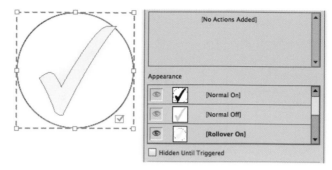

The Appearance area for check boxes and radio buttons contains separate On and Off states for Normal, Rollover, and Click.

You're not likely to need all the states for radio buttons and check boxes, but it's nice to know they're there if you do.

Checks and bullets   When you create a check box or a radio button, a default object is inserted into the button frame. This is a check mark for check boxes and a bullet for radio buttons. These are path objects that can be selected and modified just like any path in InDesign.

The default check mark and bullet that are applied when you convert an object to a check box or radio button.

To modify the check mark or bullet, click once on the field. The dashed line appears, indicating that the form field itself is selected. Position the cursor over the check mark or bullet and click again. A regular frame appears around the object; this indicates that the path is selected. You can change the size, shape, fill, stroke, or effects applied to the path, using the Selection tool or the Direct Selection tool.

A form field that has been selected (left), and a path within the field that has been selected (right). Notice that the bounding box for the form field is larger than the bounding box for the path within the field.

Once the check mark or bullet is selected, you can delete them from the field. You can then use the Place or Paste Into commands to add custom graphics to the form field. This makes your form more enjoyable.

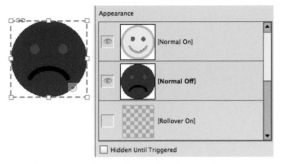

Use custom graphics for the Normal On and Normal Off states of a check box or radio button.

Sample Buttons and Forms

In addition to creating your own buttons or forms, you can use the library of premade buttons and forms that Adobe has generously provided. The buttons already have Rollover states, as well as actions to go to pages and web addresses. There is even a navigation bar with four buttons that go to each page of a four-page document. The sample forms are sets of radio buttons, check boxes, and combo boxes with a variety of appearances.

TIP The sample buttons can be customized with new states, actions, and events, just like other buttons.

Using the Sample Buttons And Forms library

Choose Sample Buttons And Forms from the Buttons panel menu. The library panel opens. If you choose the Interactive for PDF workspace, the library panel also appears docked next to the other panels.

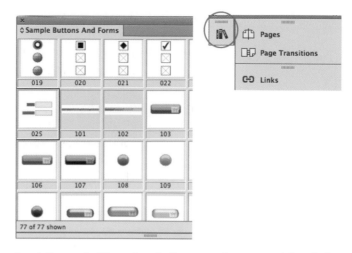

Choose Sample Buttons And Forms from the Buttons panel menu, or switch to the Interactive for PDF workspace to access the Sample Buttons and Forms library panel.

Once you have the sample library open, you can easily add those buttons and forms to a document. Drag the item onto your document page, or select the item in the library and choose Place Item(s) from the panel menu.

There are four types of actions assigned to the sample buttons: Go To Page, Go To Next Page, Go To Previous Page, and Go To URL. There are three types of sample forms: check boxes, radio buttons, and combo boxes.

Working with
the buttons

The buttons in the library are pretty basic. They each have only one action. But they have very nicely designed Normal and Rollover states with 3D effects and drop shadows. We use them for more than the simple actions already applied.

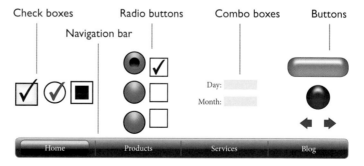

The types of buttons and forms in the Sample Buttons And Forms library panel.

Working with the
check boxes

There are nine sample check boxes in the library. Each check box contains the artwork for at least one state: Normal On. However, not all the check boxes have artwork for the Normal Off state. And none of the sample check boxes contain artwork for any of the other states.

Some of the sample check boxes display a large check or cross for each state. Although they may look like the elements in a dingbat typeface, they are not a font—they are vector artwork that does not rely on a typeface.

The check boxes from the library all have a button value of "Yes." You need to change that entry for your own form data.

Working with the radio buttons

There are 13 sets of three radio buttons. While most people think of radio buttons as dots inside circles, the samples contain all sorts of artwork. Only two of the button sets contain artwork for all the states. The rest have artwork for only the Normal On and Normal Off states.

The radio button sets all have a value of "Choice." You can change that value for your own purposes. The Normal On state is selected by default for the top button in the set. The other two buttons have that option turned off.

Working with the combo box forms

We're delighted to see the set of two combo boxes included in the sample forms. These are labeled for days and months.

The form for the days of the month has a list of the numbers 1 through 31. This makes it easy to set up a form that can be used to pick a day of the month. The form for the months has a list of the numbers 1 through 12, which makes it easy to create a form that can be used for the months of the year. However, the months form does not have the names of the months. This is because every language version of InDesign uses the same library and English months would not be appropriate for foreign-language versions of the software.

Animations

In This Chapter

IT'S HARD TO FIND ANYONE UNDER **65** who didn't grow up watching cartoons on television. Kids have fun watching cartoon characters run, jump, and fly around the screen. It's the same creating animations for presentations and displays. Images and text can magically appear and disappear on the screen. Objects can jump up and down for emphasis. Illustrations can come to life.

Even if you've never created any sort of video or animation, it's easy to apply motion effects to InDesign elements. We like this better than leaving InDesign to work with Adobe Edge Animate. However, the output options for animated elements are limited. (See the sidebar "Exporting InDesign animations" on this page.)

Basic Animation Settings

Most of our favorite animations simply move a text frame or image onto a page. You can apply animations only to whole frames. You can't have just a single paragraph, such as a bullet point, move onto the page; each bullet point in the text would have to be in its own frame. However, as you will see, there are a wealth of ways to move objects around the page.

Objects can be animated to fade into view as they move onto a page.

Exporting InDesign animations

Today, the main use of InDesign animations is for fixed layout ePubs. With animations, childrens' books can have animated characters, travel books can show routes along maps, and textbooks can show various articles on a single page. We wish we could use them in DPS apps. Unfortunately that is not possible at this time. However, there is a terrific plug-in called in5 from Ajar Products that lets you turn InDesign animations into HTML code that can be easily added to DPS projects. See Chapter 5, "Tablet Apps" for more information on using this option.

Applying motion presets

The easiest way to animate objects is to use the animation presets that ship with InDesign. After you have applied a preset, you can then modify the actions of the animation. The primary controls for animations are applied using the Animation panel.

To open the Animation panel, choose Window > Interactive > Animation. Select the object or group that you want to animate. The object can be on or off the page.

TIP You can select more than one object to animate. However, the animation preset will be applied individually to each object. You can group the objects so they animate as a single object. This is not the same as having two separate objects animate together, which we cover on page 97.

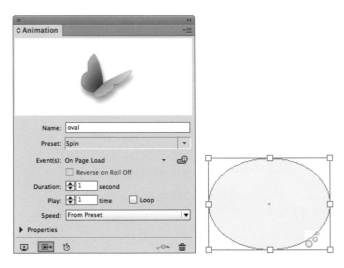

The Animation panel and an object with the animation icon visible.

With the object selected, choose one of the animation presets from the **Preset** list. This applies an animation to the object, as indicated by the animation icon displayed in the lower right of the frame.

Most of the presets are well described by their names. For example, Fade In applies the effect of the object fading into view. But the effect of a preset such as Pulse may not be immediately understood. You can preview its effect by applying the preset to the animated object. The picture of the butterfly in the Animation panel then animates according to that effect.

Naming the animation

When you apply a preset to an object, the object's **Name** field fills in with a generic description of the object. An empty rectangle frame is called *rectangle*. A text frame is named with the first few words of text. A graphics frame contains the name of the placed image. If you work with many animated objects, you will likely want to change these generic names to something more explanatory. Select the text in the Name field and replace it with a more descriptive name.

Setting the duration and speed

The **Duration** field controls how long (in seconds) the animation plays. The motion presets apply a default setting that you may find too short. You can lengthen the animation by increasing this setting.

The **Speed** menu controls whether the animation accelerates or decelerates as it plays. Applying these settings makes the animation look more realistic. (Think of a car that starts, builds up speed, slows down, and then stops.) You can choose from the following options:

- **From Preset** uses the speed control that is applied by default to the animation preset.
- **None** keeps a constant speed throughout the animation. This is useful for animations that move in a single place, such as rotations.
- **Ease In** starts slowly and speeds up. Think of a car starting at slow speed and accelerating. Since you don't want the car to stop abruptly, you will most likely want the object to move off the page.
- **Ease Out** starts at a constant speed and slows down at the end. This is like a car that is moving slowly down to a stop. Since you wouldn't want the object to start up suddenly, at full speed, it is most useful when the object starts off the page, and then moves into view.
- **Ease In and Out** starts slowly, remains constant for a period of time, and then slows down. This is most useful when the object is visible throughout the duration of the animation.

Playing the animation multiple times

Use the **Play** field to choose how many times the animation repeats. For most animations that move onto a page, you will want to set them to play only once. But for presets such as Gallop, which moves the object up and down, setting the Play field to more than 1 causes the object to jump several times.

Select **Loop** to repeat the animation endlessly. Setting an animation to endlessly play on a page is distracting. But that doesn't mean you can't loop objects such as the wheels on a car that moves across a page. The wheels should loop in that situation.

Playing Animations

Animations are like movies on a page. They need some sort of prompt to start the show.

Setting events to play animations

The **Events** list lets you choose which mouse or page actions trigger the animation. The default is to have the animation play when the page comes into view, or is loaded.

Choose a trigger option from the Events list. A check mark appears next to its name. You're not limited to just one event prompting an animation. For instance, you can have an animation play automatically when the page loads but also play when the viewer clicks the animated object. To add a second event for an animation, open the Events list again and choose another event. A second check mark appears next to that name. This indicates that two separate events can start the animation.

- **On Page Load** starts the animation when the page is visible. This can be when the viewer moves either forward or backward to view the page.
- **On Page Click** starts the animation when the user clicks anywhere on the page.
- **On Click (Self)** starts the animation when the object is clicked.
- **On Roll Over (Self)** starts the animation when the mouse moves over the area of the object.
- If you choose On Roll Over (Self), you can select **Reverse on Roll Off** to play the animation backwards when the mouse moves away from the object.

TIP Don't use the two rollover events if the document will be viewed on a tablet. Rollovers aren't supported on tablets.

Creating a button to play an animation

You can also create a button to play an animation. The InDesign team figured (rightly) that people would want to quickly make buttons to play animated objects. So they made it very easy.

Start by applying a motion preset to the object. Then create the object that you want to use to trigger the animation. You don't have to turn this object into a button. That will happen automatically as you follow these steps.

Select the animation object, and then click the **Create Button Trigger** icon in the Animation panel. A tool tip instructs you to click the object that you want to start (trigger) the animation. This converts the object into a button and also applies the action to play the animation. You now have a button that will play the animation. You can also click a button that is already on the page to add playing the animation to the actions for that button.

TIP When you set a button to play an animation, On Button Event appears in the Events list for the animation, indicating that the animation can be triggered by a button.

Create button trigger

Click the Create Button Trigger icon and then an object to convert that object into a button that plays the animation.

TIP The default event, Play on Page Load, will most likely still be applied to the animation. If you want only the button to prompt the animation, deselect Play on Page Load in the Events list.

Animation Properties

The changes to the animation settings we've discussed so far are pretty basic. You can further refine animations by using the **Properties** controls in the Animation panel. (This part of the Animation panel is hidden by default; Adobe doesn't want to overwhelm you with options.) Click the Properties triangle (officially called a *twistie*) to open the Properties area of the Animation panel.

The Properties controls in the Animation panel.

Setting the animation appearance and location

You can customize how the animation starts or ends. From the Animate list, choose one of the following:

- **From Current Appearance** uses the object's current position and appearance as the start of the animation. But you use the Properties panel to set the final appearance of the object. The object then animates to match those settings. This is the most common setting.

An object set to animate From Current Appearance in the Properties area. Notice how the motion path indicates that the object will move to the right into a new position.

■ **To Current Appearance** uses the object's current properties as the end of the animation. This allows you to set a specific end point for the animation; this setting is helpful when you want an object to animate onto a page but need the object to be visible when printing the page. If you don't select this setting, the object will be off the page when not animated.

An object set to animate To Current Appearance in the Properties area. Notice how the motion path indicates that the object will move to the left into its current position.

■ **To Current Location** uses the object's current properties as the start of the animation and the object's position as the end of the animation. This option is similar to From Current Appearance, but the object finishes in its current location and the motion path is offset. Adobe recommends using this option for certain presets, such as blurs and fades, to prevent the object from appearing in an undesirable state at the end of the animation.

Setting the Rotate controls

Use the **Rotate** controls to specify the rotation degrees that the object completes during the animation.

Use the Origin proxy box to specify the origin point of the motion path on the animated object. For instance, if the top-left point is selected, the object will move from that point. This is similar to the proxy points selected for transformations using the Scale or Rotate tools.

Origin proxy box

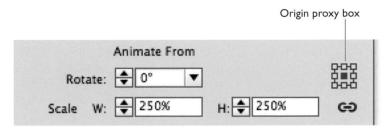

An object set to animate To Current Appearance in the Properties area. Notice how the motion path indicates that the object will move to the left into its current position.

Scaling an object during an animation

Use the **Scale** fields to specify the percentage by which the object size increases or decreases during the animation. You can see how this works, for example, in the Grow animation preset, which increases the object size from 100% to 200%.

The default for this setting maintains a uniform scale for both horizontal and vertical scaling, but you can unlock the link setting to have the object scale disproportionally. We've created a very primitive animation of a bird flapping its wings by using a Scale setting that decreases horizontally only. Use the proxy box to choose at which point on the object the scaling will occur. Our bird scales from its center.

A simple horizontal scale can create the effect of a bird flapping its wings.

Setting the opacity for an animation

There are two animation presets, Fade In and Fade Out, that set an object to slowly appear or disappear on the page. But what if you want the object to appear or disappear as part of a move across the page? The **Opacity** menu is a separate setting that can be applied as part of other animation presets. Choose one of the following from the Opacity list:

- **None** uses no opacity setting, so there is no change in the visibility of the object.
- **Fade In** causes the object to gradually become visible.
- **Fade Out** causes the object to gradually become invisible.

Setting the Visibility options

You may want to control whether an object is visible before it starts its animation or remains visible on the page after it finishes its animation. These settings are very useful when you want multiple objects to follow the same animation path but disappear to let the next object be seen. There are two visibility options:

- **Hide Until Animated** keeps the object invisible until it starts the animation.
- **Hide After Animating** makes the object invisible after it finishes the animation.

Using the animation proxy

Without actual motion on the page, it can be difficult to imagine how the animation will appear. The animation proxy is a gray shadow that shows where the actual object will move from or to as part of the animation. Turning on the animation proxy creates a gray box or outline of the shape that indicates the start or end of the animation.

TIP Text frames always display a gray rectangle for their proxy. Use Type > Create Outlines to see the actual text in the proxy.

The gray animation proxy helps you see how the actual animation will appear. In this example, the type has been converted to outlines.

Click the **Show Animation Proxy** button in the Animation panel so it is highlighted. This turns on the display of the animation proxy. Click again to hide the proxy.

Show Animation Proxy

Click the Show Animation Proxy button to display a gray shadow that shows the first or final position of an object along a motion path.

Saving custom settings

If you spend time customizing the motion presets and have put in all that time and hard work, you will want to save the preset for future work.

With the custom animated object selected, choose Save from the Animation panel menu. This opens the Save Preset dialog. Name the preset and click OK. The custom preset appears in the Preset list in the Animation panel for all InDesign documents. Use the Manage Preset dialog to duplicate presets or delete custom presets. You can't delete the default presets.

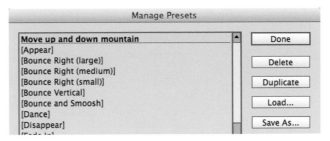

The Manage Presets dialog is where you save custom presets. It also lets you duplicate and delete presets.

Motion Paths

When you apply an animation that involves motion, a green motion path line appears when you click the object with the Selection tool. This line controls the position and direction of the object's motion. A circle indicates the starting position of the animation; an arrow indicates the direction and the ending position. You can edit this motion preset line to customize the move. For instance, you can lengthen the line to have the object move along a longer path.

Most of the preset motion paths are straight lines. To create a more natural effect, we like to add curves to these paths so they move slightly up or down into position.

Editing the motion path

Select the animated object. The motion preset line appears as a green line. An arrow indicates the direction of the animation.

The green line indicates the direction and length of the object's path.

Click the motion preset line. The line changes from a motion path to a regular InDesign path. Use the Direct Selection tool to modify the points on the path. Use the Pen tool, the Pencil tool, or the Smooth tool to add, delete, or modify the points on the path. Deselect the object to apply the changes.

Creating a custom motion path

Instead of modifying the built-in motion paths, you can draw your own motion paths for an animated object. Start by using the Pen tool or the Line tool to draw the open path that you want to use as a motion path. Select both the path and the object you want to animate. Click the **Convert**

to Motion Path icon in the Animation panel. This converts the path into a motion path and opens the animation controls for the object.

You can also swap a custom-drawn motion path for one already applied to an animation object. Select both the drawn path and the animation object. Click the Convert to Motion Path icon. The new path is applied as the motion path to the animation. The original motion path is deleted.

Convert to Motion Path

The Convert to Motion Path icon allows you to use your own paths as the motion paths for animations.

Removing animations

If you no longer want an object to be animated, you can convert it back into an ordinary object. Select the animated object, and in the Animation panel click the **Remove Animation** icon.

Remove Animation

The Remove Animation icon converts an animated object into an ordinary object.

The Timing Panel

Just as in comedy, when working with animation, timing is everything. So in addition to the duration controls in the Animation panel, you can use the Timing panel to control how an animation plays. The Timing panel has three important features. The first allows you to delay the start of an animation. The second changes the order in which objects are animated. The third causes animations on different objects to start at the same time.

Setting the delay for animated objects

Open the Timing panel (Window > Interactive > Timing). All the animated objects for that spread are listed.

TIP You don't add items to the Timing panel. They appear automatically when you create animated objects.

The Timing panel lets you control the length and sequence of how animations play.

In the Timing panel, not on the page itself, click the name of the object you want to control. Use the **Delay** field to set the length of time (in seconds) that the object's animation will be delayed.

Your animation may be triggered by more than one event, such as On Page Load as well as On Button Event. You can set different delays for each event. For instance, you might want a slight delay after the page loads to give the user a moment to get accustomed to the look of the page before the start of the animation. But you might want no delay if the user clicks a button to start the animation, assuming that the user will want a prompt response to his or her action.

Changing the order in which objects are animated

The Timing panel also lets you control the order in which objects are animated. Drag the name of the object up or down in the list in the Timing panel. Objects are played from the top of the list down, and are added to the panel in the order in which you create them on the spread.

Playing objects together

Each object in the Timing panel plays individually. However, you can link objects so they play at the same time. This is very helpful when you have two objects with separate motion paths or presets that you want to animate together.

Select the names of the objects in the Timing panel. Click the **Play Together** icon in the Timing panel. A bracket appears around the selected items, indicating that they will play together.

Play Together   Play Separately

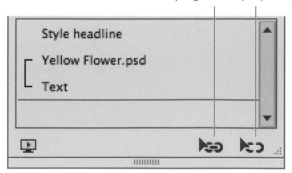

Use the Play Together icon to set separate animations to play at the same time. Brackets indicate that those objects that will play together.

If you have items linked to play together, you can use the Play field and the Loop control to control how many times they play.

TIP Click the Play Separately icon to release the items from playing together.

Timing is everything!

Even the slightest change in timing can make an enormous difference in the effectiveness of an animation. While we can't anticipate every timing situation, here are some general rules we try to follow:

Take a moment: When items are set to play on the loading of a page, you may want to set a slight delay before they play. This gives your viewers a moment to get accustomed to the appearance of the page.

Up the pacing: Nothing is more boring than elements that move too slowly onto the page. This means that the speed of the animation, as set in the Animation panel as well as the Timing panel, should be short. Your audience can anticipate where an object is moving, so don't bore them by making them watch it happen.

Overlap events: Start the next animation just a moment before the previous object settles into place or finishes a fade. Your viewers have already digested the motion of the first object and are eagerly anticipating the next.

Previewing Animations

Applying motion presets and modifying animations can feel like working in the dark, because animated objects don't move around the InDesign page. So you may feel a little lost as to whether or not the settings are working properly. You can, of course, keep exporting to ePub, PDF, or DPS. But that's going to slow you down and get in the way of your creative process.

Fortunately, there are two panels that allow you to preview the interactive objects, videos, audios, and animations on your pages: the EPub Interactivity panel and the SWF Preview panel. As you can guess, the

EPub Interactivity Preview panel displays those elements that are used in ePubs—primarily fixed layout ePubs. (*See Chapter 6, "Fixed Layout ePubs."*) The panel can even be used for a quick preview of most of the interactivity in PDF documents.

TIP Prior to InDesign CC 2014.1, the SWF Preview panel was the only way to preview animations. However, the EPub Interactivity Preview panel can preview more interactivity than the SWF Preview panel, so we don't use the SWF Preview panel anymore.

The EPub Interactivity Preview panel will preview all the animation presets, except Smoke and Fly In-Pause-Fly Out. It can also show the interactivity of object states (MSOs) that are controlled by buttons.

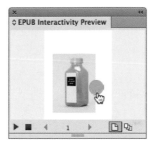

The EPub Interactivity Preview panel lets you preview animations, buttons, and other interactive elements in documents.

But the EPub Interactivity Preview panel has some limitations. It doesn't show the interactivity of PDF forms.(*See Chapter 2, "Interactivity."*) It also doesn't show some of the interactivity for DPS apps, such as a slideshow, that is applied using the Folio Overlay panel. (*See Chapter 7, "Tablet Apps" for working with the Folio Overlay effects.*) The SWF panel doesn't support these either, so you have to export to PDF in the case of forms, and use the Adobe Content Viewer for previewing slideshows in DPS apps.

Working with the preview panel

Open the panel by choosing Window > Interactivity > EPub Interactivity Preview panel or use the keyboard shortcuts Opt-Shift-Return (Mac) or Alt-Shift-Return (Windows) The preview area in the panel can be expanded by dragging the lower-right corner to expand the size of the panel. This is especially important when working with small interactive elements such as hyperlinks.

The panel controls let you preview a single spread as well as move to other pages in the document.

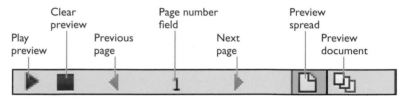

Use the EPub Interactivity Preview panel controls to play and move through the selected document.

Use the EPub Interactivity Preview panel controls as follows:

■ **Preview Spread** sets the panel to display the currently selected spread. Use this when you need to preview a single spread.

■ **Preview Document** sets the panel to display the entire document. This mode is the only way you can preview interactivity that goes from one page to the next, such as a Go To Next Page button or a cross-reference.

■ Click the **Play Preview** button to display the page with the animation and interactive objects. If there are any animations set to play on page load, they will play automatically.

■ If you edit the document, use the Clear Preview button to delete the previous version of the document from the panel. Then click the Play Preview button again to see the new version of the page.

■ Use the **Go to Next Page** and **Go to Previous Page** buttons to move through the document.

■ Enter a number in the **Page Number** field to jump to a specific page. This is faster than clicking the Go to Next/Previous Page buttons over and over in long document.

Move your mouse over the preview area of the panel and click the interactive objects. Buttons and other elements react to the mouse as they would in an exported document.

Using the preview panels from other panels

Once you start refining animations, you'll want to preview the results. However, you might be working with the Animation panel and don't want to go all the way to the Workspace menu to open the EPub Interactivity Preview Panel. The InDesign team has made it more convenient to open either of the two preview panels by adding Preview icons at the bottom of the Animation panel, the Buttons panel, and the Timing panel.

Click the Preview icon at the bottom of those panels and choose either Preview Spread: EPUB or Preview Spread: SWF. This opens the preview panel and automatically clears the previous preview.

Preview icon

Look for the Preview icon in the Animation panel, the Buttons panel, or the Timing panel.

TIP Because the Preview Spread command also clears the preview panel display, these preview buttons are faster than opening the panel, clearing the preview, and then pressing Play.

Creating Slideshows

Most people think motion when they hear animations; but it's very simple to create slideshows that play automatically when the page comes into view. Slideshows can be set so that as one objects fades out of view, the next object fades into view. You can also create buttons that give the user control over when a slideshow plays or stops.

Creating a cross-fade slideshow

A cross-fade slideshow is one where as the first object fades off-screen the next one fades on. You can accomplish this using the animation presets for Fade In. For instance, let's say you're creating a children's book where you want the letters of the alphabet to appear one by one.

Objects can be made to fade into each other using the Fade In animation preset.

1. Select all the objects for the slideshow; in this example, separate letters of the alphabet. Stack them on top of each other by using the Align panel to center them horizontally and vertically. The letters should be graphics, or if text, in a frame with a white fill so that each object hides the one below it. Choose the Fade In preset from the Animation panel. Leave the Event setting to On Page Load.

2. Set the Duration to 1 second and set the Speed menu to Ease In and Out. That gives a more natural appearance to the fades.

3. In the Timing Panel select all the objects and apply a Delay of 2-4 seconds. This gives more time for each letter to be seen. Make sure

the order of the objects in the Timing panel is the order that you want them to play. If not, drag the objects into the correct position.

4. Use the EPUB Interactive Preview panel *(see page 98)* to preview the slideshow.

5. If you want the last letter to fade out of view at the end, place a rectangle with a white fill after the last object in the series.

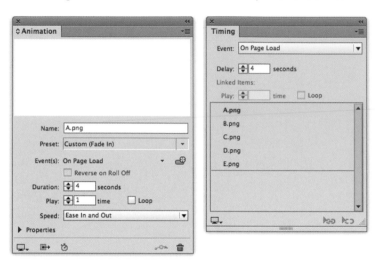

The Animation and Timing panels set to create a slideshow. The order that the objects are listed in the Timing panel is the order that they will play.

Using a button to prompt a slideshow

The slideshow in the above exercise is set to automatically play on page load. Instead, you might want to click or tap a button to play the animation.

1. Repeat steps 1 through 5 in the previous exercise. You'll notice that the Event setting in the Animation panel is set to On Page Load. You need to change that into a button event.

2. Create the object that you want to be the button. Then, with all the objects selected, in this example, letters of the alphabet, click the Create Button Trigger icon in the Animation panel. Then click the object that you want to be the button. All the slideshow objects will be listed in the Buttons and Forms panel set to play each animation. The animations don't play simultaneously. They play in sequence in the order that they are listed in the Actions area.

3. Look at the Animation panel. You'll see that the animated objects are set to play On Page Load as well as On Release. Choose On Page Load from the Events panel to deselect it. This leaves On Release as the only prompt for the animation.

4. Click the button in the EPUB Interactive Preview panel (*see page 98*), to preview the slideshow.

TIP It is possible that the objects will be listed in the Timing panel and Buttons and Forms panel in the wrong order. Drag them into the correct positions.

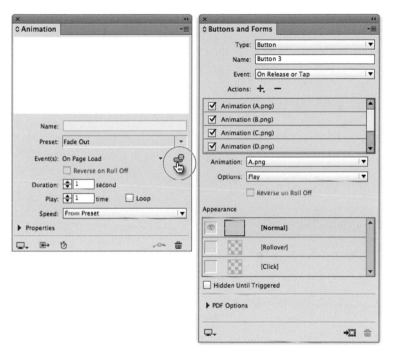

Use the Create Button Trigger icon to add all the objects in the animation to play when a button is clicked.

SWF Export Options

SWF (pronounced swiff) is a format that, like PDF, can be used for the presentation of the entire InDesign file, with transitions from page to page.

In addition to the movies, sounds, and buttons found in PDF files, SWF files (commonly called Flash files) can contain the animations of page items from InDesign. SWF files cannot, however, contain PDF forms. As easy as it is to create these SWF animations and pages, you are somewhat limited as to where you can use them.

- The native animation effects won't play in exported PDF files. They have to be exported as SWF videos and then placed on the InDesign page (*see Chapter 8, "Interactive PDFs"*).
- Apple doesn't support the SWF format for its iOS devices, such as the iPad and iPhone.

- Adobe no longer makes the Flash Player that runs SWF files on Android devices.
- InDesign animations need to be converted to HTML5 in order to be used in DPS apps.

Despite these limitations, there are still legitimate reasons to convert InDesign documents to SWF files.

- They are very easy to create, without the need to learn any code.
- They create exciting presentations that can be played on a desktop computer or on a website. One of us worked with a client who created a private URL for a SWF presentation pitch to a client. The presentation used InDesign's animation effects with great success.

To export an InDesign document as a SWF file, choose File > Export and then choose the Flash Player (SWF) format The Export SWF dialog appears.

TIP As you move your cursor over the different controls in the dialog, the Description field displays tips that help you apply the settings.

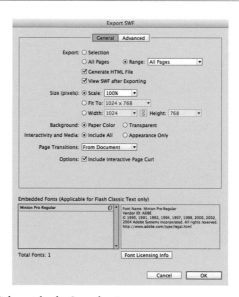

The Export SWF dialog set for the General options.

General tab Click the General tab to display the first half of the Export SWF dialog. These are the basic options, most of which will be familiar from other InDesign export dialoges.

Export: controls how many and which pages you want to export. Choose **All Pages** or **Range** to export all the pages in the document or a range of pages. In addition to exporting pages, you can convert just the selected objects on a page into a SWF file by clicking the **Selection** radio button.

As mentioned, SWF files are great for web pages. However, in order to be seen within a computer's web browser, they need to be inserted into an HTML page. The **Generate HTML File** command creates a separate HTML file that contains the code necessary to insert the SWF into a web page.

Once you choose to generate the HTML file, you can then select the option **View SWF after Exporting**. You can't select that option without generating the HTML file. The HTML file will always be used to open the SWF in the default browser on your computer. (Your default browser is whatever browser you selected in your computer or browser settings.)

The browser must have the Flash Player extension installed in your browser to play the SWF file. If you have trouble playing SWF files, go to http://get.adobe.com/flashplayer/. That page will read your operating system and browser and display the correct download for your computer.

Size (pixels): lets you change the dimensions of the SWF. You can choose to **scale** the animation by entering an amount in the **percentage** field or you can use the **Fit To** menu to choose from some of the more common monitor dimensions, such as 1024 x 768 or 1280 x 800. You can also use the **Width** and **Height** controls to pick a specific size. Changing the dimensions of the SWF is very helpful when you need a presentation to fit precisely in a specific monitor resolution.

Background: controls what is behind the elements of the SWF file. **Paper Color** uses the color Paper from InDesign's Swatches panel. Use this setting when you want the animation to be easiest to read or to stand out from the browser. **Transparent** allows the background color of the web page to show in the empty areas of the animation. Choose this when you want the animation to blend in to the rest of a web page.

Interactivity and Media: is the same as the one for exporting a PDF (*covered in Chapter 8, "Interactive PDFs"*). Select **Include All** to keep hyperlinks, buttons, and media active in the SWF. Choose **Appearance Only** to keep only the graphics for those items, without the interactivity.

Page Transitions: allows you to control the transitions applied to pages in the document. (*For more on page transitions, see Chapter 8, "Interactive PDFs."*) **From Document** keeps the transitions applied to the document. The **None** option turns off any transitions that were applied. You can also choose a new option from the transitions list to change the transition applied to all the pages.

Advanced tab
The Advanced tab of the Export SWF dialog lets you control additional options, including timing, text conversion, image resolution and compression, and font embedding.

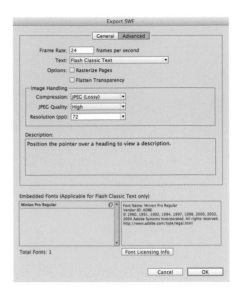

The Advanced tab of the Export SWF dialog.

Frame Rate: controls the smoothness of the animation. The higher the number, the more smoothly the animation will play.

TIP Although raising the number may make the animation look smoother, it also increases the size of the file. This can cause download speed issues if the file is viewed online. Your goal is to balance the smoothness of the animation with the size of the document.

Text: lets you choose one of three settings for how text is handled in the exported SWF. When you choose **Flash Classic Text**, the text is kept as font (vector) information, which makes the file size small. However, there may be times when the font information doesn't translate correctly to the exported SWF. This causes certain characters to be dropped from the text or to be converted to the wrong glyphs.

In those situations, choose one of the other options in the Text menu. **Convert to Outlines** converts the fonts to their vector shapes. This option increases the file size slightly. Most likely this will solve your missing characters or glyph problems.

However, if you still have problems, choose **Convert to Pixels**. This rasterizes the text from vectors to a bitmapped image, which results in a larger file. This option should only be used as a last resort, when converting to outlines doesn't work correctly.

Embedded Fonts (Flash Classic Text only): If you've got text in your document, you'll see a list of the fonts at the bottom of the dialog that have been embedded in the file. Most of the time, this will be a complete list of all the fonts in your document. However, some font publishers put code in their fonts that prevents them from being embedded in a file for export in a streaming animation. If that happens to your text, you need to change the font. Check the licenses of the fonts you are using for more information on what you can and cannot do with the font. For instance, you may be tempted to convert the font to vectors or pixels to avoid font licensing problems. But even that may be prohibited by the font licensing agreement.

> TIP Click Font Licensing Info to go to an Adobe web page that provides more information on font licensing.

Options: If you want a bitmapped picture of your animation that doesn't move, doesn't respond to mouse clicks, and basically just sits there like a bump on a log, select **Rasterize Pages**. The option removes all interactivity from your exported SWF. It is used for multi-page documents that are going to be presented using Flash Player. And even then, you should only apply the setting if you can't get the SWF to work correctly without the option applied. Basically, it's a last-resort measure to get the SWF to export. Because the option converts vector objects into bitmapped images, the option also increases the file size of the SWF.

The same warnings apply to the **Flatten Transparency** option. This setting removes all motion and interactivity from the document. It should be used only if the transparency effects, such as drop shadows or transparency PSD files, aren't exporting correctly in the SWF. It can't be used for motion animations, but it can be used for multi-page presentations.

> TIP A yellow alert symbol in the Export SWF dialog indicates that the setting will remove all interactivity from the SWF.

Image Handling: for exported SWF files are the same as the options for exporting images in a PDF. (*See Chapter 8, "Interactive PDFs" for more information on these settings.*)

Previewing without exporting

You may want to check the result of various options as you apply them in the Export SWF dialog. If you export a file each time, you will constantly have to go through the steps to create a SWF, and you may also litter your desktop with files as you test the export settings.

As discussed earlier in this chapter, you can use the SWF Preview panel to preview animations or presentations. You can also choose Test in Browser from the SWF Preview panel menu. This opens your default browser and displays the animation without creating a file.

Exporting FLA Files

There is one more option for working with animation files. Instead of exporting as a SWF that is ready to be placed into a web page or PDF, you can export the document as a native Flash (FLA) file. This is the format that Flash developers use to create their Flash web pages and games.

Choose the Flash CS6 Professional (FLA) from the export format menu. The Export Flash CS6 Professional (FLA) dialog appears. These are the same settings as the Export SWF dialog with two differences. An additional option for text, **Flash TLF (Text Layout Framework) Text**, is offered for the Flash developer. If you choose the Flash TLF option, **Insert Discretionary Hyphen Points** is available. This prepares your text so it can be hyphenated.

Now before you get too excited about exporting as FLA files, be aware that the presets, timing, and actions for the animation are not converted as expected. Each spread is mapped to a new keyframe, and animations are visible in the Flash Library only as movie files that are set to loop continuously. This makes the file extremely complicated to edit.

TIP Most Flash developers would rather have the InDesign file exported as an image that can be used as the background for the Flash animation area.

The future of InDesign animations

Up until the release of CC 2014.1, we felt the future of using animations in InDesign was bleak. Since animations were SWF only, and it is difficult to get SWF files to play in PDFs, we didn't see them getting much use.

Today it's a different story. Fixed Layout ePubs support so many of InDesign's animation features. And we hope that some of the Folio Overlay effects (*see Chapter 7, "Tablet Apps"*) will be added to fixed layout ePubs.

We also hope that at some point InDesign's animations can be exported as part of DPS apps. In the meantime, companies like Ajar Productions make it possible to turn InDesign animations into HTML5 output for DPS apps. So we're thrilled to be able to say that the future of animations in InDesign is bright.

Layout Controls

In This Chapter

UNLIKE PRINT BOOKS AND MAGAZINES, which tend to have a constant page size from one copy to another, digital publications can morph from one size to another depending on the device the reader is using.

Consider the different sizes of iPads, Kindle Fires, Nooks, Android tablets, and smartphones. Each one needs its own layout size. To add to those sizes, those devices may allow the reader to rotate the device from vertical to horizontal layout. Suddenly there are quite a number of different layout sizes and orientations to handle. This is where the layout tools for working with a design on different page sizes come into play. Fortunately, they're also helpful for the occasional print layouts that change size.

Alternate Layout is a set of commands that means that one document can have several different page sizes and orientations within the file. It also means that elements from one layout can be linked to elements in the other layouts. So if you change the text on the vertical layout, it updates on the horizontal one.

Liquid Layout is an intelligence that you can specify for objects on a page when the size changes. It causes the elements on that page to automatically change their shape and/or move into new positions to fit the new layout when you change the size and orientation of the InDesign page.

You also can use various tools and commands to further control how text and images are modified as their frames change size and orientation. These are *Auto-Fit* options for images, *Auto-Size* for text frames, and *Flexible Width* for columns.

Setting Page Sizes

When you design for print, you need to know the size of the paper your document will be printed on. Similarly, when you design for digital publications like tablet apps or interactive PDFs, you need to know the size of the device that your document will be viewed on. This isn't as simple as working in print.

The "page size" (size of the screen) is different for the iPad versus the Kindle Fire or the Android devices. You need to know which device your application is going to be used on and set the screen size accordingly.

Finding tablet and smartphone sizes

Most manufacturers list two different sizes for their devices. The *device size* is the size of the entire tablet, including the frame and any hardware around the screen. The *screen dimensions* are the number of pixels of the actual area of the screen. The manufacturer will often also list the *resolution* of the device. Just as with a computer screen, the higher the resolution, the more detail there is on the device screen. You need to enter the screen dimensions when designing digital publications.

When you create tablet applications for the iPad or for Android devices, you will want to create individual document sizes for the various screen dimensions of those devices. You may also want to create a horizontal and a vertical version of the documents. This allows the document to change orientation as the user rotates the device. (*We cover the details of creating DPS apps in Chapter 7, "Tablet Apps."*)

Fortunately, Adobe ships InDesign with page sizes for some common tablets. When you choose Digital Publishing from the Intent menu in the New Document dialog, the Page Size menu displays the sizes, in pixels, for the iPhone, iPad, Kindle Fire/Nook, and Android 10" devices. The Android 10" label denotes tablets from many different manufacturers that all use the same Android operating system and screen dimensions.

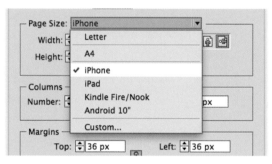

The Page Size menu of the New Document dialog shows a few of the most common devices for digital publishing.

These are the dimensions of the four default tablet sizes in the New Document dialog along with the resolution information from the original tablet specs.

Device	Dimensions	Resolution
iPhone	960 x 640 pixels	326 ppi
iPad	1024 x 768 pixels	132 ppi
Kindle Fire	1024 x 600 pixels	169 ppi
Android 10"	1280 x 800	149 ppi

But these default sizes are very out of date. For instance, Apple no longer sells iPhones or iPads with those resolutions. And Amazon no longer sells that version of the Kindle Fire. There are much newer versions with larger or smaller screens and much higher resolutions. Here is a sample of other tablets that are available as this book is being written:

Device	Dimensions	Resolution
iPad (retina display)	2048 x 1536 pixels	264 ppi
iPad Air (retina display)	2048 x 1536 pixels	264 ppi
iPad Mini (retina display)	2048 x 1536 pixels	326 ppi
iPad Mini	1024 x 768 pixels	163 ppi
iPhone 6	1334 x 750 pixels	326 ppi
iPhone 6 Plus	1920 x 1080	401 ppi
iPhone 5, 5s, 5c	1136 x 640	326 ppi
iPhone 4, 4s	960 x 640 pixels	326 ppi
Kindle Fire HD	1280 x 800 pixels	216 ppi
Kindle Fire HDX (7")	1920 x 1200 pixels	323 ppi
Kindle Fire HDX (8.9")	2560 x 1600 pixels	339 ppi
Samsung Galaxy S 8.4	2560 x 1600 pixels	360 ppi
Nexus 7	1920 x 1200 pixels	323 ppi

You're not expected to keep up with all the devices and their many different resolutions. The bottom line is go to the manufacturer's website to get the size of the specific device you're designing for. That includes pixel dimensions as well as resolution.

Understanding resolution

Understanding resolution and the screen dimensions are the most important part of designing for digital devices. (Skip this section if you totally understand resolutions.)

The dimensions of the iPad Mini are 1024 x 768 for a resolution of 163 pixels per inch. The dimensions of the iPad Mini with Retina Display (high-definition display) are 2048 x 1536 with a resolution of 326 pixels per inch. The screens for the two devices are the same size. They are different resolutions because there are twice the number of pixels for the Retina Display device. 326 ppi is exactly two times 163. That's what makes the device high definition. The pixels in the Retina Display are smaller so they can show more details.

Understanding
aspect ratio

Resolution isn't the only element you need to know to design for digital devices. The *aspect ratio* is just as important.

Look at the resolutions for the various iPads. Even though they have different resolutions, they have the same aspect ratio of 4:3. The resolution for the three iPads with Retina Display is 2048 x 1526. This is exactly twice the size of the resolution of 1024 x 768 of the iPad. So one design created for any of the iPads will scale up or down correctly for any of the others.

Kindle Fire HD tablets are shaped differently from the iPads. They all have an aspect ratio of 16:9. So any design created for one of the Fire HD devices will scale up or down correctly for any device with a 16:9 aspect ratio.

What happens when you put one design on several devices that have different aspect ratios? The images will scale to try to fit the screen, but there will be black bands where the design can't fill the screen. This is called letterboxing in television broadcasting. In that case, you will probably want to create different-sized pages for devices with different aspect ratios.

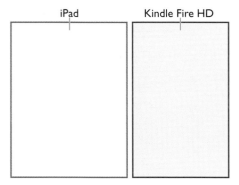

The different screens for the iPad or Kindle Fire HD are shaped differently due to their aspect ratios. Notice that the Kindle has more height compared to its width. The iPad screen is closer to a square. You may want to design to accommodate these different aspect ratios.

Keeping up with the tablets

It's impossible for us to list all the different iOS and Android devices and their sizes. Apple, Google, Samsung, Barnes & Noble and all the other phone and tablet makers change their models faster than award shows change hosts.

The only advice we have is to design for what's out there and try not to worry about what's coming down the pike.

Setting and saving custom page sizes

If your device is not listed in the New Document dialog, use the Height and Width fields to enter its dimensions in pixels. (The unit of measurement automatically changes to pixels when you choose the Digital Publishing intent.)

TIP You don't have to calculate the aspect ratio for a specific screen size. As soon as you enter the screen dimensions, you have automatically set the correct aspect ratio.

As new tablets enter the market, you will most likely want to save those sizes as custom pages. Enter the width and height measurements, and then choose **Custom** from the Page Size menu. This opens the Custom Page Size dialog, where you can name the custom page.

In addition to creating page sizes for new devices, you may also want to create custom page sizes for the horizontal or vertical orientations. Click the orientation icons to change from horizontal to vertical pages and then save that custom size.

TIP Deselect Facing Pages when creating layouts for digital publications. There are no left- or right-hand pages on a screen.

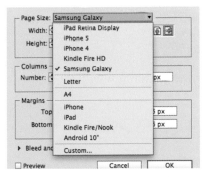

The Custom Page Size dialog lets you define and store screen dimensions for devices that are not listed in the New Document dialog. These sizes then show in the Page Size menu in the New Document dialog.

Working with Alternate Layouts

The ability to create different-sized pages within a single InDesign document was introduced in InDesign CS5. It was, however, a bit of a hassle to quickly create new sets of pages with a different layout size and orientation. With the Alternate Layout feature, introduced in CS6, you have easier ways of creating the new page sizes as well as managing the layouts in the Pages panel.

Setting up the Pages panel

There are three different views for the Pages panel: **Horizontally**, **Vertically**, and **By Alternate Layout**. The Horizontally and Vertically settings are used primarily for print layouts. By Alternate Layout is used for working with digital publications, such as dual-orientation tablet apps. It allows you to see the alternate layouts in the document side by side in the Pages panel.

When you choose **Digital Publishing** from the Intent menu for a document, the Pages panel is automatically set to the By Alternate Layout display. The panel is also changed to By Alternate Layout when you choose Digital Publishing from the Workspace menu. Or you can change the setting by going to the Pages panel menu and choosing View Pages > By Alternate Layout.

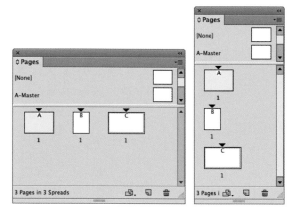

The Pages panel different-sized pages shown, set to View Horizontally (left) and View Vertically (right).

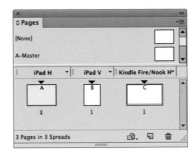

The Pages panel, set to View By Alternate Layout, labels the different layouts with the devices they are being designed for. Notice that the page displays for the alternate layout pages have different sizes, orientations, and aspect ratios.

TIP If you have a document set for a Print or Web intent, the Pages panel automatically switches to View By Alternate Layout when you add an alternate layout to the document.

To create an alternate layout

To create an alternate layout, choose Create Alternate Layout from the Pages panel menu or the Layout menu. This opens the Create Alternate Layout dialog.

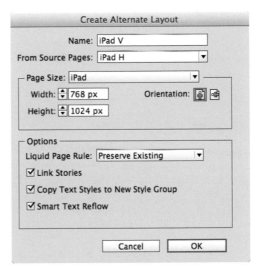

The Create Alternate Layout dialog lets you set the options for new layouts added to the document.

Name field: This is where you enter a name for the alternate layout. By default, the alternate layout is named from the source pages with a change in the orientation. So if you have been working on a horizontal iPad layout, the default name for the alternate layout is "iPad V."

TIP InDesign recognizes the orientation of the alternate layout and adds a V (for vertical) or an H (for horizontal) after the name.

From Source Pages: This lets you specify which pages the new layout should take its information from. For instance, it will automatically set the new layout to the same size as the original layout, but in the opposite orientation.

Page Size menu: This menu lets you pick the from the same sizes that are available in the New Document dialog. If you want to enter your own sizes, use the **Width** and **Height** controls to apply custom dimensions to the alternate layout.

Orientation: Click the appropriate icon to specify whether you want a horizontal or vertical orientation for the alternate layout. It also gives you a quick way to swap the width and height settings.

Liquid Page Rule menu: lets you choose if or how objects on the pages will be resized or repositioned to accommodate the new page sizes. (*See the next section, "Using Liquid Page Rules."*)

TIP Unless you choose Preserve Existing, the Liquid Page Rule setting in the Create Alternate Layout dialog overrides the settings applied to the individual pages.

Link Stories: creates a link between the text in the original layout (the "parent") to the text in the alternate layout. Then, edits done in the parent layout are sent to the other layouts. See the section "Linking Items" on page 129 for more information on using this feature.

Copy Text Styles to New Style Group: creates a separate style group of paragraph styles that are applied to the alternate layout text. This makes it easy to use different point sizes and leading for smaller or larger alternate layout pages. For more information on copying styles between alternate layouts, see the section "Linking Styles" on page 132.

Smart Text Reflow: automatically adds pages to the alternate layout if an overset is created. This is the same as turning on Smart Text Reflow in Preferences > Type Preferences.

Alternate layout master pages

As you create each new alternate layout, a new master page is added for that alternate layout. The pages created by the alternate layout are automatically based on the new master.

If you need to change the size of the alternate layout pages, don't select the document pages. Instead, select the master page with the Page tool and change the page size there.

TIP Choosing File > Document Size, and changing the size in the dialog, will only change the size for the first layout in the document, not for the alternate layouts.

Liquid Layouts

When you create alternate layouts, you'll often need to adjust the size, shape, and location of the elements to fit the size of the new pages. Liquid Page rules are settings that control how these elements change. Liquid Page rules help automate the process of producing alternate layouts, but each page will likely require some manual adjusting afterwards.

How much to expect from Liquid Layout adjustments

It is very tempting to expect that Liquid Page Rules will completely automate the process of creating an alternate layout. With just a click of the mouse, elements would resize, reshape, and rescale to create a perfect new layout.

Sadly, that is not the case. Even a simple layout with a few basic elements won't necessarily translate perfectly when the alternate layout is created with a particular Liquid Page rule. Think of the Liquid Layout feature as the starting point for converting one layout into another. But don't be disappointed if you need to tweak one or two elements in the new layout.

Applying Liquid Page Rules

You apply Liquid Page Rules using the menu in the Liquid Layout panel. Choose Layout > Liquid Layout to open the panel. This selects the Page tool in the Tools panel. If a page in your document is not selected, choose it with the Page tool. Then if you want to apply Liquid Page Rules to several pages, use the Pages panel to select more than one page, or apply the rule to the Master Page.

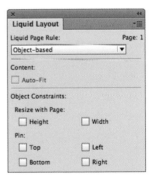

Use the Liquid Layout panel to choose a type of Liquid Page Rule.

TIP If you select a page in the Page panel, selecting the Page tool will also display the Liquid Page Rule menu in the Control panel.

The Liquid Page Rules are explained in the following chart.

Liquid Page Rule	Description	Comments
Off	Turns off the Liquid Page Rules for the page. Objects do not change their size or shape when the page size or orientation is changed.	
Scale	Objects are scaled as the page changes. Text and images are scaled to fit within the new frame size and shape.	This is the only rule that scales text and images.
Re-center	Objects do not resize but are kept in the center of the page. Whitespace is added around the objects.	No whitespace is added, and images are not affected if the page size is made smaller.
Object-based	Allows you to set whether the width or height of objects should change. Also allows you to maintain the relative space between the object's sides and the sides of the page.	Requires individual settings for each object.
Guide-based	Uses guides to set whether an object's width or height should change. The position of the guides controls which objects are affected.	Requires slightly less work than the Object-based page rule.
Controlled by Master	Uses the setting that has been applied to the master page governing the page.	Allows you to quickly apply a Liquid Page Rule to multiple pages in the layout.
Preserve Existing	Uses the setting that has been applied to each page.	Is available only in the Create Alternate Layout dialog (*see page 116*).

TIP You cannot combine different Liquid Page rules on the same page. Each page can have only one Liquid Page rule applied to it.

Using the Scale rule
The **Scale** rule is the easiest to apply and understand. When the Scale rule is applied to a layout, the objects shrink or expand to fit in the new page size and shape. This is similar to grouping the elements on a page and dragging with the Free Transform tool. Text point sizes change, as well as the size of images within frames.

Let's say you start with a vertical layout for the iPad. The size of the page is 768 x 1024. You then use the Scale rule to create an alternate layout for the vertical layout of the Fire/Nook. This page is 600 x 1024. The height of the page remains constant, but the width needs to shrink.

When the Scale rule is applied, the objects scale down to fit the new width, but that leaves a lot of whitespace at the top and bottom of the page. The Scale rule gives the best results when the source page and the new layout have aspect ratios that are identical or very similar.

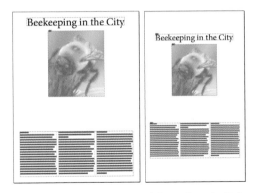

An example of how the Scale rule changes the size of objects from the iPad to the Fire/Nook. The point size of the text as well as the size of the image are reduced to fit the smaller width. However, there is whitespace added at the top and bottom of the layout.

Using the Re-center rule

The **Re-center** rule adds or removes space for the new page size without changing the size of the elements on the page. As space is added to the page, the objects are repositioned so they stay centered on the page.

This rule may create satisfactory results if the page increases in size. But if the page is made smaller, you need to set the objects far enough from the edges of the page so that they don't get cropped as the page edges move inward.

An example of what happens when the Re-center rule is applied to change a layout from iPad H to iPad V. Elements are centered horizontally on the page, but they extend vertically off the page because the Re-center rule does not change the size or shape of the elements.

Using the Guide-based page rule

The **Guide-based** page rule uses guides to designate which objects on the page should resize and in what direction. It uses special guides called Liquid guides.

To create a Liquid guide, switch to the Page tool and use the Page tool cursor to drag a guide out from the horizontal or vertical ruler. The Liquid guide appears. Liquid guides are indicated on the page by dashed lines (rather than the solid lines of Ruler guides). When you set a page to the

Guide-based page rule, the liquid guides and ruler guides display special icons that indicate which type of guide they are. Click the icon to turn a Liquid guide into a Ruler guide and vice versa.

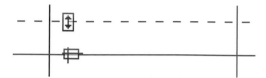

Selecting a Liquid guide (top) or a Ruler guide (bottom) displays the icons for the guides. Notice that the Liquid guide is dashed and the Ruler guide is solid.

Liquid guides control the objects they touch on the page. Vertical Liquid guides "lock" the vertical size of the object, and allow it to expand or contract from left to right. Horizontal Liquid guides allow the object to expand or contract from top to bottom.

Position the Liquid guide so that it crosses the items on the page that you want to resize. The Liquid guide does not have to cross through the center of an object; it only has to touch the object.

TIP Liquid guides can also be placed on the master for document pages. This makes it much simpler to apply the Guide-based page rules to multiple pages.

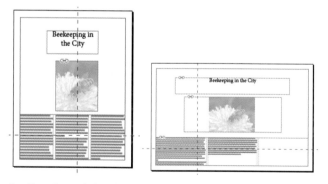

An example of how the Guide-based page rule changes objects from one orientation to another. In this case, the bottom text and image are set to change both their height and width, but the top text frame adjusts only horizontally, changing two lines to one.

Using the Object-based page rule

The **Object-based** page rule provides the most control over how items change as the page size changes, but it is also the most complex. Unlike the Guide-based page rule, which controls only the height and width of an object, the Object-based page rule lets you apply six adjustments to an object to control its location and size when the page size changes.

With the Page tool selected, choose Object-based from the Liquid Page Rule menu in the Control panel or the Liquid Layout panel. Then click the object that you want to control. The object-based controllers appear over the item.

On the top, bottom, left, and right sides of the object are the controls that govern whether the space between the edge of the page and the edge of the object is flexible or pinned. By default, the edge is set to flexible, displaying an open circle next to the edge of the object. This will allow the space between the object and the page edge to adjust when the page is resized. Click on the open circle to set the edge to be pinned, which will maintain the exact spacing between the object and the page edge. To set the edge to be flexible, click again on the small circle icon.

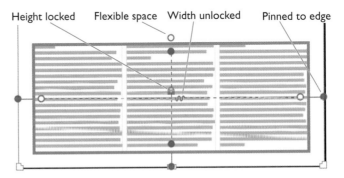

The Object-based page rule controls.

The edge controls let you keep an object in a specific area on the page. For instance, if you pin the bottom edge controller to the page, that edge of the object will maintain its position relative to the bottom edge of the page.

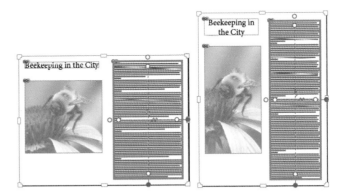

An example of how the Object-based page rule controls the change from one layout to another. In this case, the text frame on the right of the page is pinned to the bottom and right edges of the page. This allows the frame to adjust its height and width while maintaining the same distance from the bottom and right edges of the page.

TIP When you choose the Object-based page rule, the Liquid Layout panel shows check boxes for Resize with Page and Pin. These are the same controls as the icons that appear over and next to the object.

Inside the object are the controllers to set whether the width or height of the object adjusts. A spring icon indicates that the height or width can change as the page size changes. A lock icon indicates that the height or width is fixed.

The controls need to be applied to each object on the page, but instead of manually setting them for each object, for some layouts, you can apply the controls to objects on the master page. Those settings are then applied to the master page objects on the document page. If there are objects on the page that are not controlled by the master, you need to set those controls on the document page.

TIP You can set only two out of the three settings on each axis. For instance, if you pin the left and right edges to the page, then the width of the object has to be unlocked. If the height and top edge are locked and pinned, then the bottom edge has to remain flexible.

Tips for using Liquid Page Rules

Liquid Layout is a sophisticated feature, and setting the rules requires a certain amount of experimentation. Here are a few techniques we suggest for getting a handle on Liquid Page Rules.

- After you set a Liquid Page Rule to the page, resize the page by dragging one of the handles on the page with the Page tool. Watch how the objects resize and reposition. This will give you a better idea of how the Liquid Page Rule will affect the page. When you release the drag, the page snaps back to its original dimensions. Hold the Opt/Alt key as you drag if you want the page to resize when you release the mouse.

- Crop images so there is extra image outside the frame. If the image frame expands, this ensures that there is more of the image to be displayed. For instance, if the image frame expands horizontally, you will be able to fill that horizontal area without changing the visible area on the top and bottom.

- Choose Flexible Width from the Column menu (*covered on page 137*) so that text frames automatically add or delete columns as the page width increases or decreases.

- Use the Auto-Size settings for text frames (*covered on page 136*) so that the text frames expand or contract to fit the text.

- Use the Auto-Fit Content Fitting options for image frames (*covered on page 135*) to control how images expand or contract as the frame adjusts.

Using Layout Adjustment

Liquid Layout is not the only technique for adjusting page items when you change page sizes. InDesign also has a feature called Layout Adjustment. This is a very primitive technique compared to Liquid Layout, but some people are more comfortable with the simple controls of Layout Adjustment. If you work with layouts created in versions of InDesign before CS6, it's possible that Layout Adjustment will be turned on.

Layout Adjustment conflicts with Liquid Layout. You can't have both applied. To turn Layout Adjustment on or off, open the Liquid Layout panel. In the panel menu, select or deselect Layout Adjustment.

TIP You can also turn Layout Adjustment on or off in the Margins and Columns dialog.

Once you turn Layout Adjustment on, the Layout Adjustment dialog appears. This is where you control how objects change when the layout or page size changes.

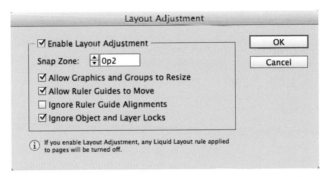

The Layout Adjustment dialog provides a simpler alternative to Liquid Layout adjustments.

Click the Enable Layout Adjustment to turn on the feature. Then choose any of the following options:

Snap Zone: This option sets how close an object needs to be to page edges or margins before it resizes as the guides or page change. A larger snap zone makes it easier for objects to resize.

Allow Graphics and Groups to Resize: Check this to allow objects not just to move, but to also scale up or down as the page or guide change.

Allow Ruler Guides to Move: This option allows guides pulled from the rulers to move along with any changes in the page sizes.

Ignore Ruler Guide Alignments: Normally, Layout Adjustment uses the alignment of objects against ruler guides to reposition or resize them. With this option checked, Layout Adjustment does not use ruler guides to move with changes in the page sizes. Use this if you have drawn ruler guides for purposes other than object alignment. For instance, if you've used a guide to check the baseline of text.

Ignore Object and Layout Locks: Check this option to apply adjustments to objects locked by the Lock command or on locked layers.

Using the Content Tools

When you create an alternate layout, elements from one page are automatically copied onto the pages in the second layout. You can also manually copy elements from one page or document to another using the Content tools — the **Content Collector**, **Content Placer**, and **Content Conveyor**. These give you more control over how objects are placed and linked.

Content Collector   Content Placer   Content Conveyor

The Content tools.

To collect content

Choose the **Content Collector** tool from the Tools panel. The Content Conveyor automatically appears. Unless you have previously collected content, the Content Conveyor is empty.

Click to select, and "collect," the item that you want to place elsewhere. A preview of each item appears in the Content Conveyor as it is selected. Click to continue to collect other items. Each item appears in the Content Conveyor.

You can also drag with the Content Collector to select multiple items. This creates a set. A number appears next to the preview in the Content Collector cursor, indicating how many items are in the set. All the items in a set are placed together on the page.

Number of items in set   Last item in queue

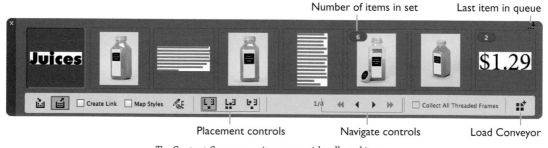

Placement controls   Navigate controls   Load Conveyor

The Content Conveyor as it appears with collected items.

TIP If you want to hide the Content Conveyor but still use the Content tools, press Opt/Alt-B. Press the keystroke again to reshow the Content Conveyor.

To place content

Once you have collected content, you can copy it to a different area of the page, on a different page, or even on a different document. The **Content Placer** is nested with the Content Collector in the Tools panel. You can also choose it from the Content Conveyor. But our favorite way to select the two tools is to tap the B key; this toggles between the two tools.

Move to the new area, page, or document where you want the content to be placed. A preview of the content appears in the cursor. If there is more than one item in the Content Conveyor, a number appears in the cursor preview, indicating how many items are in the Content Conveyor.

The Content Placer cursor with a preview of the placed item.

Click or drag to place the item. If you click, the item will be placed at the same size as its source. If you drag, the size of the area determines the size of the placed item. Dragged items are automatically constrained to the same proportions as the source. Hold the Shift key to change the proportions of the placed objects.

TIP You can quickly place items by selecting them, then choosing the Edit > Place and Link command. This loads the item into the Content Conveyor and switches to the Content Placer tool.

As you place content, the Content Conveyor highlights the next item in the queue for placing. You can skip an item by using the left and right arrow keys on your keyboard or the Previous and Next controls in the Content Conveyor. Click the escape (ESC) key on the keyboard to delete an item from the Content Conveyor.

TIP Items remain in the Content Conveyor until it is emptied or until you quit that session of InDesign.

To control the placement of items

You can control whether items in the Content Conveyor are kept or deleted as they are placed. Keeping items is helpful for those times you want to use them for placement elsewhere.

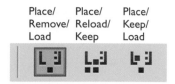

The Content Conveyor controls for how items are placed, removed, reloaded, and kept.

With the Content Placer selected, choose one of the following controls from the Content Conveyor:

- **Place/Remove/Load** places the content, removes it from the Content Conveyor, and then loads the next item. Use this setting when you want to place an item once and then delete it from the Content Conveyor.
- **Place/Reload/Keep** places the content on the page, keeps it in the Content Conveyor, and then reloads it for placement again. This is helpful if you want to keep placing the same item over and over.
- **Place/Keep/Load** places the content, keeps it in the Content Conveyor, and then switches to the next item. This setting is useful if you want to cycle through all the items in the Content Conveyor without deleting them.

Using the Load Conveyor

You can also add objects or pages to the Content Conveyor using the Load Conveyor dialog. This can be more powerful than using just the Content Collector tool. Display the Content Converyer by clicking on the Content Placer Tool. Click the Load Conveyor icon to open the Load Conveyor dialog.

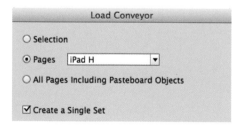

The Load Conveyor dialog lets you enter the contents of multiple pages into the Content Conveyor.

Choose one of the following:

- **Selection** adds any selected objects on the page. This automatically creates a single set if more than one object is selected.
- **Pages** allows you to choose specific pages in the document. If you choose Pages, you can then use the drop-down menu to choose All Pages or one of the alternate layouts in the document. You can also enter specific page numbers in the Pages field.

■ **All Pages Including Pasteboard Objects** adds the items from all the pages, including any items on the pasteboard. This is very helpful if you want to replicate all the items from one document in another.

Select the **Create a Single Set** check box to load all the items as a single group instead of as individual items.

Linking Items

The Alternate Layout feature and the Content tools allow you to create links between the original and copied items. This is very helpful if you make changes to the source item and want those changes applied to the duplicated items. You can create linked content with both alternate layouts and the Content tools, but the Content tools give you additional features.

Linking text and objects

To create text with links, select the **Link Stories** in the Create Alternate Layout dialog (*shown on page 117*). This links the text from the source layout to the alternate layouts. The **Create Link** setting in the Content Conveyor also sets a link between the text in the items copied into the Content Conveyor and the text in the placed items.

When you create links by choosing Create Link in the Content Conveyor, this creates two separate types of links — one for the item's content (text story or imported graphic) and another for the object itself (fill, stroke, size).

TIP The relationship between the source item and the duplicate is sometimes called a parent/child relationship.

Updating linked text

When text is linked, the frame for the copied text displays a link icon. When the source text has been modified, the link changes to a yellow alert triangle. Click the alert icon to update the alternate layout text to match the source text.

The yellow alert icon on the text frame on the left indicates that the source text has been modified. Click the alert icon to update the text. The link icon on the right appears.

You don't have to go scrolling through the document to find all the instances of the modified text. Open the Links panel. A yellow alert icon appears next to each text story. Double-click the alert icon next to each text story to update all the instances of that linked text. You can also hold the Opt/Alt key as you click one alert icon to update all the items at once.

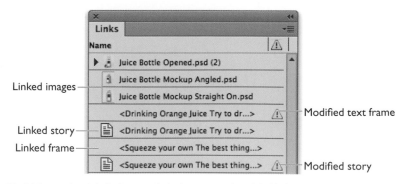

The Links panel with linked stories, linked images, and modified links. Double-click the yellow alert icons to update the modified text or objects.

Releasing linked text

There may be times when you want the linked text to be different from the source. In that case it's best to free the copied text from its linked state. Open the Links panel. The linked text is listed. Select the text and then choose Unlink from the Links panel menu. This removes the links between the text frames in the document. You can then modify either without any alert icons.

TIP You need to be careful if you edit the text that is still linked to its source. If you then update the child text to match the parent, those edits will be lost. This is why we recommend editing only the parent text, or unlinking the child text from the parent.

Once you have links for objects, you can change the parent object's size, shape, appearance, or other attributes and then have those changes applied to the child objects. For instance, if you change the stroke color of the parent object, you can then update the stroke color of the child object by simply clicking the yellow alert icon, either from the listing in the Links panel or on the object itself.

Setting the Links options

You can modify which attributes of a linked item are part of the parent/child relationship by using the Links Info dialog. Select the linked item (or items) and choose Link Options from the Links panel menu. Depending on which type of links you have chosen, either the **Link Options: Story** dialog or the **Link Options: Story and Objects** dialog appears.

The Link Options: Story dialog controls text stories that have been linked by using the Content tools or by creating an alternate layout. It allows you to set the following attributes:

- **Update Link When Saving Document** automatically updates a modified link when the Save command is applied to the document.
- **Warn if Link Update Will Overwrite Local Edits** shows an alert if the child story has been modified to be different from the parent story.

- **Remove Forced Line Breaks from Story** removes any forced line breaks when updating the parent and child text. This is useful when the lines in the parent text have been forced to rag a certain way but the child text lines don't need those changes.
- **Define Custom Style Mapping** lets you choose how styles with one name in a document can be mapped to styles with a different name. (*For more information on this command, see the section "Mapping Styles" on page 133.*)

The Link Options: Story dialog controls how linked stories are updated between the parent and child text.

If you have chosen the link for an object created using the Content tools, you have additional options in the Link Options: Story and Objects dialog. This lets you choose to **Preserve Local Edits while Updating Object Links**. The following attributes can be maintained in the child object, even when the link is updated to match the parent object:

- **Appearance** maintains the fill, stroke, effects, and corner effects.
- **Size and Shape** maintains the transformation settings for size, shape, rotation, scaling, and skewing of an object.
- **Interactivity** maintains the attributes for buttons, forms, object states, animations, and timing.
- **Frame Content** maintains the settings for items within a group, for HTML code, and for Media panel settings applied to movies and sounds.
- **Other** maintains the settings for text wrap, hyperlinks, text frame options, and object export.

TIP The Size and Shape option is automatically selected if you drag with the Content Placer tool when placing to create a custom size or shape for a linked object.

Link Options: Story and Objects

☐ Update Link When Saving Document
☑ Warn if Link Update Will Overwrite Local Edits

Preserve Local Edits while Updating Object Links

☐ Appearance   ☐ Interactivity   ☐ Others
☑ Size and Shape   ☐ Frame Content

The Link Options: Story and Objects dialog adds settings for objects. This lets you preserve local edits applied to the child object when updating it to match the parent setting.

Linking Styles

You may find that the text styles applied to a story in one layout or page need to be adjusted for an alternate layout or page. For instance, the point size used for a print layout may be much too small when used for a tablet device.

There are two ways to control how text styles (paragraph, character, table, and cell styles) are applied to linked stories. The first is using *style groups*, which are created for alternate layouts; the second is using *style mapping*, which is applied to items linked using the Content tools.

Using style groups

As mentioned in the section on creating alternate layouts (*see page 116*), you have the option to select **Copy Text Styles to New Style Group** in the Create Alternate Layout dialog. This copies the text styles from the first layout into a new style group folder. These second styles are then applied to the alternate layout. Once you have these two style groups applied to the linked text, you can modify the style definition in one group without changing the appearance of the text in another group.

The new style group allows you to have different style definitions depending on the page size of the alternate layout. Creating a new style group lets you modify the styles for a tablet device so the text is bigger. We have also seen situations where the horizontal layout for a digital magazine looks like the pages for a typical print magazine, with images, but the vertical layout has larger text without images. By creating new style groups, you can define the style for the horizontal layout with a certain point size and font while switching to a totally different size and font for the vertical one. Even though the two layouts have totally different styles, their content is still linked.

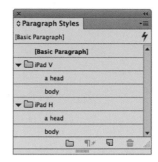

Style groups for each layout as they appear in the Paragraph Styles panel. Notice that the styles have the same name but are contained in different style group folders.

Mapping styles

Mapping styles creates a similar result to style groups, but it gives you a little more flexibility.

When you use the Content Conveyor to duplicate items, you have the option to map the text style names from one story to different style names in the document or in other documents. This is especially helpful if you use the Content Placer to duplicate a text story in a separate document that already has a set of styles.

The style mapping controls in the Content Conveyor.

Choose **Map Styles** in the Content Conveyor. Then click the **Edit Map Styles** icon. This opens the **Custom Style Mapping** dialog.

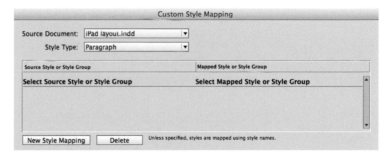

The Custom Style Mapping dialog without any styles mapped.

In the **Custom Style Mapping** dialog, use the **Source Document** menu to choose the document that contains the styles you want to map. Choose a style from the **Style Type** menu; the options are Paragraph, Character, Table, and Cell.

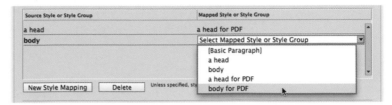

Source Style or Style Group	Mapped Style or Style Group
a head	a head for PDF
body	Select Mapped Style or Style Group

[Basic Paragraph]
a head
body
a head for PDF
body for PDF

New Style Mapping   Delete   Unless specified, st...

Choosing the mapped styles in the Custom Style Mapping dialog.

Click the **New Style Mapping** button. The Select Source Style or Style Group controls appear. Click the Source Style or Style Group control (on the left) and choose a style from the list. Then click the Select Mapped Style or Style Group control and choose the alternate style that you want mapped to the source. Repeat these steps for additional styles that you want to map.

TIP If you place items between documents, you need to switch to the second document in order to map to the styles found in that second document.

Comparing Layouts

As you work with alternate layouts, you will probably want to compare how one layout looks next to another. The Split Window feature makes that easy to do.

Split window

Unsplit window

Split window icon

Using the Split Window feature to compare two layouts.

Choose Window > Arrange > Split Window. This converts the document window into two parts. Each part displays a different alternate layout. Click a side to choose which alternate layout you are controlling. You can then use the Pages panel to choose different layouts for each side.

Choose Window > Arrange > Unsplit Window to restore the document to a single layout.

TIP You can also click the Split Window icons in the lower-right corner of the document window to split or unsplit the layouts.

Creating Flexible Image and Text Frames

With the exception of the Scale Liquid Page rule, the text and images within frames normally are not affected by changes in the size and orientation of pages. However, Liquid Page rules do change the size of the frames that contain the images and text. InDesign has several features for adjusting the text and images within frames as the page size changes. For instance, what happens to the text and images when frames become wider? How does the text rewrap to fit the new column width? What happens to the image inside a frame? This is where you can use the **Auto-Fit** options for images, **Auto-Size** for text frames, and **Flexible Width** for columns.

TIP These features are not limited to working with Liquid Page rules for creating alternate layouts; they can be useful when manually modifying frames.

Using the Auto-Fit options for images

Set the Auto-Fit options by choosing Object > Fitting > Frame Fitting Options. The Frame Fitting Options dialog appears. When you select the Auto-Fit check box, the Fitting menu automatically changes to the default selection, Fill Frame Proportionally. This is the most useful setting for most images.

The Frame Fitting Options dialog lets you control how an image is treated when the frame resizes.

With Auto-Fit applied, the vatious Fitting options will be applied to an image frame no matter how the frame is changed , whether in the process of creating an alternate layout or manually resizing the frame. For example, if the frame becomes wider, the image will be refitted within the frame to still honor the Fitting option, usually Fit Frame Proportionally.

Fill Frame Proportionally: This resizes the image so that it completely fills the frame without any distortion. The image will be scaled so that it fits the frame exactly either vertically or horizontally, but leaves no whitespace in the frame. The image will usually be cropped in one direction or the other. But no matter how much the proportions of the frame change, the image will always fill the frame completely.

Frame resized

Original image

The Fill Frame Proportionally option applied to a frame. When the frame is resized, the image is scaled and cropped to fill the frame. Notice that there is less image above and below the little girl.

Use the **Align From** reference box to set from what point the image fitting and cropping appears. Click the center point to keep the image centered in the frame.

Use the **Crop Amount** settings to specify the position of the image in relation to the frame. Positive numbers crop the image. Negative numbers add space between the image and the frame.

There are three additional Fitting menu options to choose how the image will automatically adjust.

None: Applies no resizing to the image.

Fit Content To Frame: This resizes the image to fit in the frame. If the proportions of the frame change, this setting will distort the image. We almost never choose this option.

Fit Content Proportionally: This resizes the image to fit in the frame while maintaining the proportions of the image. If the image and the adjusted frame have different proportions, there may be some whitespace within the frame.

Applying the Auto-Size text controls

One of the worst things that can happen to your cherished text is that some of it disappears in an overset. The Auto-Size controls help you avoid that problem as text frames change size, whether as the result of creating an alternate layout, or from simply typing more text into an existing text frame.

Select the text frame that you want to control. Choose Object > Text Frame Options to open the Text Frame Options dialog.

Click the **Auto-Size** tab to display its settings. Choose one of the following from the **Auto-Sizing** menu:

- **Height Only** expands the top-to-bottom dimension of the frame.
- **Width Only** expands the left-to-right dimension of the frame.
- **Height and Width** expands both dimensions of the frame. This can change the frame's proportions.
- **Height and Width (Keep Proportions)** expands both dimensions but keeps the original proportions of the frame.
- **No Line Breaks** is available when you choose Width Only. It prevents the text from wrapping to a second line.

Use the Alignment reference box to set from what point the auto-sizing is applied. For instance, click the upper-left corner to have a frame that resizes its height and width down and to the right. Click the top middle point to have a frame that resizes its height downward.

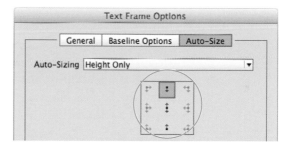

The Auto-Size controls of the Text Frame Options dialog let you choose which dimensions of the frame change and from which position in the frame.

You can also set **Minimum Height** or **Minimum Width** to maintain the minimum amount for either dimension. For instance, if the leading for your text is 12 points, a minimum height of 24 points ensures that at least two lines of text are always visible. This is very helpful to ensure that the frame doesn't collapse when the Liquid Layout adjustments are applied.

Setting Flexible Width columns

What happens to a multi-column text frame when you change the orientation of a page from vertical to horizontal? Depending on the Liquid Layout rules applied, the width of the frame may expand. This can make the columns of text too wide to read comfortably. One way to correct this is to increase the number of columns in the frame.

Instead of manually changing the number of columns when a text frame is resized, you can use the **Flexible Width** option. InDesign will adjust the column widths for you automatically.

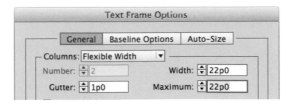

The Text Frame Options dialog set to the Flexible Width option for columns.

To set Flexible Width columns, select the text frame and choose Object > Text Frame Options. With the **General** tab selected, choose **Flexible Width** from the Columns menu.

The values in the dialog will initially be set according to the text frame you have selected. The number of columns of the selected frame will be in the grayed-out Number field. It's grayed out because this number will change as the frame width changes. The **Width** and **Maximum** fields are set to the width of the column(s) in the selected frame.

The value in the **Width** field specifies the minimum width a column can be as a frame is resized. As the columns become narrower, one will be deleted if the remaining columns are below this value.

The **Maximum Width** value specifies the width at which additional columns will be created within the text frame. As the frame width continues to expand, additional columns are created as needed.

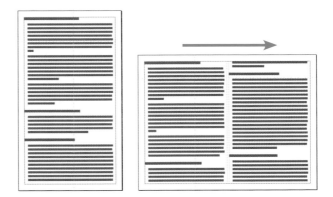

The Flexible Width option adds new columns as the width of a text frame increases.

TIP You don't have to start with multiple columns to apply the Flexible Width option. A text frame with one column can still expand to multiple columns.

Reflowable ePubs & HTML Export

In This Chapter

ONE OF THE MOST PROFOUND CHANGES in our digital world has been the rapid rise in the acceptance and embrace of ePubs, also known as eBooks, by the general reading public. Those stacks and shelves of beloved printed volumes, with their dog-eared pages, have been replaced by a single, sleek eReader that can contain hundreds of books and takes up almost no shelf space at all.

You can see the change anywhere you go — on airplanes and subways, in waiting rooms, and even at the beach. You're as likely to see a Kindle or Nook as you are a paperback or hardcover book. And as the years go by, ePubs make up an increasing percentage of publishers' sales. (Are you reading this book on paper or a screen?)

It turns out that another aspect of our digital world—viewing information on websites coded with HTML—has a lot in common with certain types of ePubs, called "reflowable" ePubs. Under the hood of every reflowable ePub is actually HTML and CSS code. In fact, many of the options for exporting InDesign files to reflowable ePub are the same as those for HTML. There are, of course, some significant differences, including the way in which the files are ultimately viewed, but understanding one format will help you understand the other.

Understanding Reflowable ePubs

An eBook is an electronic book — any book that can be read on a tablet device, desktop or laptop computer, or a smartphone. Technically, when we talk about an *eBook*, we're referring to all kinds of electronic books in different formats, which could include PDF or HTML files. But *ePub* is a *format* for eBooks, and in this chapter we'll specifically explore the features of the ePub format, and specifically, the "reflowable" ePub format.

The ePub file format is an open eBook standard developed by the International Digital Publishing Forum (IDPF). It was first established in 2007 and replaced the Open eBook standard.

An ePub file can be read on a variety of hardware ePub readers, like the Amazon Kindle, the Barnes & Noble Nook, or the Kobo eReader. It can also be read by software running on many platforms: the iBooks application on an iPad, iPhone or Macintosh computer; Adobe Digital Editions or Kindle readers on iOS, OS X or Windows; Aldiko Book Reader on Android devices; and dozens more.

Since the original ePub standards were established, ePubs have evolved a great deal. There are two distinctly different types of ePubs: the older, and more common format, called "reflowable" ePub, and the newer format, called "fixed layout." We'll discuss reflowable ePubs in this chapter, and cover fixed layout ePubs in the next chapter in this book.

What distinguishes reflowable ePub files is that the way they will be viewed on different devices varies greatly, because the text and layout adjust to the screen size available. Furthermore, most ePub readers allow the user to adjust the font family and size of the text.

Readers of ePub files can change the font family and size of the text. These are the options available in the iBooks application on an iPad.

Fixed layout ePubs, on the other hand, are more like print layouts, and similar to a PDF in the sense that the layout, along with the type size, is fixed.

Because a reflowable ePub file is so different from the fixed format you create in InDesign, it requires a steeper learning curve to create than does a file format like interactive PDF or fixed layout ePub, where the print layout is maintained. You'll need to learn what information you'll lose when you export a reflowable ePub file, along with how to prepare your file in InDesign before exporting.

InDesign Feature	Supported by Reflowable ePub
Animations	Not supported
Hyperlinks	Yes, all types
Buttons	Not supported
Forms	Not supported
Audio	Yes, MP3 files, EPUB 3 only
Video	Yes, MP4 files with h.264 encoding, EPUB 3 only
Bookmarks	Not supported
Cross-References	Yes
Page Transitions	Not supported

Reflowable content can display only one stream of text and anchored graphics, so it can be a mind-blower seeing your carefully laid out print-layout page seemingly fall apart the first time you export an ePub file from InDesign!

Like creating a
mini website

When you create an ePub file, it's helpful to visualize the process as being similar to creating a mini website. In fact, the settings in the EPUB - Reflowable Layout Export Options dialog are very similar to those in the HTML Export Options dialog, though they are organized a little differently. That's because an ePub file is a compressed package (a ZIP file) that consists of HTML or XHTML files, CSS (Cascading Style Sheets), and some XML files.

As on a website, the HTML indicates the structure, such as identifying a top-level heading. The CSS formats the heading to a particular size and weight and indicates how much spacing will appear on all sides of it. We'll give you an introduction to the structure of an ePub file, and a few basics about working with CSS, later in the chapter. (*see "Going Under the Hood," later in this chapter, on page 175*)

When InDesign creates a reflowable ePub file, it performs a conversion. It exports the objects in your document (text and graphics primarily) in a particular order. It translates the formatting that you have applied to text and graphics into a CSS style sheet. Other information you have added to the document, like a table of contents and *metadata* (information about the book), is exported as well.

Losing information
when exporting

Because you're converting from a fixed layout to a reflowable one and translating InDesign styles into CSS styles, you'll lose much of the InDesign document's formatting in the process of creating a reflowable ePub. Much of it can be retained by carefully preparing your InDesign file before ePub export.

Only the text and graphics on your document pages are exported. Any objects on your master pages, including headers, footers, and page numbers, are skipped during the export. (Since the pages of a reflowable ePub file will flow very differently on a laptop than on a smartphone, your fixed-layout page numbers won't be useful.)

In a print book, you might start each part of your front matter (title page, acknowledgments page, and so on) on a separate page. Because page breaks in your fixed layout will be discarded, they must be re-created in a different way when exporting an ePub.

The exact positions of unanchored images or sidebars will be lost. To be retained, they need to be anchored in the text.

And some kinds of InDesign formatting are lost altogether. Any InDesign-created objects (lines, frames with no content, and so on) will be ignored unless you rasterize them. Paragraph rules are discarded.

Can I read an ePub on my Kindle?

Sadly, the popular Kindle eBook readers don't support reading ePub files directly. They use a much simpler, HTML-based format called *MOBI* or *KF8*.

In the section "Converting to Kindle Files" on page 180, we'll tell you some ways to turn an ePub file created in InDesign into these formats. One of the best conversion tools is the free Kindle Previewer app.

Reflowable ePub workflow

Creating a reflowable ePub requires following a workflow to capture the maximum amount of information from the InDesign document. This requires you to establish the export order of the text and anchor any graphics or sidebar text. You also need to format your text with styles. You may need to make adjustments to graphics formatting and add information such as a table of contents or metadata.

After making the correct settings in the EPUB Reflowable Layout Export Options dialog, you'll preview your ePub file in an ePub reader. For example, you can download and use the free Adobe Digital Editions ePub reader.

It's a good idea at this point to do an initial *validation* of the ePub, which means running a version of EpubCheck or other validator. This ensures that it meets the requirements of the ePub specification required for your eBook to be published. We'll discuss this further in the section "Proofing and Validating ePubs" on page 173.

Prepare InDesign File → Proof ePub → Edit ePub (optional) → Validate ePub → Publish ePub

Creating an ePub file from InDesign requires following a series of steps. These include preparing your InDesign file, proofing, and validating the ePub before publication. You may also need to edit the CSS or HTML files.

Often, you'll discover that corrections need to be made in the InDesign file. For example, you may discover that some of your images aren't named correctly, which will cause validation to fail. Images need to be named as they would be in a website, so exclude spaces and certain special characters.

While InDesign is quickly improving on the quality of its reflowable ePub export, there may be times when other changes or corrections need to be made in an HTML editor. Some formatting, for example, may not come through correctly when viewed in an ePub reader. Not all readers will display your ePub in the same way. Other formatting — for example, paragraph rules — has to be added to the CSS style.

The last step is the final validation of your file. Once it passes, you'll be ready to publish your ePub, either through a bookstore or on your own website.

Creating Reading Order

As we described, you can't just use the ePub export function in InDesign and expect that it will instantly produce a perfect ePub. You have to set the order of export, style your text carefully, work with your images, and add some additional information to your document.

InDesign uses its own export order, which is rarely what you want! It looks at the objects in the document, starting with those closest to the left edge and beginning at the top, and then it exports objects farther down at the same vertical position. It then moves to the right, adding other objects from top to bottom.

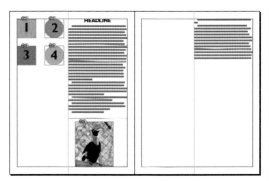

When the InDesign layout (left) was exported to ePub, InDesign's default export order kicked in, top to bottom and left to right. The results are shown in the Adobe Digital Editions ePub reader (right).

A story is considered a single object, and all text in the story is exported before going to the next object — even if this means going all the way to the last page of the document and then back to an earlier page. There can be only one text flow, so any sidebar objects or graphics that aren't anchored would be dumped at the bottom.

Layout order The most basic way to create a proper reading order when exporting to ePub is to use layout order. If you are building a very simple document, like a novel, you can simply create the objects (such as text frames) in the document in the order in which you want them exported.

This is the only method to use when the text in your document flows as a long story in one thread. The key is to anchor images and other blocks of text in the main story flow so they will appear in the anchored location. Anchoring objects is simple: Simply drag the blue icon on the object's frame to the location at which you want it to appear in the text. You may want to create an extra paragraph return so the object is anchored on its own line, depending on how you want the final object to be positioned.

In the General pane of the EPUB-Reflowable Layout Export Options dialog, choose **Based on Page Layout** under the Content section of the dialog. The document will be exported with the images and other anchored objects positioned in the main text flow.

XML structure   A second method uses InDesign's somewhat obscure XML structure panel. Select the **Same as XML Structure** option in the Content menu. Creating XML is beyond the scope of this book, but Cari Jansen describes this method in a blog post: http://carijansen.com/2010/09/18/moving-print-publications-to-epub/.

Articles panel   For complex documents with many elements, an easier and more intuitive method for ordering the content is to use InDesign's Articles panel (Window > Articles).

The empty Articles panel will give you instructions for what to do. Drag your first object onto the Articles panel, and you'll be prompted to name your article.

TIP You can name the article anything you like, because it is not exported to the ePub file.

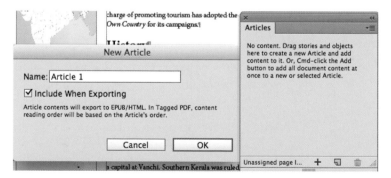

Drag one or more objects onto the Articles panel to begin establishing the export order for the article.

To set the export order, reposition the objects in the Articles panel in the order in which you want them to appear. This overrides InDesign's left-to-right, top-to-bottom order. You don't have to move any objects around on your pages or anchor any objects to set the order. This is a great way to keep your elements in their original position from a print layout. When you export, choose **Same as Articles Panel** in the Content menu.

You can create a new article by clicking the New Article button at the bottom of the panel. Having multiple articles makes it easier to move large groups of objects up or down the list. Any article that has **Include When Exporting** selected will be exported to the ePub file in the order in which it is listed on the panel.

TIP You can also hold down Cmd/Ctrl and click the + button at the bottom of the panel to add all objects in the document to the current article.

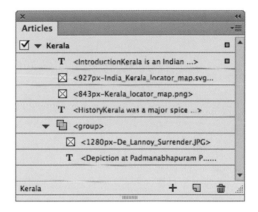

Once you have added text frames, graphics, images, and groups to an article, you can drag them up and down to rearrange them. You can delete an object by selecting it and clicking the Delete All Items (trash can) button.

Preparing Text

There are a few things you can do to prepare the text in your print file for successful export to ePub. Many of the good practices for your print layout — things like avoiding double spaces and paragraph returns, and applying paragraph and character styles correctly — are also good, and necessary, practices for ePub export.

Spacing text

There are are several kinds of spacing issues that you need to keep in mind as you're preparing your text for ePub export.

First, if your text is in separate text frames, InDesign will ignore the separate frames and export them in one text flow, with no space between them. For example, let's say you have a title page where the title text is in one text frame and the author name is in another text frame an inch lower on the page. In the ePub export, the author name will be immediately below the title, with no extra space between.

In order to create vertical space between text in separate frames, you need to apply Space Before and Space After as part of the paragraph style. It can be easier to see the result of these settings if you thread all the frames into one first, but it's not necessary to get the desired results.

In addition, keep in mind that double paragraph returns and double spaces are ignored by ePubs, and reduced to a single occurrence of the character. That means that vertical spacing with multiple returns will be ignored, as will horizontal spacing with multiple space characters.

Further, tab characters are ignored completely, so they can't be used for paragraph indents or tabular text. Set a First Line Indent in your paragraph styles instead, and convert tabular text to tables.

It's a good idea to clean up all these extra characters before you export your ePub, so you can see more closely what the result will be. You can use a series of Find/Change queries to do this or you can use a script that ships with InDesign that lets you clean them up in a single pass. See the sidebar that follows for more information on using this script.

Quick Clean Up

To rid your publication of double spaces and paragraph returns that are not exported to ePub, clean them all up at once by using a script that ships with InDesign: FindChangeByList. You'll find it by choosing Window > Utilities > Scripts > Application > Samples. It's listed under both AppleScript and JavaScript. It uses a support file, called "FindChangeList" text that can be edited to add additional queries.

To display the FindChangeList text file, find it in your Scripts panel, then right-mouse click and choose Reveal in Finder/Explorer. It can then be edited to add additional queries. Finding the right syntax can be a little tricky, but refer to the examples in the comments portion of this file. It's a great little time-saver!

Paragraph and character styles

Another important process in preparing your document for ePub export is consistently applying styles. While styles are always important in formatting text and objects consistently and quickly in InDesign, it turns out they are essential for ePub export. Creating and applying styles is a basic skill that we don't cover in this book, but if you need to learn how to work with styles, we recommend the *InDesign CC Visual QuickStart Guide (2014 release)* by Sandee Cohen.

When you export a document as an ePub file, InDesign's paragraph and character styles are converted into CSS. We can't stress enough that it is best practice to do all the styling in your document via paragraph and character styles. While we could get away with not using text styles in our print documents, that is no longer true when it comes to creating reflowable ePubs.

For example, if you have a Heading1 paragraph style that is defined as Minion Pro Bold 18/19 with 12 points of space before and 5 points of space after, all that information is converted into the CSS. The CSS can then be edited further, if necessary, to give you the desired result. If you don't apply a paragraph style, the text will not have a CSS style applied to it, and will not be formatted properly.

Some elements, like paragraph rules, do not get written into the CSS, and have to be coded in later, as discussed in "Going Under the Hood" on page 175.

```css
h1.heading1 {
    color:#000000;
    font-family:"Minion Pro", serif;
    font-size:1.5em;
    font-style:normal;
    font-variant:normal;
    font-weight:bold;
    line-height:1.056;
    margin-bottom:5px;
    margin-left:0;
    margin-right:0;
    margin-top:12px;
    orphans:1;
    page-break-after:auto;
    page-break-before:auto;
    text-align:left;
    text-decoration:none;
    text-indent:0;
    text-transform:none;
    widows:1;
}
```

When InDesign converts the Heading1 style definition into CSS that is applied to h1 elements with the class heading1, the font family, size, leading, and color become CSS properties.

It's also important to use character styles correctly, too. If you rely instead on "local" formatting, or overrides — formatting done with the Character panel instead of via Character Styles — you may get unexpected results in your ePub. Further, if you apply character styles, InDesign will write CSS for the style and you can better control its appearance if you decide to edit the CSS yourself.

If you have used local overrides instead of styles, such as creating bold text using the Character panel, select the **Preserve Local Overrides** option on the CSS panel of the EPUB-Reflowable Layout Export Options dialog, and InDesign will attempt to write CSS attributes to reflect the relative sizes, weights, and spacing. However, this will create very messy and difficult-to-edit CSS and again, is *not* recommended. Using paragraph and character styles consistently is definitely the way to go.

TIP If you're converting an InDesign-created ePub file to Kindle format, be aware that the Kindle may discard the local formatting that has been applied to paragraphs. Using styles in this case is critical.

Table and cell styles If you need to include tables in your ePub, it is essential to work with table and cell styles. Because tables are anchored by default, they'll usually appear in the correct location in your ePub export.

However, if you apply formatting to your table manually, you'll still get a table when you export to ePub, but virtually all the formatting will be missing. If you use Table Styles and especially Cell Styles efficiently, your ePub table can look very similar to or even identical to the version in your print layout.

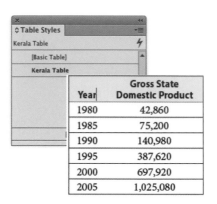

An InDesign table formatted using a Table Style, which includes several Cell Styles, (left) produces good results in the ePub export (right), maintaining the formatting.

Not all table attributes carry over, even if applied via styles. Alternating Strokes and Alternating Fills used in Table Styles are ignored. Instead, use Cell Styles to apply these attributes. Since a Table Style can be made up of Cell Styles, it doesn't mean you have to apply Cell Styles to each cell individually.

Cell styles applied to a table are converted into HTML table tags and CSS. Border color, border style, border width, and background color are retained. Be sure and have your Cell Style point to a Paragraph Style, so you can use the CSS to control the appearance of the text, too. Use cell indents to force the table in the ePub to have padding on the left and right; otherwise, it defaults to a column width of the longest string of text, with no padding between the text and the cell stroke.

Mapping styles to tags By default, InDesign maps all paragraph styles to HTML <p> (paragraph) tags. But HTML is designed to give semantic meaning to content. It's a good idea to leave the <p> tags for body copy, but it's a good idea to map your paragraph and character styles, and even object styles (discussed later in this chapter) to the correct HTML tag. For example, map a "header" paragraph style to HTML header tags —<h1>, <h2>, and so on. Mapping styles to tags creates cleaner CSS and HTML code that will make it easier to edit, and some eReaders rely on tagging to display text correctly.

You can map styles in the Export Tagging pane of the Paragraph Style Options dialog. Choose the paragraph style you'd like to tag (for example, "heading"), and choose Style Options from the Paragraph Style Options panel menu. In the Export Tagging pane, select between <p> and heading tags; for example, for a Heading1 (first-level head), apply an <h1> tag.

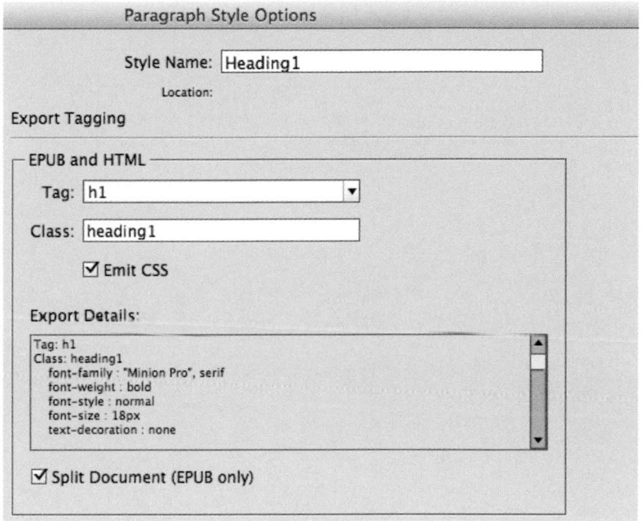

Mapping paragraph and character styles to HTML tags creates better code, making it easier to edit and more likely to be read correctly by ePub readers.

It's also helpful to apply the name of the paragraph style (with hyphens instead of spaces) to the class name. A class helps pinpoint which elements the CSS is being applied to. A tag can be associated with several different classes, each applied to different elements.

Similarly, character styles can be mapped to tags in the Character Style Options dialog. For italic, you would usually apply an <em> (emphasis) tag; for bold, you would apply the <strong> tag. Although entering a class name of *italic* or *bold* is not required, it creates clearer CSS. These are applied as classes in an HTML <span> tag to a range of words inside another tag.

TIP You can edit the mapping of all your paragraph and character styles at once by choosing Edit All Export Tags from the Paragraph Styles panel menu.

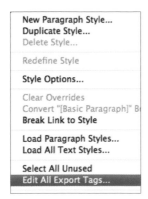

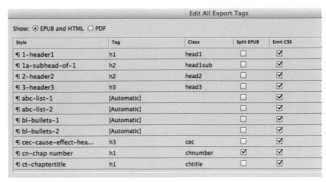

Use the Edit All Export Tags dialog to set tags and classes for all the paragraph styles in your document at once.

How much code do you need to know?

How much does a print designer need to know about CSS and HTML to be successful with reflowable ePubs? Whether you are a freelancer doing all your own work or working for a large company that has a several different players, you should *at the very minimum* know how to set paragraph styles, character styles, and object styles in InDesign.

If you're working on a simple book with a single story and no special graphics, you can simply apply paragraph and character styles and map them to tags.

But if you're going to work on anything more than the simplest of documents, you really should understand how those styles come through in CSS format, and you should at least be familar with what CSS looks like. Beyond that, you may either edit the CSS yourself or have a more experienced person do it for you. It is not trivial to become fluent in coding, but some designers and creative professionals choose to do so because they're interested in it or because their job requires it. See the section "Going Under the Hood" on page 175.

Preparing Graphics

Exactly how a graphic will appear in an ePub very much depends on the device on which you're viewing it. eBook readers vary widely in their device resolution and size of display, and some may not display in color. The traditional Kindle with the E Ink display or the Kindle Paperwhite will show the graphic only in grayscale. Other readers, such as the Kindle Fire and the iPad, can display beautiful color at full resolution.

The good news is that you don't have to prepare your graphics differently for different devices. Instead, format your graphics for the highest-quality device and let the other readers display them as best they can.

Anchoring graphics   As discussed earlier in this chapter, InDesign follows a specific layout order when it exports to ePub. Text frames that contain stories threaded to other frames are exported as one block of text. Just because a graphic is positioned in the middle of a story in your layout doesn't mean it will get exported in that location.

The Articles panel won't let you place a graphic *within* a story, so if you want a graphic to appear in the middle of a story, you must anchor the graphic within the story. This is true, too, for any other elements that are separate objects like pull quotes or sidebar frames.

When viewed with frame edges turned on, every frame has a little blue square (called an adornment) in the upper-right corner of the frame. To anchor a frame, drag that square to the location in the story where you'd like the frame to be anchored. Choose View > Extras > Show Text Threads to display a line connecting the bounding box of the frame and its anchor location.

TIP If you have trouble moving the object anchor point to a specific position, view the text in the Story Editor. The anchored graphic is represented by an anchor icon, and you easily drag it to reposition it.

There are differences in how the object is anchored when you drag the blue adornment into the text. If you drag the adornment without any modifier keys, the object gets anchored to that position in the flow of the text, but it doesn't change its position on the page. It might even keep its position on the pasteboard.

If you drag the adornment while holding the Shift key, the object moves into position in the paragraph. This is an inline anchored object. If you hold the Opt/Alt key while dragging the adornment, you open the Anchored Object Options dialog which lets you choose the settings for the object.

Once an image is anchored, it doesn't really matter where it's located on your layout; InDesign exports it according to the position where the image is anchored.

TIP If you need to change the position of an object, choose Object > Anchored Object Options, to display the Anchored Object Options dialog, or Option/Alt click on the anchor adornment as a shortcut to the dialog.

When you export an ePub from InDesign CC and later, choosing the Inline option for an anchored image creates some limitations on output. Inline images will ignore any custom Object Export Options that you set (discussed in the next section). Instead, use Above Line or Custom Anchored Object options when you export to ePub. You can keep images inline for your print layout, but change them before exporting. Applying an object style to your images, discussed on page 158, makes this a simple task.

Sometimes it can be easier to create an empty line and anchor the image in front of the return character. You can even apply a paragraph style to this return character, such as "anchored_graphic," and apply alignment, space before and space after attributes that will be honored when the file is exported.

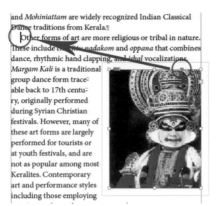

To anchor a graphic, drag the square to the location in the story where you want to anchor it (left). You can tell that a graphic has been anchored when it displays the anchor adornment. Choose View > Extras > Show Text Threads to display a line connecting the bounding box of the frame and its anchor location (right).

Object Export Options

The EPUB and HTML tab of the Object Export Options dialog lets you set custom rasterization options, alignment, and spacing for text frames and graphics on an object-by-object basis.

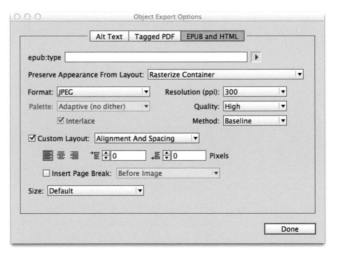

The Object Export options dialog lets you specify custom settings for how each image will be handled when exported.

Many of the settings in the Object Export Options are duplicated in the EPUB-Reflowable Layout Export Options dialog. The export options set the default settings for all of the graphics and rasterized objects in the ePub file. The Object Export Options dialog lets you customize those settings for individual objects.

There are many different reasons you may want to customize the export settings for objects. For example, if you have anchored objects drawn with InDesign's drawing tools, you'll need to rasterize them in order for them to export. Or, you may have an image that you want to export in higher resolution than other images in your file.

TIP The Object Export Options dialog is non-modal. That means you can leave it open as you apply custom settings to images — a great time-saver!

Here are the options you can specify in this dialog:

epub:type: If you are interested in creating semantically correct ePub files, this field offers a menu of various attributes that can be entered, such as Document Partitions, Document Divisions, or Titles and Headings, for example. While it can improve the accessibility of your ePub, depending on the reader, setting these attributes is not essential to successful ePub export.

Preserve Appearance From Layout: These options work in conjunction with some of the options in the Conversion Settings pane of the EPUB - Reflowable Layout Export dialog. The **Default** setting means the way the object will be handled on export is determined by the settings in the export dialog. (*See "Conversion Settings pane" on page 169.*)

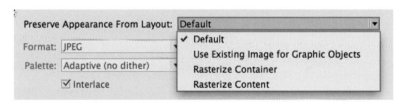

Preserve Appearance From Layout options control whether your images will be exported as they appear in your layout or not.

Use Existing Image for Graphic Objects is the best option to use when you don't want InDesign to sample or process your image. If you've optimized your image already, and imported it at 100%, you may want to use this setting.

Rasterize Container is the same as checking Preserve Appearance from Layout in the Conversion Settings pane of the export dialog, where both the frame and its content are rasterized. Note that frames containg text will be rasterized and the text will no longer be live text.

One of the most important uses of this option is to rasterize objects drawn in InDesign. Earlier in this chapter, we said that InDesign-created objects (lines, empty frames, and so on) are ignored during export to ePub. There are a couple of ways to overcome this limitation.

One way is to use the Articles panel to select the export order for page objects, any InDesign-created objects you include in an article will automatically be rasterized. They are turned into images at the default image resolution in the EPUB-Reflowable Layout Export Options dialog. If you group these objects before adding them to the Articles panel, they will be rasterized and included in the ePub as one object.

If you choose instead to anchor an InDesign-created object, you can use Rasterize Container the Object Export Options dialog to choose settings to rasterize the object.

Rasterize Content rasterizes what's inside the frame, but not the frame itself. This may yield different results than the appearance of the object in your layout.

Format: The various options for custom rasterization controls the image format used for images when exported. They are the same as those in the Conversion Settings pane of the EPUB-Reflowable Layout Export Options dialog, and are discussed later in this chapter, starting on page 169.

Custom Layout: This section controls options related to the spacing and position of an object. It allows you to specify if an object is aligned left, right or centered, and it allows you to float an object, which essentially creates a text wrap around an object.

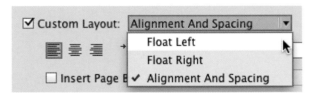

Create text wrap around an object using Float Left or Float Right alignment.

To wrap text around a graphic on the left or right, apply a custom Float Left or Float Right setting in the Object Export Options dialog. The command places the graphic where you have anchored it and maintains the text wrap you have applied.

Start by selecting an anchored graphic. Use the Text Wrap panel to apply the Wrap Around Bounding Box setting, with an offset from the text. In the EPUB and HTML tab of the Object Export Options dialog, select the Custom Layout check box and choose Float Right or Float Left from the menu on the right.

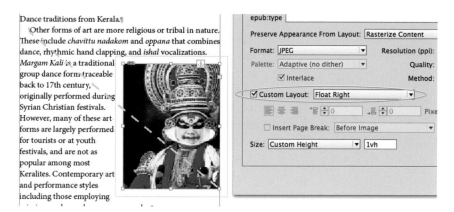

Other forms of art are more religious or tribal in nature. These include *chavittu nadakom* and *oppana* that combines dance, rhythmic hand clapping, and *ishal* vocalizations. *Margam Kali* is a traditional group dance form traceable back to 17th century, originally performed during Syrian Christian festivals. However, many of these art forms are largely performed for tourists or at youth festivals, and are not as popular among most Keralites. Contemporary art and performance styles including those employing mimicry and parody are more popular.

Kerala's music also has ancient roots. Carnatic music dominates Keralite traditional music. This

The Custom Layout option Float Right (top) creates a text wrap object in the ePub, as seen in Adobe Digital Editions (below).

You can also set whether you want space before or space after an object, by adjusting the values in those text fields. Check **Insert Page Break** to apply a page break before, after or before and after an object.

Size: InDesign now allows you to size objects using CSS, using settings under the **Size** menu. This is a really nice feature, because it means that an image, for example, can be one size in your layout for your print document, but you can set it to be a different size in your ePub export.

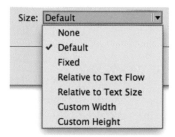

The Size settings allow you to customize the sizing of objects, including setting custom width and height.

These settings allow the CSS to size your images. Leaving the size at **Default** allows the image size to be controlled by its size in the layout, relative to the width of the text frame it's in, and the relative or fixed sizing controls set during export, discussed later in this chapter.

If set to **None**, InDesign will write no CSS for this object, and it will appear at 100% of screen width on the viewing device.

You can set the width to **Fixed**, which will not resize if the device screen size changes, or **Relative to Text Flow**, which will resize the object if the device screen gets larger or smaller. Your device screen size can change when you simply turn your device, your iPad or Kindle, from a portrait to landscape orientation. These are the same sizing controls available in the Object pane of the EPUB - Reflowable Layout Export Options dialog, and this allows you to set one object to be sized differently from the settings specified during export.

The setting **Relative to Text Size** will size the object by measuring the height of the object in points, then converting it to ems at 12 pts/em. Because the height is now in ems, if the reader increases the size of the text, the graphic changes size accordingly.

You can also specify a **Custom Width/Height** for the object size. Enter a value in cm, mm, inches, pixels or %. If you set one, the other is set to the same value. For example, you could set an image to size to 25% of its default size. The image can remain full size in your layout, but be resized when exported to ePub.

Object styles There are several good reasons to create and apply object styles to images and other frames in your layout before export to ePub.

Using Object Styles can help you apply custom rasterization and other attributes more quickly. Using Object Styles also helps create cleaner CSS and HTML code.

Use the EPUB and HTML pane of the Object Styles dialog to set Custom Rasterization options for images. For example, if you have some images that need to float left and others that need to float right, you can create an object style for each and quickly apply the custom rasterization, without having to open the Object Export Options dialog each time. Or you could have an object style that uses CSS width and height to resize a graphic in ePub export without it affecting its size in the InDesign layout.

Object styles can also control anchored object options. This means you can have an object style for images that would set them to inline for your print layout. But you can simply change the object style definition to above line or custom for ePub export. As discussed earlier in this chapter, inline graphics ignore any custom Object Export options applied, so it's best to set images to above line or custom anchored.

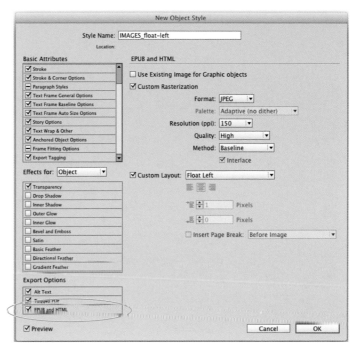

EPUB and HTML options in object styles allow you to set custom rasterization and positioning options for images.

Another benefit of using object styles is they help create cleaner CSS and HTML coding in your files. When you are including frames containing graphics or sidebars in an exported ePub, InDesign designates each of them with an HTML `<div>` tag. A `<div>` tag simply divides the HTML code into a section that controls more than one attribute for the elements and applies CSS styles to many elements at once. InDesign will attempt to include the frame formatting (background color; border weight, color, and style; and the spacing inside and outside the frame) into the CSS for the particular `<div>` tag.

However, by default InDesign gives each `<div>` a generic name, which makes it difficult to identify them. By applying an object style with a descriptive name, you can better identify it in the HTML code.

For example, you can define the Sidebar object style with a background color, a stroke width, and a stroke type and color, and then apply it to the sidebar frame. When you look at the HMTL code in an HTML editor, you can more easily identify the `<div>` because it contains the style name. The CSS reflects the size of the frame as well as the border style and width, the fill color, the padding (inset on text frame), and the margin (on text wrap).

Managing Document Pages

There are two kinds of table of contents (TOC) in an ePub. One, a *navigational* TOC, is "built-in" and is part of a device's eReader. All ePub files must have a navigational table of contents (TOC). The other, an *internal* TOC, is more like the TOC in the page of a book, and is optional.

Each eBook reader displays the navigational TOC in a different way. Shown here is the iBooks application on an iPad (left) and the Adobe Digital Editions application on a computer (right).

In the iBooks application on an iPad, the navigational TOC is displayed when you select the TOC icon at the top left of the page. In the Adobe Digital Editions application, the TOC is automatically displayed in the navigation pane on the left, although it can be turned off.

Creating a TOC

To create a navigational TOC in a relowable ePub, you need to create a TOC style. You can learn how to do this in the "Creating a Table of Contents (TOC)" section of Chapter 2.

When you export from InDesign, the default setting in the General panel of the EPUB - Reflowable Layout Export Options dialog is to create a navigational TOC from the File Name of your InDesign documents. This doesn't usually give very satisfactory results.

Instead select **Multi Level (TOC Style)** from the Navigation TOC menu. Select the name of your TOC style from the TOC Style menu. If you have created a book file, the TOC style must be defined in the style source document (*as discussed on page 163*).

Many ePub files also include an internal TOC, which looks like the TOC page in a printed book. In an ePub file, this is not required, but it provides readers with another way to find content if the navigational TOC is not visible.

In a printed book, the TOC would include page references that tell you where a section or chapter begins. Because there are no fixed-size pages in a reflowable ePub file, the internal TOC will not contain page numbers; instead, it will have hyperlinks to sections or chapters.

You create an internal TOC by placing the TOC you have created for your book onto a page of your document (*see Chapter 2*). If you have page numbers in the original layout of your document, they will not be included in the ePub file, but hyperlinks will be created that lead to the referenced section or chapter.

TIP An internal TOC is not required in an ePub file. However, if you later convert your ePub into a Kindle file, an internal TOC *is* required.

Creating a cover

Every ePub file needs a cover. There are two kinds of cover images. One is the internal cover image, which is the image that appears in your eReader device's library, such as the bookshelf in iBooks. The other image is that required by publishers to display the book in their bookstore. We're going to discuss options for creating the internal book cover. Check with individual publishers regarding requirements for cover images to display in various eBook stores.

TIP When you're designing a cover image, keep in mind that it's just a thumbnail. Covers that are fine on a bookshelf or on a website may not be readable in an ePub bookshelf. Avoid small type and images that can't be displayed well.

Regardless of which eReader your targeting, the cover image has to be a single flat image in a supported format, like JPEG or PNG. When you're exporting your ePub file, in the General pane of the EPUB-Reflowable Layout Export Options dialog, you can choose between None, Rasterize First Page, or Select Image.

The **Rasterize First Page** option both creates a correctly sized cover image and displays the cover as the first page in the ePub file. If you have a cover page in your InDesign file, and it is created from multiple objects, such as a backround image with type, group the objects first. Then choose Object > Object Export Options. On the EPUB and HTML tab, select the Custom Rasterization check box. When you select the Rasterize First Page option, the cover will be exported correctly. If you don't group the objects first, InDesign will just rasterize the first object it finds on the page, not the entire page.

If your InDesign file doesn't have a suitable cover page, you can choose **Select Image**, then navigate to a properly sized file in the correct file format, such as JPEG or PNG. In this case, the file doesn't have to be in your InDesign document, or even created in InDesign. Different publishers have different requirements for the size of cover images, so check the specifications first. For example, Apple recommends that the shorter dimension of your cover (usually the width) be at least 1440 pixels across. Apple also has a maximum size limit of 3.5 million pixels per image, so do the math and make sure your cover image is not too large.

The **None** option substitues a generic cover in the tablet library.

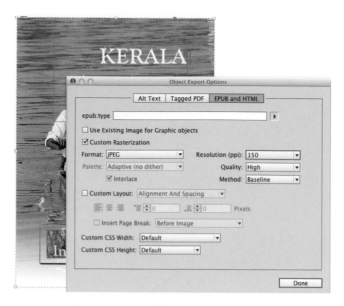

To create a cover page from your InDesign file, group all objects first, then set them to rasterize in the Object Export Options dialog.

Making page breaks

Just because you have started a chapter or a book title on a new page of your InDesign layout doesn't mean that those page breaks will export as separate pages in your ePub file. Most likely, they won't. To create a page break that will display in an ePub reader, you need to break your document into separate HTML files. There are several ways to accomplish this. Creating paragraph style-based page breaks: You can use paragraph styles to create page or section breaks in the ePub file. You can select as many paragraph styles as you like to create new page or section breaks in an ePub file. You can do it for an individual paragraph style by choosing the style in the Paragraph Styles panel and selecting Style Options. In the Export Tagging panel, select the Split Document (EPUB only) check box. When you export, in the Advanced panel of the EPUB Export Options dialog, choose Split Document > Based on Paragraph Style Export Tags.

TIP If you're selecting more than one style to apply a break to, choose Edit All Export Tags from the Paragraph Styles menu. This shows you a list of all the paragraph styles in the document. You can then select the Split EPUB check box beside each paragraph style for which the break should occur.

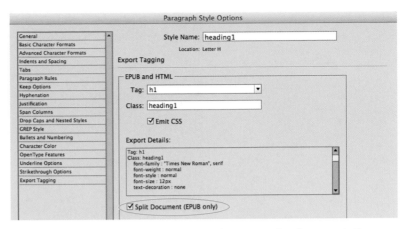

Use the Paragraph Style Options dialog to specify that a paragraph style automatically start a new page wherever it occurs.

Creating image-based breaks: If you want all the images in your document to start on a new page (such as illustrations at the start of each chapter), select the Insert Page Break check box in the Image pane of the EPUB Export Options dialog. Then choose Before Image, After Image, or Before and After Image from the menu.

If you want an single image to be on a separate page, select it and open the Object Export Options dialog. Select the Custom Layout check box and choose Alignment and Spacing from the menu. Then select the Insert Page Break check box and choose Before Image, After Image, or Before and After Image from the menu.

Working with book files: Breaks work differently in book files. When you export an ePub from a book file, each chapter automatically starts on a new page by default. This can be very helpful when designing your finished ePub.

Working with book files

When creating an ePub file from an InDesign document, you can either place your chapters in one document or organize your chapters in a *book* file. Create a book file by choosing File > New > Book. Use the + button at the bottom of the Book panel to add chapter files to your book. Place the chapters in the order you desire by dragging their names up or down in the book file list.

Click the column to the left of a file's name to make that file the *style source*. The style source is the file that contains the styles, swatches, TOC style, and other attributes that you want your chapters to share. You can synchronize your book's styles by deselecting all the chapter names (click in the gray area at the bottom of the panel) and choosing Synchronize Book. When the sync is finished, InDesign may display a message that the synchronization was successful and files may have changed. Save the individual files and choose Save Book from the Book panel menu.

Style source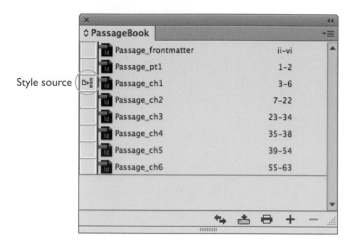

A book file can be used to number pages and coordinate the styles between documents. A book file can also be used to divide an ePub into separate sections.

TIP When using book files, you should place your TOC style and any metadata associated with the book in the style source document. Otherwise, it won't appear in the ePub file.

Adding metadata

It's important to include your book's metadata. Most eBook readers use information contained in the ePub file to display the book's title and author. You don't want the filename of the ePub to appear in a library as the book's title, which is what happens when there is no metadata. In some online eBook libraries, other metadata may be displayed as well.

To add metadata to your InDesign file directly, choose File > File Info to open the File Information dialog. At minimum, enter the book title, the author, a description, keywords, and copyright information.

You can add the necessary metadata to your InDesign file, or you can specify it when you export the file, using the EPUB-Reflowable Layout Export Options dialog. In addition, two pieces of metadata should be added in the export dialog: Publisher and Unique ID. These are described in "Metadata pane" on.

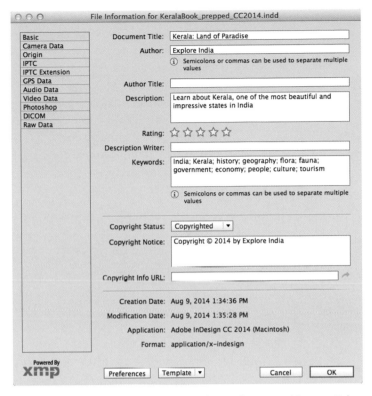

The File Information dialog lets you enter some of the metadata required for your ePub.

Export Options for Reflowable ePubs

As you can see, there's a fair amount of preparation work to be done before your InDesign file is ready for final export to ePub. Preparation steps include specifying the export order, preparing your text by applying text styles, anchoring graphics, and applying objects styles where appropriate. You also need to make decisions about what text will appear in your TOC, how you'll create a cover, and where you want new pages to appear in your ePub.

When you're ready to look at a rough proof of your ePub, you'll need to export your document to ePub format. You choose the settings to accomplish this in the EPUB-Reflowable Layout Export Options dialog. From the File menu, choose Export and select EPUB (Reflowable) from the Format menu at the bottom of the dialog.

General pane The General pane allows you to set the ePub version and choose settings for the cover image, whether or not to include a navigational TOC style, the export order, and how to split files.

Version: There are two choices in the Version menu. The version of the ePub standard that is used by most ePub readers is **EPUB 2.0.1**. This is the version that was ratified in 2007 by the International Digital Publishing Forum (the IDPF is the organization that develops and maintains the standards for the ePub format).

A second standard, **EPUB 3.0**, was approved by the IDPF in 2011. ePub 3.0 is based on HTML 5 and CSS 3. It adds extra features for including video and audio, exporting placed HTML and Adobe Edge HTML animations, and including external JavaScript. EPUB 3.0 has been adopted by most ePub readers such as iBooks, but is not yet universally supported by all eReaders.

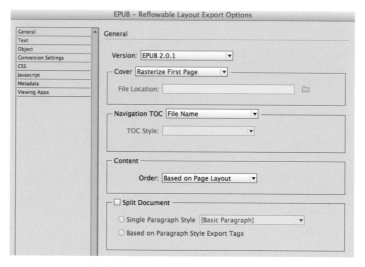

The General pane of the EPUB-Reflowable Layout Export Optons dialog is where you set the ePub version as well as options for the cover, TOC, and content order.

Cover, Navigation TOC, Content: We have discussed the decisions to be made about the **Cover** of your ePub earlier in this chapter, see "Creating a cover" on page 161. The **Navigation TOC** is discussed in "Creating a TOC" on page 160.

The basis on which the order of objects in your InDesign file will be exported is controlled by the **Content** setting and is discussed in the section "Creating Reading Order" on page 145.

Split Document: With this setting, you can specify that InDesign will split your file into separate XHTML files based on a specific style, by selecting **Single Pargraph Style** and choosing the style. Or you can use the settings you defined in setting Export Options in your paragraph styles by selecting **Based on Paragraph Style Export Tags**. See "Making page breaks" on page 162.

Text Pane The Text pane includes options for how Forced Line Breaks, Footnotes, and Lists are treated in the export.

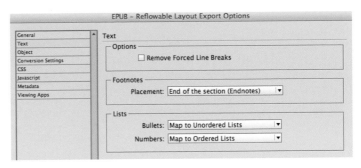

The Text pane controls how footnotes and lists are treated.

Options: By checking this setting, InDesign will remove all Forced Line Break characters, sometimes called soft returns, that have been inserted into the document text. These characters are often used by designers to create better-looking line breaks in text, but they are not honored by ePub readers.

Footnotes: If your document contains footnotes, this setting lets you control where they are positioned in your ePub. The **End of the section (Endnotes)** converts footnotes to endnotes. **After Paragraph** will position footnotes at the end of the paragraph that references them. **Inside a Pop-up (EPUB3)** is only for ePub version 3.0 export, and will position the footnotes inside a pop-up window. At the time of this writing, iBooks is the only eReader that supports pop-up windows.

Lists: In the **Bullets** menu, choosing the default option, **Map to Unordered Lists**, converts bullets created using InDesign's bulleted list feature into lists formatted with the HTML `<ul>` tag. Choose **Convert to Text** to format using the `<p>` tag, with bullet characters converted to text. This may work better when you're using custom glyphs, but will almost always require custom modification in the CSS file.

The **Numbers** menu works similarly to InDesign's numbered list feature. **Map to Ordered List** is the default and converts to formatting with the HTML `<ol>` tag. **Map to Static Order List** creates list items using the `<ol>` tag but assigns a `<value>` attribute based on the paragraph's current number in InDesign. **Convert to Text** uses the `<p>` tag and converts the number into text.

Object pane In previous versions of InDesign, there was one control area for images, the Images pane of the EPUB Export Option dialog. In InDesign CC 2014 and later versions, the image options are split between the Object pane, which controls the size and spacing of images, and the Conversion Settings pane, discussed next.

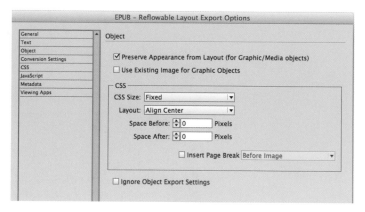

The Object pane controls the size and spacing of images.

Preserve Appearance from Layout: This is a good default to leave selected. It preserves all transformations or effects you have applied to your graphic in InDesign, including scaling, positioning or cropping the image within the container frame. If you deselect this, the graphic appears in the ePub as if you had just placed the image fresh into InDesign.

Use Existing Image for Graphic Objects: This option will export your images with no processing of any kind by InDesign. You might use this if you have optimized your JPEG or PNG images, placed them at 100%, and don't want any further processing done on them at export.

CSS Size: This option sets the sizing options for objects when they are exported. The default is **Fixed**, which means that your objects will not be resized, regardless of the screen size of the viewing device. The better choice is usually **Relative to Text Flow**, which means your image will resize relative to the width of the device your viewing it on, or if the orientation changes. If, for example, your image is 75% of the width of the main text frame on your InDesign page, it will resize in the ePub to be 75% of the text width on whatever device it is viewed on.

Layout: This option allows you to set the alignment of images, to **Align Center**, **Align Left** or **Align Right**. You may have set the alignment options already for certain images using the Object Export Options, but this will set the alignment for all images that don't have custom settings.

You can set all the images in your document to have **Space Before** or **Space After**, specified in pixels. And you can use **Insert Page Break** to have InDesign insert a page break **Before**, **After**, or **Before and After** an image. InDesign does this by inserting a break code that not all eReaders may honor, so be sure and test it first.

Ignore Object Export Options: If you have customized any of the settings for images in the Object Export Options dialog, selecting this check box overrides those settings.

Conversion
Settings pane

The Conversion Settings pane controls the file format and resolution used for converting images when they are exported. These settings are also available in the Object Export Options dialog, where they can be applied to individual images.

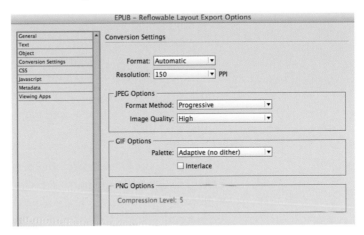

Conversion Settings control the conversion file format and resolution for images.

Format: Your choices are Automatic, GIF, JPEG, and PNG. If you choose Automatic, InDesign will decide on a case-by-case basis which format is best for which type of image. Most of the time, it will export images in the JPEG format, unless they are GIFs or PNGs to begin with. However, flat art from Illustrator is converted to PNG, maintaining its appearance.

If you choose **GIF**, you can select from the Palette menu under **GIF Options**. These options are **Adaptive (no dither)**, which creates a palette of colors from the image with no dithering; **Web**, for web-safe colors; **System (Win)** and **System (Mac)**, which uses a palette from those respective systems. Remember, GIF images use a limited palette of 256 colors. You can also choose **Interlace**, which allows the image to load progressively. Otherwise, the image will be blurry until it is completely loaded.

If you choose **JPEG**, you can select from the **Format Method** and **Image Quality** menus under **JPEG Options**. InDesign's default JPEG setting is at the High setting, which is usually a good compromise between quality and file size. The JPEG format is a lossy format that compresses images to reduce the file size. The JPEG format supports millions of colors in the file.

The **PNG** format is a lossless format that supports transparency. Choosing PNG for all your images could make your ePub file very large. Resolution (ppi): Choose an image resolution of 72, 96, 150, or 300 ppi for your graphics. 150 ppi is a good average choice.

CSS pane

CSS, or Cascading Style Sheets, control the appearance of the text in your ePub. See "Going Under the Hood" on page 175 later in this chapter. The

CSS pane in EPUB-Reflowable Layout Export Options contains options related to the CSS that InDesign writes out, and lets you add other CSS files as well.

In previous versions of InDesign, most of these options were under the Advanced pane. The Advanced pane options from previous versions have been separated into here and the JavaScript and Metadata panes, which are discussed next.

Generate CSS: Check this option to allow InDesign to generate a CSS file. You will usually leave this option checked on.

Page Margin: The settings here allow you to set margins, in pixels, on the top, bottom, left and right of your pages in the ePub. This is not the same as the margins in your print layout, because most eReaders have their own margins built into their screens. Be sure to check — and test — on the target device before increasing the values above zero.

Preserve Local Overrides: If you choose this option, any local attributes you've applied (such as italic or bold) will be included in the CSS. However, it is best practice to turn this option off, and to style your document cleanly with paragraph and character styles, as discussed earlier in this chapter.

Include Embeddable Fonts: This option will include any fonts that are embeddable in your ePub export. Some fonts contain code that allows them to be embedded. It's usually a good idea to leave this option on, so your ePub will look as close to your layout file as possible. If you've used fonts that are not embeddable, the text will display in the eReader's default font.

Additional CSS: Click **Add Style Sheet** to select an external CSS file that you want to have applied to your XHTML files. For example, you may have CSS files that have been written by someone else, or which help define elements that are part of a series of books. Delete any CSS files you no longer wish to export with your file by clicking the **Remove** button.

TIP You may want to hire a CSS expert to define a custom CSS style sheet. A custom style sheet will give you maximum control over how the ePub file displays. Any custom attributes will override matching attributes in the InDesign-created CSS file.

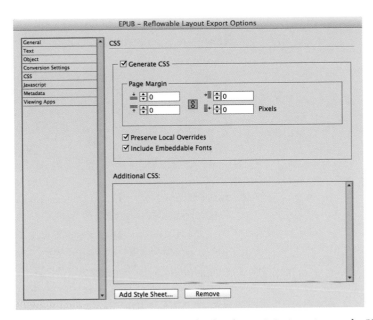

The CSS pane lets you control various settings related to the way InDesign writes out the CSS code, including those for page margins and whether or not local overrides are written out.

JavaScript pane   The JavaScript Options area works only with EPUB 3.0 files. Click **Add Script** to select one or more JavaScript files to use on export. JavaScript can be used to add various kinds of interactivity to your ePubs, but of course requires programming skills or access to them. iBooks is currently the only eReader that supports JavaScript in reflowable ePubs.

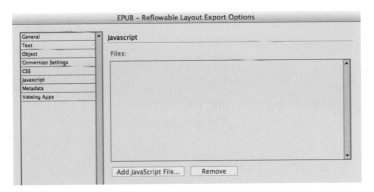

The JavaScript pane allows you to add JavaScript to your ePub.

Metadata pane   As discussed earlier in this chapter, certain information is required to be included in your ePub. You can add some of the information in the File Info dialog, as discussed in "Adding metadata" on page 164, or you can include it all at the time of export, using the Metadata pane. If you do not include this information, InDesign will fill it in for you. It's almost always better to include this information yourself.

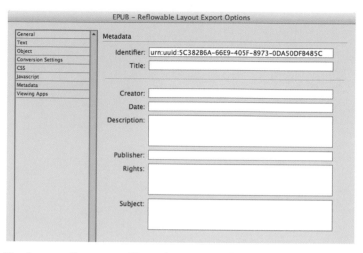

The Metadata pane allows you to add metadata to your ePub.

The only exception is the Identifier, which is a unique code InDesign generates for you. The Title is the name you want to appear in the library and across the top of the pages of your book in an eReader. If you don't inlude this title information, the filename will be used. The Creator information is usually the author. You may find some ePub sellers require the author to be inserted in the File > Info dialog. The Date information must be entered in a specific format, namely yyyy-mm-dd. The other information is optional, but it's a good idea to fill it in anyway.

When you open your ePub on a device, the only information that shows is the title. The other information is stored in the OPF file that is part of the ePub, and can only be viewed if the ePub is unzipped and viewed in an ePub editor. (*See "Going Under the Hood" on page 175.*)

Viewing Apps pane

In previous versions of InDesign, you could only preview your ePub in whatever application was set as your System default. The Viewing Apps pane lets you specify other apps to preview in as well.

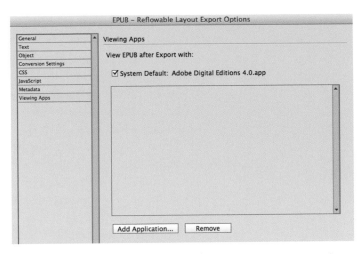

The Viewing Apps pane allows you to select the application you want to use to preview your ePub.

You may opt to use Adobe Digital Editions (ADE) as the default preview app. But there are other preview apps you can set as well, as discussed in the next section. You can even set an ePub editor as the preview app. If you have multiple apps listed, it's a good idea to just have one checked at any given time, as otherwise, all checked apps will attempt to open your ePub at once.

Proofing and Validating ePubs

As we've discussed, it's a good idea to set a preview app to preview your ePub. Proofing and validating your ePub file are critical steps in the ePub workflow.

Proofing ePubs   There are several ways to proof an ePub on your computer. The most common proofing application is the free Adobe Digital Editions. It can be installed on both Mac and Windows computers. Download it from http://www.adobe.com/solutions/ebook/digital-editions.html.

There are other options available for proofing your ePub:

- **iBooks** is Apple's ePub reader app for the iPad and iPhone, and is now available for Macintosh computers. If you are running OS X Mavericks or later, iBooks is installed automatically.
- **EPUBReader** is an add-on that allows you to view ePubs in the Firefox browser on either Mac or Windows. It can be found at https://addons.mozilla.org/en-US/firefox/addon/epubreader/.
- Readium is an extension for Chrome browsers that also works on Mac and Windows. It was especially developed for previewing

EPUB 3 files, but can also be used for EPUB 2.0.1 files. Download it from http://readium.org.

Validating ePubs The EPUB 2.0.1 and 3.0 standards were developed and are maintained by the International Digital Publishing Forum (IDPF). These standards are sets of rules for how an ePub should be interpreted so it can be viewed consistently by different ePub readers. .

The actual specifications are detailed on the IDPF website (http://idpf. org), but they are a bit complicated to read and understand. The rules are also built into an open source application hosted by Google (https:// github.com/IDPF/epubcheck), but you must be able to run Java from the command line and be familiar with command-line tools to use this tool effectively. Fortunately, there are easier solutions available, too.

For the less technically inclined, a much easier way to validate files that are 10 MB or less is the IDPF's online ePub Validator (http://validator. idpf.org/). Just click Choose File, browse to select your ePub, and click Validate. If it passes, you'll get the message "Congratulations! No problems were found in *<name of ePub>*." If there are errors, they will be listed by file and line number in the code, which can help you identify the problem. There is a 10 MB file size limit, however.

Two other good options for validating ePubs are:

- **EPUB-Checker**, available for Mac and Windows, is an application that will validate your ePubs. It has an easy-to-read list of warnings and errors. Download it from http://www.pagina-online.de/ produkte/epub-checker/.

- **epubcheck**, available for Macintosh only, is an app version of the Google ePub checker. Simply install it and drag and drop your ePub over it. If there are warnings or errors, they will be listed for you. Download it from http://www.mobileread.com/forums/ showthread.php?t=55576.

If you get errors or warnings, like the IDPF's online validator, these apps will also list the line number and sometimes the characters that are in violation of the IDPF standard. In that case, you'll need to go back to InDesign and make adjustments, then re-export your ePub, or you'll need to make edits in the HTML or CSS files directly.

It's a good idea to validate your ePub after you first export from InDesign, and before you are going to edit the HTML or CSS in a text editor, if that will be part of your workflow. That way, you can fix any problems before you introduce new errors in your editing. For example, you might discover that some of the filenames of the graphics you've placed don't follow the ePub standard because they include spaces or special characters not allowed in the HTML.

Going Under the Hood

If you set up your InDesign file properly, chances are you'll be able to export an ePub that looks exactly the way you want it to. Sometimes, however, you may need to edit the CSS rules or the HTML files to get the desired result. For example, InDesign does not export paragraph rules, so you may wish to add them by editing the ePub's CSS rules.

If you are not familiar with editing CSS and HTML, you may decide to find someone who can do it for you. Or, you may decide to jump in and learn it on your own. But even if you opt to have someone else adjust your CSS, it's a good idea to familiarize yourself with the basics.

Cracking open the ePub

If you need to edit the ePub, the first step is to uncompress the ePub file, which is really just a special form of ZIP archive. This process is quite easy in Windows. On a Mac, it is a bit more challenging but can be accomplished with the right tools.

Windows: On a Windows computer, start by putting your ePub file into its own folder. (You do this because you'll end up with several files, which you don't want loose on your Desktop.) Then change the file extension from .epub to .zip, and extract the file using any ZIP archive utility.

After viewing or editing the resulting set of files (discussed in the next section), you can use the same utility to recompress the folder into a ZIP archive. Then change the extension back to .epub.

Macintosh: On a Mac, the problem isn't in unzipping the archive, it's in correctly re-creating the ePub again after opening it. Because the Mac adds hidden data that makes the ePub invalid, you need to use a Mac-specific method. If you simply unzipped and then zipped the file, it wouldn't validate.

One method is to use the OS X Terminal commands to unzip and zip the ePub file. A much easier way is to use a free AppleScript, ePub Zip-Unzip. You can find this at http://www.mobileread.com/forums/showthread.php?t=55681. This tool uses the script to unzip the ePub, and after editing, to zip it again in a way that meets the ePub specification.

Understanding ePub structure

What do we see when we crack open the ePub? A structure of folders and files, including XML, HTML (or XHTML), and CSS files. You'll find the ePub's images in the Image folder.

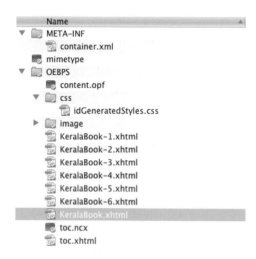

After unzipping the ePub file, you find a structure of folders and XML, HTML (or XHTML), and CSS files. Images are in the Image folder.

As mentioned at the beginning of the chapter, the ePub is like a mini website. Here's a short rundown on what the folders and files are used for, and whether you'd have any need to edit them.

META-INF folder: This usually contains only the *container.xml* file. It could also contain an *encryption.xml* file if you've embedded fonts. You won't need to edit the contents of this folder.

Mimetype: This is a single XML file that identifies the package as an ePub file. You won't edit this.

OEBPS folder: This acronym stands for Open eBook Publication Structure. This is where the good stuff lives. It contains the XHTML (or HTML) files that make up the text contents of the book: the CSS folder, which contains Cascading Style Sheets; the Image folder; and two XML files, *content.opf* and *toc.ncx*.

<chaptername>.xhtml: These files are like the body of the ePub file. They contain the structured XHTML code containing the content of your chapters or sections. You might edit these to change the content if necessary.

Image folder: This folder contains the optimized images exported by InDesign. You can view these in an image editor, such as Adobe Photoshop.

CSS folder: This folder contains the CSS files generated by InDesign as well as other CSS files you might have chosen to include when exporting the ePub. You'll edit these to change the formatting of your book.

TOC.ncx: This XML file is the navigational TOC that we described in the "Creating a navigational TOC" section on page 194. It displays in every ePub reader. Normally, you won't need to edit this.

Content.opf: This XML file could be considered the control center of the ePub file. It has three required parts and one optional part: The *metadata* contains information about your book, which we discussed in the section "Adding metadata" on page 164. Behind the scenes, InDesign adds the required "date" attribute to this part. The *manifest* is a list of the files contained within the ePub. The *spine* lists the order in which the text files should appear in the eBook. The optional *guide* describes the role that each XHTML file plays in the eBook. For example, roles could include title page, dedication, and so on. Apple iBookstore requires this section for ePub files submitted to it. Kindle files require changes to the *guide* section.

Working with an ePub editor

To work with the files described in the previous section, you'll need to use an ePub editor. You could use any text editor, but it's better to use one specialized for working with code. (Don't use the Mac's Text Edit, which adds rich text format information to its files. Also, don't use Microsoft Word, which saves files in a proprietary format. You want to save files in plain text format.) A good ePub editor will include the ability to search and replace code, will display tags with color coding, and will show the code in a structured way.

If you work with ePub files frequently, you may want to purchase a more powerful editor, like BBEdit for the Mac or Oxygen for Windows or Mac. These applications let you edit the ePub file without having to manually uncompress and recompress the file; the application takes care of that behind the scenes.

There are many ePub editors, and no agreement about which is best. Some can be used without unzipping the ePub first.

- **Adobe Dreamweaver** (Mac and Windows), is one of the best ePub editing tools, and, assuming you have a Creative Cloud subscription, you already have access to it. Simply download it via your CC subscription. Dreamweaver opens XML, HTML, and CSS files. It has a Code view and a Split view, and it quickly previews in a browser. It also gives you a menu of CSS properties that can be added to a style, so you can select the exact property you want, without having to remember how to type it in (www.adobe.com/products/dreamweaver.html).
- **Oxygen XML Author** (Mac and Windows) has all the characteristics of a good editor, but it also has some unique capabilities: It can open an ePub file on the fly, make changes to any of its files, validate it, and then just as easily save it as an archive again, with no unzipping/zipping required (www.oxygenxml.com/xml_author.html).
- **TextWrangler** (Mac) is the free version of BBEdit. It supports soft wrap of lines, multifile search, and GREP pattern matching (www.barebones.com/products/textwrangler/).

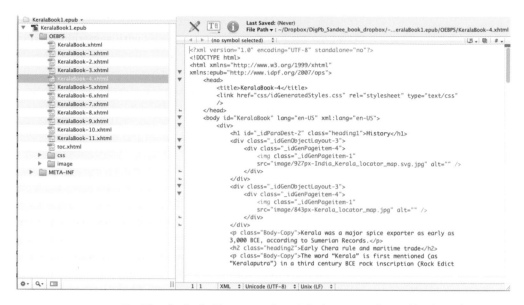

TextWrangler for the Mac is an excellent ePub editor. Notice that it adds color to the HTML tags and indents the text to make it more readable. It also has panels that show open files and recent documents.

Editing the ePub CSS

While you may use your ePub editor to edit any of the component files of an ePub, the ones you're most likely to need to edit are the CSS files. We can cover only a few basics about Cascading Styles Sheets and give a few examples. We'll point to a couple of resources at the end of this section.

CSS basics: As an InDesign user, you have an advantage because you're already familiar with using styles.

In CSS, a *style* is a rule that describes how to format a particular piece of HTML. In the CSS generated by InDesign, this HTML is most commonly a paragraph <p> tag; a heading tag, like <h1>; or a <div> or <img> tag for a sidebar frame or graphic.

For a <p> or heading tag, you set properties such as color, font-family, font-style, font-weight, and so on. For a <div> tag, you set properties such as margin, padding, text-align, height, and so on.

Types of styles: A *tag style* applies globally to an individual tag that has a particular semantic meaning (like the top level, <h1>).

A *class style* is attached to text or a tag. A class helps to pinpoint to which elements the CSS is being applied to. A tag can be associated with several different classes, each applied to different elements. Class styles are most similar to InDesign's paragraph styles. For example, a <p> tag might have the class bodytext associated with it.

The box model: A web browser thinks of an `<img>` tag or a `<div>` tag as a box. To a browser, any tag is a box with something inside it — for example, an image or text.

Surrounding the content are the properties that make up the box:

- **Padding** is the space between the content and the content's border. The InDesign equivalent is inset spacing.
- **Border** is a line that's drawn around each edge of the box. This is like the stroke on a frame in InDesign.

TIP Unlike InDesign's stroke, you can choose on which sides the border will appear in CSS. If you select the top or bottom edge, you would create what InDesign calls a paragraph rule. This is similar to applying strokes to table cells in InDesign.

- **Background-color** is what InDesign would call the fill. It extends to the border.
- **Margin** is what separates one tag from another. It's the space around the `<img>` or `<div>` tag. The closest InDesign equivalent is the space before or space after attribute.

Adding new properties to the CSS

Because InDesign doesn't export all style attributes, sometimes you have to edit the HTML in some way, or add properties to the CSS, using an ePub editor. For example, InDesign does not export paragraph rules to ePub. If you want your ePub headings to have paragraph rules, you'll need to add them to the CSS style definition.

Let's say we have an InDesign document that uses a Heading1 style with a paragraph rule above the text. This is an attribute that InDesign doesn't export.

In the CSS, you can edit the `h1.heading1` style to add other properties. To create the appearance of a paragraph rule, you can add the `border-color`, `border-style`, and `padding` properties, as well as individual `border-width` properties for the four sides.

```
orphans:1;
page-break-after:auto;
page-break-before:auto;
text-align:left;
text-decoration:none;
text-indent:0;
text-transform:none;
widows:1;
border-top-color: #0C9;
border-top-width: 3px;
border-top-style: dotted;
padding-top: 6px;
```

Flora and fauna

Much of Kerala's notable biodiversity is trated and protected in the Western Gha most a fourth of India's 10,000 plant spec found in the state. Among the almost 40 ering plant species (1272 of which are en Kerala and 159 threatened) are 900 speci medicinal plants.

Adding several properties to the `h1.heading1` style in the CSS restores the look of a paragraph rule.

Learning more about CSS

There are many sources of information to learn more about CSS. Elizabeth Castro has written several excellent books about the basics of creating eBooks. One of them — *EPUB Straight to the Point* — goes into great depth on CSS (www.elizabethcastro.com/epub).

Converting to Kindle Files

Amazon's Kindle devices hold the largest market share of eReaders in use today. Ironicially, Kindle devices do not support the standard EPUB format, but use a proprietary format instead.

Many of us wish that Amazon would adopt the EPUB standard, but so far they have insisted on staying with their Kindle file format. It was enhanced somewhat with the release of the Kindle Fire, but it still doesn't follow the EPUB specification. This means that if you want to offer your ePub on Amazon's Kindle Store, you'll need to convert your file to the Kindle format. The original Kindle format is called MOBI. With the release of the Kindle Fire, a new file format is supported, called Kindle Format 8, or KF8.

Amazon provides a tremendous amount of information about creating Kindle files on their Kindle Direct Publishing (KDP) portal. This is definitely the first place to get started. There, you can download the Kindle publishing guidelines and tools for converting your ePub to Kindle's format (https://kdp.amazon.com). You can simply sign in with your Amazon ID, or create one if needed.

The KDP portal contains all the tools and information you'll need to publish a book for Kindle. It is also where you will finally upload your file to be listed in the Kindle store.

There are three primary ways to create a Kindle file from an InDesign file. The easiest and often the best way is to download and install Kindle Previewer, which you can use to convert your ePub to Kindle format, as well as preview it. We'll discuss this method in the next section.

A second method is to download the free KindleGen application (available for Mac and Windows), which you can run from the command line to convert an ePub to a Kindle file. We don't use it, because we're not very fond of using command-line controls. Use the Kindle Previewer instead.

Finally, Amazon provides a Kindle plug-in for InDesign. The plug-in allows you to export your InDesign document directly to Kindle format. Unfortunately, as of the time of this writing, it is only updated for use through InDesign CS6. It gives pretty good results, but isn't available to InDesign CC or higher users. Also, if you intend to publish to other platforms, you'll need to create an ePub version as well, and it's much easier to do that first, then convert the ePub to Kindle format using Kindle Previewer.

All three tools can be found on the Kindle Direct Publishing portal at https://kdp.amazon.com/help?.

Using Kindle Previewer The Kindle Previewer was created by Amazon as a way to preview what an ePub would look like on the various Kindle documents. But it is also the best way to convert your InDesign document to Kindle format. Kindle Previewer will convert your ePub to KF8 format, with the older MOBI format embedded as well, so the file can be viewed on any Kindle device.

Start with an ePub exported from InDesign that you have previewed and validated. Open Kindle Previewer and select the ePub you wish to convert. Click OK, and Kindle Previewer will automatically open and convert the ePub file and then show it in the Previewer window.

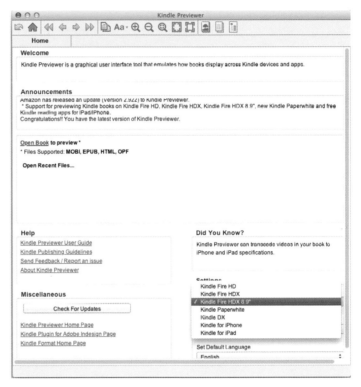

Use Kindle Previewer to convert an ePub exported from InDesign into the Kindle format. The converted file can be viewed on all Kindle devices.

When it's done, you can click on the progress bar to display a window of everything that's been done to the file. Much of it is information that you don't need to be concerned with, but it will also list warnings about any potential problems with the file. There are a few differences in requirements for a standard ePub. For example, Amazon requires that Kindle books have an internal TOC as well as the built-in navigational TOC. (*See "Creating a TOC" on page 160.*)

After conversion, Previewer will save the Kindle file in a new folder. From the Devices menu, you can choose from among various types of Kindles to preview what it will look like on each device. You'll usually see a big difference between the display on an old E Ink Kindle and the newer Kindle Fire devices.

After converting the ePub file to Kindle format, Kindle Previewer allows you to select which Kindle device to preview it in. Shown are the E Ink Kindle (left) and the Kindle Fire (right).

Evolving ePubs

The world of ePubs is changing and growing with great speed. What was true last week may have changed this week with new devices, evolving ePub standards, and even new forms of ePub files. Here's a glimpse of the changes coming to ePub files.

Changing standards

Since the ePub file format is controlled by the IDPF, their site is the best place to read about the evolving EPUB 3.0 specification, first approved in 2011 (http://idpf.org/epub/30/spec/epub30-overview.html).

Switching to this new standard has taken some time. Most vendors now support EPUB 3, but it remains important to test your ePub on any actual device on which you want to publish your book. And especially before you add multimedia (video and audio) and interactivity (using JavaScript), be sure and check the vendors' respective guidelines as to whether or not these are fully supported.

Fixed layout ePub

The EPUB 2.0.1 and 3.0 specifications are both for reflowable ePub, the kind described in this chapter. But there are books for which a reflowable format doesn't work such as children's books with lots of illustrations or coffee table art books. These require eBooks in which the pages are static and objects have a fixed position.

To get around this limitation, individual ePub readers (including iBooks, Kobo, and Nook) have initiated the creation of what is called a *fixed-layout ePub*. This is a fast-developing area, and the use of fixed layout ePubs has been greatly accelerated by the fact that InDesign does such a great job of exporting them. See the next chapter in this book, where we dicuss fixed layout ePubs in detail.

InDesign and HTML Export

As we mentioned earlier in this chapter, under the hood of every reflowable ePub is a mini website. Exporting InDesign files to reflowable ePub can be a pretty satisfying endeavor. With the right file preparation beforehand, and sometimes a bit of massaging afterward, the ePub export controls in InDesign produce a result that, well, looks like an ePub.

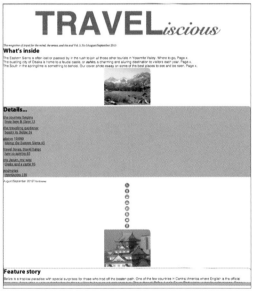

A print layout (left) and the resulting HTML export (right), with default export option settings.

With HTML export, the result most of us would like to have is a web page (or pages) that looks like our print layout, with columns, colors, and images in at least roughly the same position. Unfortunately, this is not what happens, and if you're reading this section hoping to learn about one-click conversion from your print document to a web page, read no further. It simply doesn't exist.

InDesign's HTML export feature is not designed to give you instant web pages. It is designed more to extract *content*, not page geometry.

But just because you can't create a finished web page, that doesn't mean HTML export from InDesign isn't useful. After all, moving the content from a print document to a web page is important, because so much information in print also appears on the web. And much of what we read in print today was created in InDesign.

How (and whether) you'll use InDesign's HTML export options really depends on your workflow and the skill level of your resources. You will almost never get a result that you can use on a website without extensive work on the code. So the question becomes, who will do the coding? Will you do it? Or are you part of a workgroup or organization that has designers to massage the basic files you provide?

TIP In order to export content from InDesign to HTML, you should have at least a basic understanding of CSS and HTML code, even if you are not coding the final website yourself.

Preparing Files for HTML Export

If you plan to export your content to HTML, there are a few things you can do to prepare your InDesign document. They are similar, though not identical, to the steps required for ePub export. Remember, a reflowable ePub is like a mini-website, with CSS and HTML under the hood. So many of the good practices for preparing a document for export to reflowable ePub are good practices for exporting to HTML, too.

First, if you are exporting your entire InDesign document to HTML, just as when preparing for reflowable ePub export, you need to establish the order in which the objects in your file will be exported. If your document consists of one long story thread, you will need to anchor all the images in position. If your document consists of many different stories and images, you'll probably want to use the Articles panel to order your document (*see "Creating Reading Order," on page 145*).

And just as with preparing files for reflowable ePub export, one of the most important things you can do to prepare for HTML export is to use styles in your document. Paragraph and character styles are absolutely essential; object styles and table and cell styles can be helpful, too, because they export code that can be used to format the HTML. It's also significant that InDesign allows you not only to style text, but to assign HTML tags to that text via the export tags that can be applied to styles. This helps form the content for use in a web page.

In organizations that have separate groups for print production and web production, simply adding export tags to existing InDesign styles is perhaps the single most useful thing a designer can do to create usable HTML code. The nice thing is that it does not burden the print designer with extra work, because once the tags are assigned to styles, the workflow for the designer is unchanged. For more information on using styles, see "Preparing Text," on page 147.

Images may need to be made part of the export order by anchoring them in text or by adding them to the Articles panel. In terms of optimizing them for use on a website, you can let InDesign convert them on export. However, most web designers strongly prefer to process images by using programs designed for the task of web optimization, such as Adobe Photoshop or Adobe Fireworks.

If you have just a few simple images or don't know how to use other programs to prepare images for the web, you can let InDesign convert the images for you. For more information on positioning graphics for export and using InDesign's image conversion, see "Preparing Graphics," on page 152.

Export Options for HTML

Although ePub export and HTML export are viewed quite differently, their export options are very similar. However, the EPUB - Reflowable Layout Export Options dialog is organized a little differently than the HTML Export Options dialog. This section discusses the few export options that are unique to HTML.

The table below shows which options that are available in HTML export are the same or similar for reflowable ePub, and where (which pane) in the EPUB - Reflowable Layout Export Options dialog the option is located.

General pane

The General pane of the HTML Export Options dialog contains settings for choosing the export content and format options.

HTML Export Option	Location in HTML Export Options	Location in Reflowable ePub Export Options
Export: Selection/Document	General	N/A
Content Order: Page Layout/XML/Articles panel	General	General
Formatting Options: Bullets/Numbers	General	Text
Copy Images: Optimized/Original/Link to Server Path	Image	N/A
Preserve Appearance from Layout	Image	Object

HTML Export Option	Location in HTML Export Options	Location in Reflowable ePub Export Options
Resolution (ppi)	Image	Conversion Settings
Image Size: Fixed/Relative	Image	Object
Image Alignment and Spacing	Image	Object
Image Conversion: Automatic/GIF/JPEG/PNG	Image	Conversion Settings
Ignore Object Export Settings	Image	Object
CSS Options: No CSS	Advanced	CSS
Embed CSS: Include Style Definitions/Preserve Local Overrides	Advanced	CSS
JavaScript Options	Advanced	JavaScript

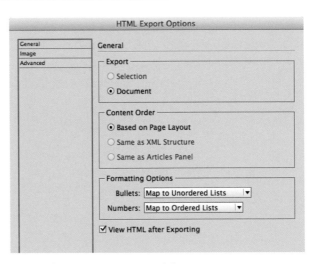

The General pane of the HTML Export Options dialog.

The **Export** area allows you to export either a **Selection** of your InDesign document or the entire **Document**. To export a selection of your document, click the objects or frames you wish to export first, then choose Selection. This option is not available for reflowable ePub export; you can export only your entire document to ePub.

The **Content Order** options control the order in which the objects in your InDesign file or selection are exported to the HTML file. These are the same options that appear on the Content Order menu in the EPUB Export Options dialog. **Based on Page Layout** will export objects in the order in which they appear in your layout, using the same top-down, left-to-right order used for reflowable ePub export. If your document uses XML markup, choose **Same as XML Structure**. You can also add objects to the Articles panel and use that for the export order by selecting **Same as Articles** panel. (*For more information on using the Articles panel, see the section "Articles panel" on page 146.*)

The **Formatting Options** area lets you control how bullet lists and number lists will be formatted. These options work identically to those in the Text pane of the EPUB-Reflowable Layout Export Options dialog (*see the section "Text pane" on page 167*).

Image pane
: The Image pane controls are, for the most part, identical to the image export options for reflowable ePub, though in the EPUB-Reflowable Layout Export Options dialog, they are divided into Object options and Conversion Settings options.

The Image pane of the HTML Export Options dialog.

The **Copy Images** menu options found in the HTML Export Options dialog, however, are not available for ePub export, but they are very useful for workflows that include HTML export.

Choose **Original** to simply copy your original images into their own Images subfolder on export. The Images folder will be included in the <*document name*>-web-resources folder that is exported along with your HTML file. You can then use a program such as Photoshop or Fireworks to optimize the images. When you choose this option, all other options in the dialog are dimmed.

The Copy Images: Original option creates a folder that includes all the images in your InDesign document.

Link to Server Path lets you enter a local URL (such as "/images") that will appear in front of the image file in the exported HTML code, with the link attribute displaying the path and extension you specify. This makes it easy to keep your images in a subfolder and optimize them in a program such as Photoshop or Fireworks.

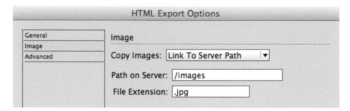

Link to Server Path lets you specify a path that will be written in the HTML code to point to your images.

If you choose **Optimized**, InDesign will optimize the images on export. All of the options in the dialog become available, and they are identical to those in the Conversion Settings pane of the EPUB-Reflowable Layout Export Options dialog (*see the section "Conversion settings pane" on page 169*).

Advanced pane   The Advanced pane controls the settings related to the CSS code that will be generated on export. Again, the options found here are similar to those found in the EPUB-Reflowable Layout Export Options dialog, including the option to have InDesign generate CSS with the HTML, or not. For those who know HTML and CSS, this is a good option, because a programmer can sometimes create cleaner code, based on the appearance of the website where the page will be viewed.

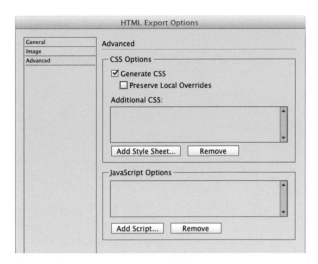

The Advanced pane of the HTML Export Options dialog.

You have the option to **Preserve Local Overrides**, which you usually want to have checked off. Click **Add Style Sheet** to link to an external CSS file. See the section "CSS pane" on page 169 for more information on these options.

As with ePubs, JavaScript can be added by clicking **Add Scrip**t under **JavaScript Options**, discussed in "JavaScript pane" on page 171.

Working with others   Even if you are responsible for exporting your InDesign files to HTML, there is a good chance you are passing those files on to someone who is ultimately responsible for getting them on the web. It's really important to coordinate with those who are posting the HTML pages, and make sure you are preparing your InDesign file in a way that will yield the best results, including setting the correct export order, and especially assigning the most useful export tags that can be used to mark the code efficiently and cleanly when InDesign exports your layout.

Fixed Layout ePubs

In This Chapter

The most common type of ePub is the one we wrote about in the previous chapter, "Reflowable" ePubs. This is the type of ePub that was established when the format was first defined back in 2007. And it is the format read today on most eReaders. This type of ePub is reflowable because the reader can change the font or type size, and completely alter the layout of the book.

When the EPUB 3 specification was developed in 2011, it included a standard for a new type of ePub, called "Fixed Layout." This ePub, as its name implies, follows the layout of a publication so that when viewed in an eReader, it looks pretty much the way it does on the printed page. While not supported by all eReaders yet, it's an exciting development for ePubs, allowing catalogs, children's books, photo books and other highly-designed publications to be viewed just as they were designed.

Understanding Fixed Layout ePubs

Fixed layout ePubs, often called FXL (eff ex ell) ePubs, share many characteristics with reflowable ePubs. Both are in the ePub format, which means they are like "mini websites" under the hood. They contain CSS, XML, and HTML or XHTML files in a compressed format. Both can be exported directly from InDesign CC 2014 or later.

We're going to talk about some of the other similarities between a reflowable ePub and a fixed layout ePub throughout this chapter. But first, it's important to understand the differences. If you haven't already, you may want to review the previous chapter in this book, which is all about reflowable ePubs (*See Chapter 5, "Reflowable ePubs & HTML Export"*).

Reflowable ePubs allow the reader to change the layout and appearance of pages. The type size and font can be changed by the reader. In fact, there is no notion of pages per se, because the end of a page on the screen may change if the font size is increased or decreased on the reader's device.

You can include images in a reflowable ePub, but you can't easily achieve complex layouts; images are usually within the flow of the text, and their position changes if the font size or style of the text is changed. On most eReaders, you can even change the background color of a page, or the color of the type on a page. You, as a designer, have lost complete control of your design.

Fixed layout ePubs, on the other hand, are more like a PDF file. They appear almost exactly the same as the page in your InDesign layout. Text, which is "live" text, and can be searched or bookmarked, and most importantly, appears in the exact font and size as it appears in your layout.

Images also appear exactly as they appear in your layout. You can easily have complex arrangements of images, include transparency, and even have text on top of images, things that are nearly impossible to achieve in a reflowable ePub.

If you're thinking that fixed layout ePubs sound pretty good, you'd be right. One thing to keep in mind, though, is that because this is a newer format than the older reflowable ePub, it is not as widely supported by the various eReaders on the market today.

The best support for fixed layout ePubs, especially those created from InDesign, is found with Apple's iBooks. iBooks has long supported advanced features, and their proprietary extensions to the EPUB 2 specifications helped form the fixed layout EPUB 3 specifications. iBooks supports almost all the features of fixed layout ePubs that are exported by InDesign.

iBooks

Apple iBooks offers some of the best support for reading fixed layout ePubs.

The Kobo eReader also has good support for fixed layout ePubs. And the Google Play Books app supports fixed layout as well. However, implementation of some features varies from device to device, and a fixed layout ePub that looks good and works well in iBooks may not work as well on other readers.

Amazon's KF8 format, for Kindle Fire and newer Kindle devices, has support for fixed layout ePubs, but in its own proprietary format. InDesign cannot currently export files to fixed layout for KF8. And unlike reflowable ePubs, which can be run through Amazon Previewer to convert them to Kindle files, a fixed layout ePub from InDesign can't be processed in Amazon Previewer and yield a fixed layout ePub that can be read on a Kindle.

Media and interactivity   Reflowable ePubs can include hyperlinks, and can also include audio and video files, though not all eReaders support them. Fixed layout ePubs, too, can include hyperlinks as well as audio and video files.

But fixed layout ePubs can be even more interesting, because they can include almost all of InDesign's interactive features, including buttons and object states (*See Chapter 2, "Interactive Tools."*) And most exciting of all, fixed layout ePubs can support animations created directly in InDesign! (*See Chapter 3, "Animations."*) These features can be previewed using the EPUB Interactivity Preview panel.

Fixed layout ePubs can include interactive features like buttons and object states, shown here on an iPad, as well as InDesign animations.

As discussed in previous chapters in this book, you can create buttons that do all kinds of wonderful things, like play movies, sounds, or link to a website. Buttons can also allow your reader to go from one state to another in an object state, or MSO. And InDesign's easy-to-use animation features can create all sorts of interesting movement and effects, limited only by your imagination.

Even Adobe's Digital Publishing Suite (DPS), discussed later in this book, does not currently support InDesign animations. You have to use Adobe Edge Animate or a third-party product to create animations for DPS apps.

This makes fixed layout ePubs a really attractive option for creating rich, interactive documents. It's currently one of the most flexible formats available by exporting your InDesign document. The following table shows which features are supported.

InDesign Feature	Supported/Not Supported by Fixed Layout ePub
Animations	Yes, except Smoke and Blur
Hyperlinks	Yes, all types
Buttons	Yes, except PDF Only actions
Forms	Not supported
Audio	Yes, MP3 files
Video	Yes, MP4 files with h.264 encoding
Bookmarks	Supported for TOC creation only
Cross-References	Yes
Page Transitions	Not supported

TIP The DPS Folio Overlays panel includes some additional interactive features, such as image sequences, scrolling frames and panoramas. These and other DPS-only features are not supported by fixed layout ePubs. However, we show how to mimic the look of the DPS slideshow in Chapter 3, "Animations."

FXL vs. PDF format

Fixed layout ePubs are very much like a PDF file. They contain pages that look just like your print layout, and include live, selectable text. But you may wonder why you should bother with a fixed layout ePub at all. After all, PDF files have been around for a long time. Almost everyone knows how to make one, and it's really easy.

One important reason to create a fixed layout ePub instead of a PDF file has to do with how you plan to distribute your book or publication. If you want to sell or distribute your book from your own website only, there's really no reason you can't just create a PDF file. However, if you want to sell your book in a public marketplace, like the iBooks store, you must make an ePub. While you can open a PDF file in the iBooks app on your iPad or computer, Apple does not accept PDF files for sale for its store, only ePubs.

Also, if you sell a book through a marketplace like the iBooks store, your publication will have a type of digital rights management (DRM) protection assigned to it. This means that one person who purchases the book won't be able to send it out (for *free!*) to all their friends. This is an important consideration if you want to make any money.

Another reason to create a fixed layout ePub from your InDesign file, rather than a PDF, is that fixed layout ePubs support almost all of InDesign's interactive features as well as animations, whereas PDF files do not. This means you can give your readers a much more engaging experience with a fixed layout ePub.

Fixed layout ePub workflow

The workflow for a fixed layout ePub is generally the same as that for a reflowable ePub. First you prepare your InDesign file. While this process for fixed layout ePubs is generally much simpler than the file preparation for reflowable ePubs, there are still a few things you need to check and keep in mind. (*See the next section, "Preparing Your InDesign File."*)

After making the correct settings in the EPUB-Fixed Layout Export Options dialog, you'll preview your ePub file in an ePub reader. For example, if you're on a Macintosh running Mavericks, you can use the iBooks app.

It's a good idea at this point to do an initial *validation* of the ePub, just as you would for a reflowable ePub, which means running a version of EpubCheck or other validator. This ensures that it meets the requirements of the ePub specification required for your eBook to be published. We discuss this further in the section "Proofing and Validating FXL ePubs" on page 206.

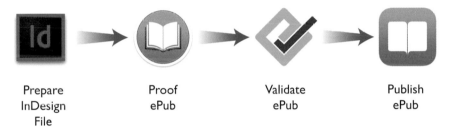

| Prepare InDesign File | Proof ePub | Validate ePub | Publish ePub |

Creating a fixed layout ePub file from InDesign requires following a series of steps. These include exporting your InDesign file, proofing, and validating the ePub before publication.

Sometimes you may find you have errors in your ePub. For example, you may discover that some of your images aren't named correctly, which will cause validation to fail. Images need to be named as they would be in a website, so exclude spaces and certain special characters.

Unlike reflowable ePubs, you'll almost never need to make other changes or corrections using an HTML editor. InDesign does a great job of exporting fixed layout ePubs, and it is usually simply a matter of exporting your InDesign file with the correct settings.

Once you're happy with the preview of your file, and it passes final validation, you'll be ready to publish your ePub, either through a bookstore or on your own website.

Preparing Your InDesign File

If you read the previous chapter on reflowable ePubs, you know that there is usually quite a bit of preparation required before you can export your InDesign print layout file to reflowable ePub. You may have to set the content order, anchor all graphics, and apply styles meticulously.

The good news about fixed layout ePubs is that there is very little — if any — file preparation required to export a fixed layout ePubs. About the only thing you need to be concerned with is that your document uses fonts that are embeddable in ePubs.

Fixed layout ePubs rely on CSS and HTML to create pages, but the code is very different from that used in reflowable ePubs. Fixed layout ePub relies on code that positions every item in a specific location, and basically "locks" the layout into place. We'll cover more specifics later in this chapter in "Going Under the Hood" on page 207. Fortunately, you'll rarely, if ever, have to edit this code.

Checking
document fonts

The one thing that you need to check in your InDesign document before exporting to fixed layout ePub is that the correct format fonts are being used. You must use OpenType or TrueType fonts in exporting to fixed layout ePubs. You can also use fonts synced from TypeKit, a free service available with your Creative Cloud subscription. Postscript Type 1 fonts cannot be exported, and will yield an error on export. Any Type 1 font in your document will be replaced with the eReader's default font.

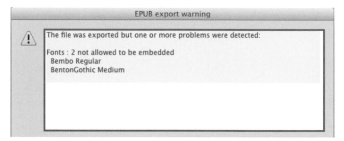

You cannot export Postscript Type 1 fonts to fixed layout ePub; doing so will produce an error message.

Thousands of fonts from TypeKit

If you've got a Creative Cloud subscription, you've also got free access to the thousands of fonts available from TypeKit. TypeKit is a service from Adobe that collects fonts from many different type foundries into a single library.

Instead of searching all over the web for a specific font or the right look, you can browse through TypeKit and use fonts without any additional costs! You can select as many fonts as you like, and sync them to your desktop for use in any Adobe application.

Of course, if you're creating a fixed layout ePub, you want to ensure that your readers see the same fonts that you used. Any of the TypeKit fonts that are licensed for desktop use can be embedded in digital publications such as fixed layout ePubs as well as PDFs and DPS apps.

It's pretty easy to check what format fonts are used in your document. Simply choose Type > Find Font. In the Find Font dialog, click the **More Info** button. At the bottom of the dialog you will see additional information about each font, including the Type of font. There's other useful information here, too, including the location of the font, indicating either the path on your hard drive or whether the font is synced from TypeKit.

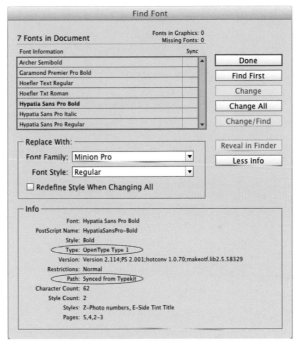

Use the Find Font dialog to check that all fonts in your document are OpenType or TrueType fonts. You can also use any font from TypeKit that is synced for use on the desktop.

Table of contents As discussed in the previous chapter, there are two kinds of Table of Contents, or TOCs, that can be used in a reflowable ePub. One is the *navigational* TOC, which is the TOC "built-in" to the eReader. This kind of TOC is required by many eReaders. The other is the *internal* TOC, which is more like the TOC page in a printed book or PDF, usually with links to pages listed. This TOC is optional for some eReaders.

Fixed layout ePubs can have both types of TOCs. The navigational TOC in a fixed layout ePub functions differently, though, than the TOC in a reflowable ePub. In a reflowable ePub, when you tap the TOC icon, you get a list of the chapters or sections in the TOC. But tapping the TOC icon in a fixed layout ePub gives you a thumbnail view of the pages in the document. You can optionally view a text list as well.

This makes sense for fixed layout ePubs because they are often highly visual books, and a visual TOC is appropriate. In fact, a navigational TOC is not required by iBooks and other fixed layout eReaders, so you don't even have to include one, unless your book is several pages, or you simply want to include it.

Tapping the TOC icon in iBooks displays a thumbnail TOC (left). Tap the list view icon in the upper-right corner to display a text version (right).

There are two ways to create a navigational TOC in a fixed layout ePub. Using a TOC style: Just as with reflowable ePubs, you can create a TOC style, and specify that as the navigational TOC when exporting. You don't even have to flow the actual TOC out on a page. You need only create the TOC style, and set it up correctly with the chapters or section titles you wish to be included. The text specified in the TOC style will display on the eReader when the list view icon of the TOC is tapped .

Using Bookmarks: Fixed layout ePubs also can use Bookmarks to create a navigational TOC. The Bookmarks will be displayed as the TOC when the list view icon is tapped.

The steps for creating a TOC and Bookmarks are discussed in detail in Chapter 2, "Interactive Tools."

To create an internal TOC, a TOC page that is part of the book with links to other pages, you simply follow the same steps you would use in your print layout: create a TOC using Layout > Table of Contents. When this page is exported to a fixed layout TOC, the links to each page will be active, and will take you to the appropriate page when tapped.

TIP We often put a button on pages inside the document that can take readers back to the internal TOC.

Export Options for Fixed Layout ePubs

Compared to reflowable ePubs, as we've discussed, there's not much preparation you need to do before exporting your InDesign file. You'll need to make sure your document uses only OpenType or TrueType fonts. You'll need to include a TOC, if you want one in your ePub. And you'll need to preview any interactivity or animation in the EPUB Interactivity Preview panel.

When you're ready to look at a rough proof of your ePub, you'll need to export your document to the fixed layout ePub format. You choose the settings to accomplish this in the EPUB-Fixed Layout Export Options dialog. From the File menu, choose Export and select EPUB (Fixed Layout) from the Format menu at the bottom of the dialog.

General pane · The General pane of the EPUB-Fixed Layout Export Options dialog allows you to set options for which pages you want to export, the cover artwork source, the navigational TOC and how you want spreads to appear.

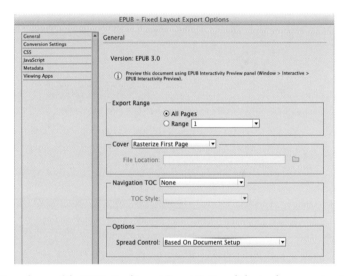

The General pane of the EPUB-Fixed Layout Export Options dialog is where you set options for the cover, TOC, and appearance of spreads.

Unlike the EPUB-Reflowable Layout Export Options dialog, there is no choice about which EPUB version you want to use. Fixed layout ePubs are part of the EPUB 3 specification, and cannot be EPUB 2.

Export Range: Unlike a reflowable ePub, but similar to printing files or exporting to PDF, you can choose to export all the pages in your document, or only a range of pages. Use the same syntax, such as "1-5," or "2-4, 5, 8."

Cover: These options are similar to those in the EPUB-Reflowable Layout Export Options dialog. The default is **Rasterize First Page**. This will use the first page in your InDesign file as the cover that appears in the eReader library. Unlike reflowable ePubs, you don't have to worry about grouping or setting any custom rasterization options. The cover, with all its objects, including type on top of images, will rasterize beautifully, with no extra steps required on your part.

You can also use an external file as your cover page. Select **Choose Image** and navigate to the file you want to use. It need not have been created in InDesign, although it could be. It should be sized the same dimensions as your InDesign document, and should be in either JPEG or PNG format. If you're using an InDesign file to create the cover, export it as a JPEG first, using Export > JPEG.

Choose **None** if for some reason you don't wish to have any cover for your iPub. In that case, apps like iBooks will add a generic cover.

A generic cover (left) and a custom cover (right) as they appear in the iBooks bookshelf.

Navigation TOC: We have discussed the decisions to be made about the Navigation TOC of your ePub earlier in this chapter, see "Table of contents" on page 199.

Options: This lets you set the options for **Spread Control**. Unlike reflowable ePubs in some readers, fixed layout ePubs do not change from a single-page display to a facing-page display when you change the orientation of your device. Facing page spreads give the illusion of a page turning when the viewer moves to the next page. They may also have a light gray line between the "pages" as if the book has a spine.

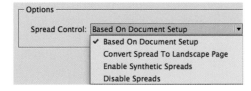

Spread Control determines whether your ePub will display as single pages or facing-page spreads.

Choose **Based on Document Setup** if your InDesign document is already set up the way you want it to export in the ePub. If your document is set up in facing pages, it will export in facing-page spreads. If your document is set up without facing pages, as single pages, then it will export as individual pages.

Choose **Convert Spread to Landscape Page** if you want the spreads in your facing page document to be combined and exported as a single landscape page.

Enable Synthetic Spreads will export your document as two facing pages in a spread, regardless of how the InDesign document is set up.

If you have a facing-page document and you want to export it as single pages, choose **Disable Spreads**.

Conversion Settings pane   The Conversion Settings for fixed layout ePubs are identical to those for reflowable ePubs. They are discussed in detail in the previous chapter, "Reflowable ePubs & HTML Export."

Since fixed layout ePubs are often graphics-intensive, you may not want them to export at the highest resolution possible, because some ePub stores may have restrictions on the maximum size of your ePub that can be submitted. Also keep in mind that the larger your ePub file, the longer it's going to take to download.

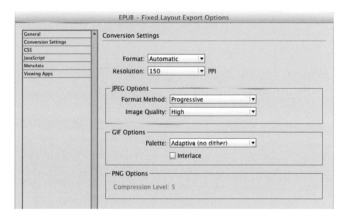

The Conversion Settings options are the same as those for reflowable ePubs.

CSS pane   This dialog is similar to that for reflowable ePubs. However, you do not have the option to prevent InDesign from exporting a CSS file. This is because with fixed layout ePubs, the CSS file controls the positioning of every object on every page. Without InDesign's CSS file, you'd have a big mess on your hands!

As with reflowable ePubs, you can add additional, external CSS files by clicking **Add Style Sheet**. Click **Remove** to detach external CSS files from being exported with the file. Adding external CSS files is not as common with fixed layout ePubs as it is for reflowable ePubs; most users will find there is no need to add additional CSS rules to what InDesign produces for fixed layout ePubs.

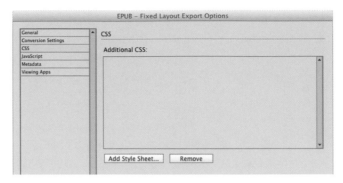

You can add additional CSS files, but you cannot prevent InDesign from generating the necessary CSS file for fixed layout ePubs.

JavaScript pane   As with reflowable ePubs, you can add JavaScript to your ePub, giving it additional features and capabilities. However, since many of InDesign's interactive features and its animations can be incorporated from InDesign, JavaScript files for those kinds of functionality aren't often necessary.

Click **Add Script** to select one or more JavaScript files to use on export, or **Remove** to remove the associated files.

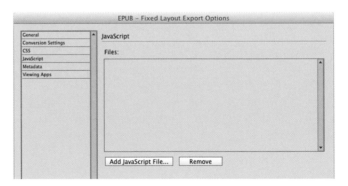

The JavaScript pane allows you to add JavaScript to your ePub.

Metadata pane   As discussed in the previous chapter on reflowable ePubs, certain information, or metadata, is required to be included in your ePub. This is true for fixed layout ePubs as well. You can add some of the information in the File Info dialog, or you can include it all at the time of export, using the Metadata pane.

This is important information for the successful publication of your ePub, so be sure and review the details on metadata, discussed in detail in the previous chapter, "Reflowable ePubs & HTML Export."

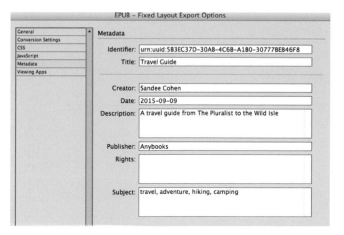

The Metadata pane allows you to add metadata to your ePub.

Viewing Apps pane   The Viewing Apps pane lets you set which application you want to use to preview your ePub. The default is that it sets whatever application is set in your system to preview ePubs.

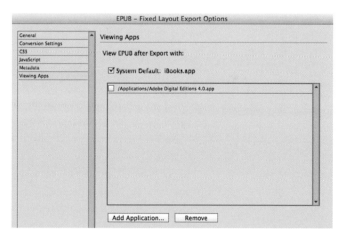

The Viewing Apps pane allows you to select the application you want to use to preview your ePub.

You may opt to use Adobe Digital Editions (ADE) as the default preview app. But there are other preview apps you can set as well, as discussed in the next section. If you're on a Macintosh running Mavericks OS or higher, you'll want to use the iBooks app to preview your fixed layout ePubs, as it can display all the interactivity and animations in the file. We discuss options for previewing your ePub in the next section.

Proofing and Validating FXL ePubs

As we've discussed in this and the previous chapter, it's a good idea to set a preview app to preview your ePub. Proofing and validating your ePub file are critical steps in the ePub workflow.

Proofing ePubs   There are several ways to proof a fixed layout ePub on your computer. If you've added media, interactivity, or animations to your file, you can preview these using the EPUB Interactivity Preview panel as discussed in Chapter 3, "Animations." But you should also proof your ePub using a proofing app, or even better, the actual device it will be viewed on.

The most common proofing application is the free Adobe Digital Editions (ADE). It can be installed on both Mac and Windows computers. Download it from http://www.adobe.com/solutions/ebook/digital-editions.HTML. In order to use ADE to proof fixed layout ePubs, you'll need version 4.0 or higher.

One of the best ways to preview a fixed layout ePub, if you are on a Macintosh computer and running the Mavericks OS or higher, is to use the built-in iBooks app. This gives excellent results and can preview media, interactivity and animations accurately.

If you're on a Windows computer or a Macintosh running an OS earlier than Mavericks, one of the best alternatives to ADE is the Readium extension for the Chrome browser. It does an excellent job of proofing fixed layout ePubs, including media, interactivity and animations. Download it from http://readium.org. Unfortunately, you can't set it as a viewing app and have it open automatically when you export your ePub, but you can deselect all the apps in the Viewing Apps pane of the export dialog, then simply open the exported ePub file from Readium running in your Chrome browser.

One of the best devices for viewing fixed layout ePubs is the Apple iPad running iBooks. You can "sideload" your ePub directly onto your iPad, and see exactly how it will look and function on an iPad. Simply launch iTunes, from either a Mac or Windows, and drag your ePub over the icon of your iPad in the iTunes sidebar. The ePub appears in the iBooks library where you can open it. This isn't as fast as previewing it on your computer, but it is a good idea to proof it this way before submitting it to be published.

Validating ePubs   The EPUB 3.0 standards, under which the format for fixed layout ePubs were specified, were developed and are maintained by the International Digital Publishing Forum (IDPF). These standards are sets of rules for how an ePub should be interpreted so it can be viewed consistently by different ePub readers. Just as with reflowable ePubs, you need to validate your fixed layout ePub to make sure that it meets these specifications.

There are several tools available that you can use to validate your ePub, including some ePub editors. Two good options for validating ePubs are:

- **EPUB-Checker**, available for Mac and Windows, is an application that will validate your ePubs. It has an easy-to-read list of warnings and errors. Download it from http://www.pagina-online.de/produkte/epub-checker/.

- **epubcheck**, available for Macintosh only, is an app version of the Google ePub checker. Simply install it and drag and drop your ePub over it. If there are warnings or errors, they will be listed for you. Download it from http://www.mobileread.com/forums/showthread.php?t=55576.

Validations options are discussed in detail in Chapter 6, "Reflowable ePubs & HTML Export."

Going Under the Hood

Just like reflowable ePubs, fixed layout ePubs are like little "mini websites." They are compressed zip files that, when expanded, contain CSS, XML and HTML files. With reflowable ePubs, you may sometimes have to use an HTML editor to add additional formatting or other information to your ePub. For example, InDesign does not export paragraph rules to reflowable ePubs, so you may need to add those in the CSS. The good news with fixed layout ePubs is that you will likely never have to crack one open and edit it in an HTML editor!

An unzipped fixed layout ePub shows a similar structure to a reflowable ePub but with some differences. There will usually be more XHTML files for a fixed layout ePub, since each page of the document is a separate XHTML file.

However, it's interesting to know how fixed layout ePubs are constructed, even if you'll never have to actually edit one. There are some important differences within the code that make fixed layout ePubs work, and work quite differently from reflowable ePubs.

Fixed layout files

If you unzip a fixed layout ePub, you'll find it contains the same basic components as a reflowable ePub, including a META-INF and OEPS folder containing a folder for CSS, images, and HTML or XHTML files. But if you compare the files inside a reflowable ePub to a fixed layout ePub, you'll see how the two formats differ.

For one, there can be many more HTML files in a fixed layout ePub than a reflowable one. A fixed layout ePub requires a separate HTML file for each page in the document. If your ePub has 50 pages, you'll end up with 50 HTML files. Reflowable ePubs don't have to be split into separate HTML files at all, but if they are, they are usually split by chapters, and certainly not by pages.

Understanding the viewport

Another difference is that fixed layout ePubs rely on special HTML position tags to create pages that look exactly like your layout. Every object is positioned within the area of each page. The page itself is defined in each HTML file by a tag called `meta name="viewport"`. This is the area, in pixels, within which each object on the page falls.

The viewport size is taken from the document size of your InDesign file. If your document is, for example, letter-size, the viewport will be 612 px x 792 px.

```
<head>
    <meta charset="utf-8" />
    <meta name="viewport" content="width=539,height=666" />
    <title>YogaBookx66-1</title>
    <link href="css/idGeneratedStyles.css" rel="stylesheet" type="text/css" />
</head>
```

The meta name="viewport" tag defines the page size in a fixed layout ePub.

Positioning objects

Another characteristic of the HTML files in a fixed layout ePub is that every object on the page is positioned relative to the position in the viewport. In fact, InDesign positions each word in a specific position. It's very precise, but it makes for some very scary code!

TIP Because fixed layout ePubs set absolute positioning for each word also allows fixed layout ePubs to have a separate narration sound track that highlights each word as it is spoken. These are very popular for children's books. Unfortunately, InDesign does not support creating these "read-along" books.

```
                              <p class="A-Spread-Intro-3-lines ParaOverride-1"><span id="_idTextSpan025'
class="CharOverride-7"
style="position:absolute;top:767.23px;left:0px;letter-spacing:1.75px;">Start </span><span
id="_idTextSpan026" class="CharOverride-7"
style="position:absolute;top:767.23px;left:455.06px;letter-spacing:1.68px;">your
</span><span id="_idTextSpan027" class="CharOverride-7"
style="position:absolute;top:767.23px;left:899.83px;letter-spacing:1.58px;">day
</span><span id="_idTextSpan028" class="CharOverride-7"
style="position:absolute;top:767.23px;left:1264.39px;letter-spacing:1.57px;">off
</span><span id="_idTextSpan029" class="CharOverride-7"
style="position:absolute;top:767.23px;left:1554.6px;letter-spacing:1.75px;">right
</span><span id="_idTextSpan030" class="CharOverride-7"
style="position:absolute;top:767.23px;left:2005.88px;letter-spacing:1.68px;">with
</span><span id="_idTextSpan031" class="CharOverride-7"
style="position:absolute;top:767.23px;left:2417.89px;letter-spacing:1.68px;">some
</span><span id="_idTextSpan032" class="CharOverride-7"
style="position:absolute;top:767.23px;left:2922.72px;letter-spacing:1.87px;">standing
</span><span id="_idTextSpan033" class="CharOverride-7"
style="position:absolute;top:767.23px;left:3703.28px;letter-spacing:1.26px;">yoga
</span><span id="_idTextSpan034" class="CharOverride-7"
```

"Start your day off right with some standing yoga," is the text (shown in black) in the InDesign document; each word is positioned precisely relative to the viewport area.

This kind of precise positioning means that line breaks and other typographic characteristics are maintained in the ePub. And, as we've mentioned, it allows the text to be "live," so that you can do things like select it and look up words in the eReader's dictionary, if that feature is supported.

In addition to the position from the position from the edge of the viewport, objects also have the notion of a stacking order. This is specified with the z-index tag. This makes it possible, for example, for text to be positioned on top of an image correctly, unlike reflowable ePubs which would require you to group and rasterize type on an image in order for it to display properly.

A stacking order also allows you to place objects that you don't want to be seen, such as the controls for audio files, behind images.

The Future of Fixed Layout ePubs

Up until now, fixed layout ePubs had to be described as simply as a file format that could be read and sold by iBooks. And since iBooks by no means has 100% of the tablet eReader market, there didn't seem to be a completely compelling case for using them. All that has changed with the release of InDesign that adds interactivity as well as animations to fixed layout ePubs. Suddenly the fixed layout format has a very exciting future.

Alternate to PDF and DPS

Fixed layout ePubs offer a terrific alternative to PDFs — especially since it is difficult to find a PDF reader on a tablet that supports all the interactivity in PDFs. Also, since PDFs have never been able to display InDesign animations, fixed layout ePubs have an additional feature in their favor.

Fixed layout ePubs offer a compelling alternative to DPS apps. Fixed layout ePubs have audio, video, buttons, and multi-state objects that can duplicate many of the features in DPS apps, though there are a few features that DPS apps have, such as images sequences, or scrolling frames, that fixed layout ePubs don't. But on the other hand, fixed layout ePubs go one step beyond DPS apps from InDesign. Fixed layout ePubs can easily incorporate InDesign animations!

It also makes fixed layout ePubs much easier to export and distribute than apps. Apps require becoming an Apple or Google developer, and then involve a rather involved technical process to get the app approved and published. When it comes to publishing fixed layout ePubs, the requirements for uploading a book to iBooks or Amazon are not nearly as rigorous, or expensive, as the requirements for publishing an app.

Further, for self-publishing, all a user has to do is create the ePub and distribute it by email, ftp, or host it on a company's server. This is the most common request we see on user forums; people want a way to make interesting presentations and distribute them to co-workers, schoolteachers, friends, or family members. Fixed layout ePubs fit that bill perfectly.

What needs to be done

There is one cloud on the fixed layout ePub horizon: the lack of widespread support among the various eReaders on the market. We believe, however, that will change with the ability of InDesign to easily create fixed layout ePubs, complete with rich, interactive features.

All in all, we are very enthusiastic about working with fixed layout ePubs. We hope you have caught some of our enthusiasm.

Tablet Apps

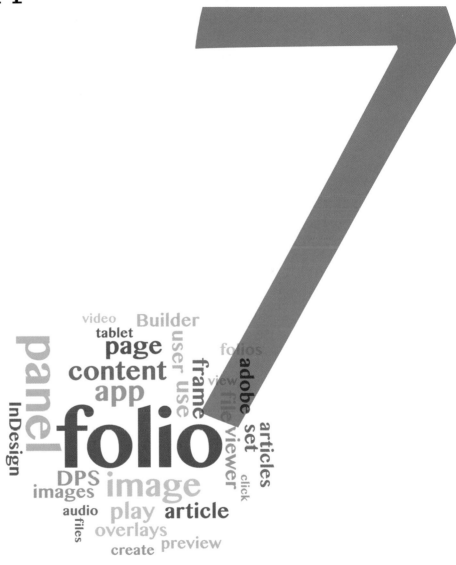

7

In This Chapter

WHEN STEVE JOBS INTRODUCED the iPad on January 27, 2010, the world expected another game-changing product from Apple. But few of us in publishing and design realized how profoundly it would change *our* world. Today, an increasing number of books and magazines are read with a swipe and a touch onscreen. Buttons and video are becoming as commonplace as editorials and classifieds. And the experience of reading is becoming much more immersive and engaging in the process.

InDesign is at the center of the publishing world for print, so it's not surprising that it has now become a key part of publishing to mobile devices, including the iPad and other tablets, as well as the iPhone and other smartphones. With InDesign and Adobe's complementary set of tools, known as the Digital Publishing Suite, a whole new world of design and interactivity has opened up to designers and publishers everywhere.

Understanding Digital Publishing Suite Apps

Several third-party products allow you to convert your InDesign layouts to tablet apps for the iPad, Kindle Fire, or Android tablets. Most of them provide a set of free plugins for creating interactive overlay elements, along with some means of converting your documents into an app. Our focus in this chapter will be on Adobe's solution: the Digital Publishing Suite, also known as DPS.

Adobe's Digital Publishing Suite consists of several components that allow you to bring your InDesign layouts to life as applications on tablets that include the iPad, the Kindle Fire, Android tablets such as the Samsung Galaxy, and even the iPhone (though our focus throughout this chapter will be on tablet apps). The DPS tools allow you to add interactive features to your publication and to publish your file in a *folio* format that allows it to be shared and published to tablet devices.

DPS tools   DPS tools include several components. Each plays a different part in the process of creating a tablet app from your InDesign layout. These components are installed automatically with Adobe InDesign CC:

- **Folio Overlays panel:** An InDesign panel that allows you to add interactive features for tablets to your layout.
- **Folio Builder panel:** An InDesign panel that allows you to assemble your files into *folios,* which are files that can be previewed and shared.
- **Adobe Content Viewer (desktop version):** A computer application that allows you to preview your content and interactivity as it will appear on a tablet.

Related components include:

- **Adobe Content Viewer (device version):** A free application that can be installed on your iPad (or other tablet) allowing you to preview your content and interactivity.
- **Folio Producer:** A browser-based application for organizing your folio files, adding metadata, and publishing folios to a development server.
- **DPS App Builder:** An Adobe AIR application that allows you to build an app that you can submit to Apple's App Store, the Google Play store, or Windows store.
- **Additional Tools:** For some DPS users (Professional and Enterprise subscribers), additional analytics and account administration tools are available. (See the next paragraph for information about these subscribers.)

To publish your app and make it available for sale requires that you sign up for one of Adobe's DPS subscription programs. At the highest and most expensive level are the Professional and Enterprise Editions, which are geared to mid-sized or large publishers. These allow publication of an unlimited number of single-issue folios or subscription-based, multi-issue folios (such as monthly magazines) on the iOS and Android platforms. Both also provide analytics, or data, about the folio downloads, with the Enterprise Edition offering additional services, such as the ability to create in-app custom navigation.

DPS Single Edition, which allows you to publish single-issue folios only, offers a more affordable entry point for small and individual publishers. In fact, the Single Edition is available to all Adobe Creative Cloud members for free. InDesign CS6 users who do not subscribe to Creative Cloud have to pay a per-publication license fee of $395. The Single Edition is currently available for iPad only.

No matter which version you use, the tools and the creation process are the same. And anyone with an Adobe ID can use these tools to create and share folios with others. In this chapter, we'll be focusing on the app design and creation process.

One important thing to note is that the components of DPS are regularly updated, so you'll want to check out the resources mentioned at the end of this chapter.

DPS workflow overview   The basic DPS workflow involves multiple steps. The diagram below illustrates the overall process.

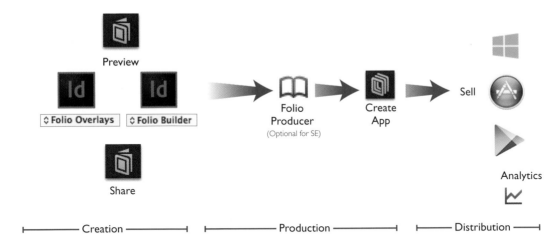

The basic DPS workflow includes adding interactivity to your InDesign layouts using the Folio Overlays panel, using the Folio Builder panel to assemble them into a folio, then using the DPS App Builder to create an app. Single Edition users can only create apps for the iPad.

The first step is to design your publication for viewing on a tablet and to add interactivity where appropriate. Design issues are discussed in the next section, "Design and Workflow Considerations" on page 217. Interactivity is added using both InDesign's built-in features (*covered in Chapter 2*) and the Folio Overlays panel, discussed in the section "Interactivity and Digital Overlays," starting on page 222.

Next, your individual InDesign documents, called *articles*, are assembled into a folio, which you can think of as the file format for a tablet app. This assembly is done using the Folio Builder panel in InDesign, which is discussed in the section "The Folio Builder Panel" on page 253. You can also import HTML articles into your folio, but we're going to focus on working with InDesign files.

Once you've created your folio, you can preview it in a number of ways. You can view it on your computer by clicking the **Preview** button in the Folio Builder panel, which opens the Desktop Viewer. Or, install the Adobe Content Viewer on your iPad or other tablet, then sign in with your Adobe ID. The folio will then be available on your tablet. Both of these options are discussed further in "Previewing and Sharing Your Work" on page 264.

If you need to share your folio with others on your team or with a client, you can do so by clicking the name of the folio in the Folio Builder panel and choosing **Share** from the panel menu. You can then enter multiple email addresses inviting others to view the folio. In order to view the folio, invitees must have an Adobe ID to sign in, and they can view the folio either on their tablet (using the Adobe Viewer) or in their Folio Builder panel in InDesign. See "Sharing folios" on page 267 for more information.

Once your folio is complete, if you are a Single Edition user, use the DPS App Builder to prepare your app for publication in the Apple App store. Or, if you're an Enterprise or Professional user, use the Folio Producer to publish it to Adobe's distribution system, the first step to getting your app in the Apple App Store, Google Play Store, or Windows Store.

DPS app navigation and user interface

Whether you create a folio to share with a few colleagues or to publish for sale to the general public, all DPS apps allow you to navigate pages in the same way, and all share a common user interface with navigation controls — icons that appear when the user taps the screen. The only exceptions are Enterprise Edition apps that can have a custom interface created by the publisher. But the vast majority of DPS apps share the same "look and feel."

When you download the free Adobe Content Viewer for your tablet, you'll find an illustrated help file that explains this basic navigation and interface. It's also common when publishing an app to include a similar help file so that users unfamiliar with the interface can fully experience and engage with your app.

Most DPS apps are set to read from page to page within an article by swiping vertically. The article may be set as individual pages or as one long, scrolling article. Swiping horizontally moves to the next article. However, a folio can also be set so that the user swipes horizontally only, much the way a print publication is read. Setting these swipe controls is covered on page 263. With horizontal-only navigation, the user basically has to swipe through every page of the publication.

When the user taps the screen, standard DPS navigation controls appear. These controls include the following icons:

- **Library:** tap to return to the app library.
- **Table of Contents:** tap to display the table of contents.
- **Previous View:** tap to go back to the previously viewed page.
- **Browse Mode:** tap to display thumbnail images of the articles.
- **Scrubber:** drag to scroll through the article thumbnails.

Table of Contents icon   Previous View icon

Browse Mode icon

Library

Library icon

Scrubber

DPS apps have a standard interface for navigation. The user taps the screen once to display the navigation controls and can then jump back to the library, to the table of contents, the previous view, or browse through the app's articles.

Design and Workflow Considerations

Although tablet apps are electronic, they still use the concept of "pages." But the design issues involved can be quite different from those encountered when designing for print. Interactive elements require a different way of thinking about how information is presented, and even about how the user is informed that elements of the page are interactive.

Another important difference is that many print publications, especially books and magazines, are really designed as facing-page spreads. Because the reader experiences both pages at once, they are effectively viewed as though they were a single page. When content moves to a tablet, there is no notion of spreads, and the overall design and design elements need to hold up in what are essentially single-page layouts. This is especially true if the original facing page layout causes elements to flip from left to right.

Page orientation: H, V, or both?

One of the first decisions you need to make when converting a print publication to a tablet app is the orientation of the pages in the app. Because the iPad and most other tablets have a built-in accelerometer, the screen rotates depending on how you hold the device. You can design your publication with pages that can be viewed in a vertical orientation only, a horizontal orientation only, or both vertical *and* horizontal orientations.

Some publications use only a single orientation. *Martha Stewart Living* (left) is vertical only, and *National Geographic* (second from left) is horizontal only. Others, like *Wired* (right and second from right), use both vertical and horizontal orientations.

There is no right or wrong decision regarding page orientation. One thing to keep in mind, though, is that creating a publication with both orientations is going to be more work than creating a single-orientation app. Features that were introduced in InDesign CS6, such as Liquid Layout rules and alternate layouts (*discussed in Chapter 4*), help with the process, but building an app with both orientations still requires extra effort. You'll find most publications today choose one orientation or the other.

Scrolling vs. individual pages

Although tablet apps don't display pages in spreads like print publications do, the content still needs to hold up on its own page. One nice thing about pages on tablet apps is that they can be set as individual pages (similar to a print publication) or as long scrolling pages (so that content is one continuous page that scrolls vertically).

The most common types of articles or pages that are set as scrolling pages are tables of contents, letters from the editor, credits, and colophons — "list type" articles. Other types of stories that are well suited to scrolling pages are articles that consist of short snippets of information, such as new product releases, new hot spots to visit, or anything that is essentially a list of items. On the other hand, long blocks of text such as feature stories can be harder to read in a scrolling view. It's usually best to set those types of articles in a page-by-page view.

Scrolling pages are easy to set up in InDesign. Simply make the InDesign page long enough to fit the article. For example, you might set a horizontal page to 1024 x 2000 pixels and a vertical page to 768 x 2000 pixels. (The maximum page size in InDesign is 15,562 pixels.) You can then set the article to Smooth Scrolling in the Article Properties dialog, discussed later in this chapter. InDesign page sizes can be adjusted by choosing the Page tool. Then, hold the Opt/Alt key as you drag the bottom of the page down. (If you don't hold the Opt/Alt key, the page snaps back to its original position.)

Whether content is set up in individual pages or as one scrolling page, it's a good idea to give the reader some visual cue that more content is available. This cue could be a graphic image that you can see only part of, or it could be an arrow or other icon that points toward the rest of the article.

Fonts and images Fonts look beautiful on tablets, especially on the Retina display iPad (2012), but that doesn't mean you don't have to make adjustments for tablet apps. When it comes to fonts, the main difference between layouts in print and on tablets is that body text that looks fine in print is often too small on the tablet version. Most publications increase the body text size by at least 1 point or more, along with increasing any smaller text in the layout.

When you're working with images for tablet apps, there are a couple of things to keep in mind. Like fonts, images look fantastic on most tablets. But keep in mind that tablets use an RGB color space, so it's a good idea to keep your images in RGB whenever possible. Check the Color Settings in your document (Edit > Color Settings). The RGB menu of your Working Space in the Color Settings dialog should be set to sRGB.

If you choose Web or Digital Publishing in the New Document dialog, your Working Space is automatically set to sRGB and the Transparency Blend Space is set to RGB. In addition the default Swatches are set in RGB values.

If you have an older, print document, you can choose Edit > Transparency Blend Space > RGB. It is not necessary to change the default CMYK swatches to RGB.

You'll also want to keep your options open when cropping an image. Avoid using images that don't have the extra space for a horizontal layout. For example, you may crop an image one way for the cover of the vertical orientation of your print publication, but if you are also creating a horizontal orientation version of your tablet app, you'll need to crop the image differently, with more of the image showing on the sides.

Use high-resolution images for all non-interactive content. InDesign will automatically sample the images correctly for the device you're designing for. Some interactive content is sampled and some is not, as we'll discuss in later sections.

Interactivity visual cues   Part of what makes publications on tablets so compelling are the interactive features that can be included. There's nothing like buttons, slideshows, or movies to spice things up! Because interactivity is such an important part of the tablet app experience, it's important that your readers know it's there.

Unlike web pages and interactive PDF files on your computer, there is no "finger" that is displayed when the user hovers over an interactive element in a DPS app. But there also isn't any hand or gripper that appears when the user taps the screen. So you need to alert your viewers how to use the interactive elements in your DPS app.

The most common way to guide users to interactive elements is to develop a series of icons that indicate different types of activity. These can be included on a help page at the beginning of your publication to let users know how to navigate and use the DPS controls.

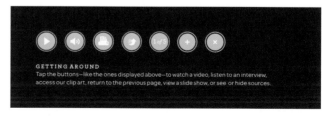

Indicate interactive elements in your app by developing a system of icons. These are the icons used in *National Geographic* (top) and *Martha Stewart Living* (bottom).

Workflow considerations   There are many issues regarding workflow when creating a tablet app publication, especially when it's in conjunction with a print version. We can't cover them all in detail here, but we'd like to mention a couple of very important things to consider.

First and foremost is the issue of resources. Whether you work on your own or are part of a workgroup, it takes time and energy to create a tablet app of your publication. Even with the tools that have been added to InDesign to make the process of creating documents in multiple sizes and orientations easier, don't underestimate the additional work that's going to be involved. As we've been highlighting in this section, the design considerations for tablet apps are quite different from those for print.

Another part of the typical workflow that is affected is proofing. How do you proof interactive content? How do you mark it up for changes? Certain elements can be output from InDesign in PDF format, but many cannot, or not very easily. Imagine you have a slideshow created with object states, each of which includes an image and text. You could make a PDF, but you'd have to make one for each state, one by one, and this can be very time-consuming.

TIP The most important step you can take in planning your workflow for creating a tablet app is this: Plan ahead!

If you know you will be creating both a print and a tablet app version of your publication, plan for both at the very beginning. Allocate resources, whether it's your own time or that of others, and right from the start, think about the assets as they relate to *both* your print version and your digital version.

Setting Up Your Document

Part of the creation process for a tablet app is to set up your file properly. If you're creating a new document for your tablet app, use the intent Digital Publishing in the New Document dialog.

The Digital Publishing intent changes several default settings in the New Document dialog, and it sets the Swatches panel to RGB when the document is created.

The Digital Publishing intent sets a primary text frame, which allows your text to reflow when you create alternate layouts. It also sets the Pages panel to display alternate layouts. Dimensions are set to pixels, preset page sizes for a number of popular mobile devices are listed, and the Swatches panel is set to RGB colors. Any of these settings can be changed, of course, and they can be modified and captured for future use with the **Save Preset** option.

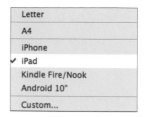

Preset page sizes in the New Document dialog include several popular mobile devices.

Keep in mind that many devices have an area that is used for navigation. For example, the iPad has a 6-pixel wide area on the right side of the screen that displays a scroll bar and crops the layout. You can download templates for the iPad that have guides to indicate parts of the screen that will be covered by the scroll bar or other parts of the interface at http://www.gilbertconsulting.com/id_templates/iPad_templates.zip.

Interactivity and Digital Overlays

Many of the interactive features for tablet apps are added to your InDesign documents using the Folio Overlays panel. These elements are called overlays because when you create a folio, all the non-interactive elements in your layout are flattened to a JPEG, PNG, or PDF file, depending on the settings you use; the interactive elements sit on top of that, as an overlay.

One of the nice things about overlays is that they are maintained in both a horizontal and a vertical orientation, with no special action required on your part. As long as the same name is used for objects in each layout, the overlay will be consistent. For example, that means that if you are viewing the second slide in a slideshow in one orientation, the same slide is displayed when the user rotates the tablet.

Some of the interactivity that you can add to DPS apps is created using InDesign's native interactive features (*discussed in Chapter 2*), which can be used in PDFs as well as DPS apps. But most of these elements require some additional settings in the Folio Overlays panel because of characteristics that are unique to tablets. For example, when you have a hyperlink to a website, you need to indicate whether the page will open directly within the tablet app or in the tablet's browser app.

Interactive elements are in an overlay that sits on top of the non-interactive elements in your layout.

Other interactive elements are unique to tablet apps, and these elements are added using the Folio Overlays panel. We'll discuss each of these in detail later in this section.

Native interactive features supported

Many, but not all, of InDesign's native interactive features are supported by DPS, as shown in the following table.

Feature	Supported by DPS	Not Supported by DPS
Animations	Not supported directly; animations must be converted to HTML5 and placed back in the InDesign file	
Hyperlinks	URL, email, Page, and Navto only	Text anchors and Shared Destination hyperlinks
Buttons	On Release or Tap event; Go To Destination (TOC-generated or Page destinations only), Go To First/Last page, Go To URL, Sound, Video, Go To Page, Go To State and Go To Previous/Next State actions	On Click and On Rollover events; Go To Destination (user-created), Go To Next/Previous Page, and Show/Hide Button, Animation actions
Forms		Not supported
Audio	MP3 files	
Video	MP4 files with h.264 encoding	
Bookmarks		Not supported
Cross-References		Not supported
Page Transitions		Not supported

The Folio Overlays panel extends the native interactive features it supports by allowing you to add options that are unique to tablet apps. But the panel also adds overlays that provide additional interactive features to DPS apps, including the following:

- Image sequencing
- Panoramas
- Web views
- Pan and zoom on images
- Scrollable frames

These features are created entirely using the Folio Overlays panel and, usually, a set of external files.

Folio Overlays panel basics

The Folio Overlays panel is essential to adding much of the interactivity to DPS apps. After you install the DPS tools from the Folio Builder panel, you can find the Folio Overlays panel under the Window menu.

The Folio Overlays panel lets you access all of the interactive features you can modify or create for DPS apps.

Think of the Folio Overlays panel as your hub for adding interactivity to your DPS apps. It provides important tools for creating engaging experiences for your publication's readers, and previewing your work as you go along, either using the desktop Content Viewer or directly on your iPad.

> **TIP** Preview the interactive features that you apply to your layout by clicking the Preview button at the bottom of the Folio Overlays panel.

Creating links with buttons and hyperlinks

Both buttons and hyperlinks play an important role in providing interactivity to DPS tablet apps. They both can provide navigation and links to the outside world. However, buttons are more versatile than hyperlinks, because they can also trigger sounds and videos, and can be used in slideshows and other multi-state objects. When it comes to links, though, either a hyperlink or a button can be used.

When to use buttons vs. hyperlinks

Both buttons and hyperlinks share similar linking functionality, and you can use either buttons or hyperlinks for these kinds of links:

- To link to websites
- To link to other pages or articles
- To send email

It can sometimes be confusing to know when to use a button rather than a hyperlink. They each have unique characteristics that when understood make it easy to choose the right feature for the job.

For one thing, only entire objects or frames can be made into a button; you can't select text within a frame and set a button, but you can set a hyperlink. Use a hyperlink when you need to link selected text within a frame.

Keep in mind, though, that the hyperlinked text needs to be large enough to be tapped with a finger when displayed on a tablet, not just the tip of a mouse. If you're converting a print document, and it already has many hyperlinks in the text, make sure your text is large enough so the links can be tapped.

> **TIP** You can create a hyperlink on text within a paragraph, but it can often be too small for a finger to tap. Instead, create an "invisible" button that is larger, and insert it as an anchored object over the hyperlinked text. Add the link action to the button, not the text.

But whether you use buttons or hyperlinks, you must use the Folio Overlays panel to set how URL links behave.

Use the Hyperlink settings to specify whether a link opens in the app (folio) or in a browser.

Hyperlink overlay settings

Open in Folio: This option opens the link inside a browser screen that is part of the app. All links on the website are fully functional inside this browser. To return to the original screen, the user simply taps the Done button in the upper-left corner of the screen. The benefit of this is that the user never changes the application that is running.

Open in Device Browser: Choose this option if you want the user to leave the original app and open the device's browser app, such as Safari on the iPad. With this option selected, the user will exit the app and go to the external browser. Always choose this option for email links, because you always want the user's email client to open to send a pre-addressed email.

TIP When setting a link to iTunes or the Apple App Store, use the Open in Device Browser option to avoid a Cannot Open Page error message.

Select the **Ask First** check box to specify that a prompt will appear, requesting permission to exit the app. It's usually a good idea to specify this prompt, so the user knows what's about to happen. Once the user is in the browser app, the DPS app has been completely exited and the app has to be brought to the foreground again. .

Jump to another article

To create a hyperlink to jump to another article in your folio, you can use a URL hyperlink or a Go To URL button with the **navto://** syntax. Then specify the name of the article as it appears in the Folio Builder panel, not as it appears in the Article Properties dialog. (Both are discussed in detail later in this chapter.) Add a page number if you wish to link to a specific page in the article.

TIP When you're linking to a specific page in an article, keep in mind that the first page in the document is counted as page 0 (zero). So, for example, if you specify #3 in the URL, the link will jump to page 4. A typical URL to link to another article on page 4 in your folio might be something like navto://*articlename*#3.

Creating buttons for DPS apps

While you can create URL links using hyperlinks or buttons, buttons are the only choice when you want the appearance of your link to change when it's tapped. And again, remember that only buttons let you jump to an object state, which is useful for slideshows, remote rollovers, or button "hot spots." And only buttons can be used to play audio and video files.

Creating a button for a DPS folio is the same as creating a button in InDesign for any other type of use, such as for a PDF file. Creating buttons is discussed in detail in Chapter 2.

However, you need to be aware that there are certain button events and actions that do not work in DPS apps and cannot be used. In fact, the only button **Event** that is supported by DPS is **On Release or Tap**. After all, an iPad doesn't have a mouse, and therefore you don't "click" on the screen. A mouse is also required for a "Roll Over/ Roll Off" events. You can't have a finger hover over an area on the screen and have the button react.

The only button event supported in DPS is On Release or Tap. The others have no effect when exported to a DPS folio.

There are also certain button **Actions** that are not supported in DPS folios, including Go To Destination (user-created), Go To Next/Previous Page, and Show/Hide Buttons And Forms. None of the PDF Only actions are supported.

DPS supports the following button **Actions**:

- Go To Destination, for destinations created by a generated Table of Contents, or a user-created Page destination (with DPS v31 and higher).
- Go To First/Last Page
- Go To Page
- Go To URL
- Sound
- Video
- Go To Next/Previous State
- Go To State [_], where the user chooses a specific state from the states shown in the Actions area.

When you use a button for a URL link to a website, use the Folio Overlays Hyperlink options to specify if the link will open in your app or in the device's browser. If you want to use a button to link to another article, use the same syntax as used when setting the URL for a hyperlink such as navto://*articlename*#3. Both of these options are discussed in the previous section.

Buttons have **Appearance** options for Normal, Rollover, and Click, but only Normal and Click appearances are utilized by DPS. The Click appearance should be called "Click/Tap," because it occurs when you tap on a button on your screen. If a button uses the Go To State action, the Click state appears when the associated object state is selected. For example, if Normal state button is black, and the Click state button is red, the red button appears until another button is tapped and another object state is selected.

Creating slideshows with object states
Slideshows are just one of the many interactive elements that can be made using object states. In DPS apps, slideshows can be navigated by using buttons or by using tablet actions (such as Tap or Swipe) that are specified in the Slideshow tab of the Folio Overlays panel.

As discussed in Chapter 2, you make an object state, also known as a multi-state object or MSO, by combining multiple objects into one. Select the objects — whether several images or a series of images grouped with text — and align them on top of each other using the alignment icons in the Control panel. Then in the Object States panel, click **New**, which groups the objects into a new object state.

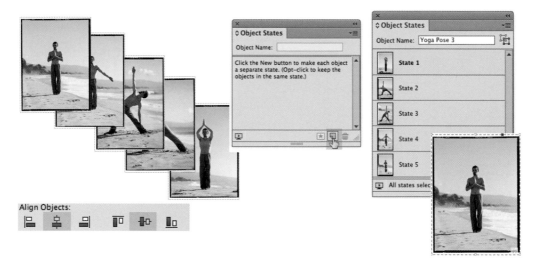

Creating an object state: Select a group of images and align them; click the Convert Selection to Multi-state Object icon in the Object States panel.

A state within a state within a state...

Object states don't have to be ordinary graphics or text. You can insert graphics, videos, audios, or any of the overlay objects covered in this chapter as individual states inside an MSO. Buttons need to be inserted as anchored objects within text frames. This gives you the mind-boggling choice of playing a slideshow that then stops at a video, that then shows another slideshow, which contains scrollable text, and so on.

Obviously you shouldn't do this just because you can. You do it because it serves a purpose; but it does let you know how deep working with MSO objects can become. So deep, in fact, that you may need help to work with all the states. If so, you should consider investing in the Object States Assistant from Automaticon (http://automatication.com/index.php?id=23).

To allow the user to view the slideshow by tapping buttons that access a specific state or by browsing slide by slide, set the buttons to the Next/Previous State action. Or, you can allow the user to view a slideshow without any buttons by selecting the appropriate settings in the Slideshow tab of the Folio Overlays panel.

Use the Slideshow tab of the Folio Overlays panel to specify settings for your slideshow.

Slideshow overlay settings

Auto Play: As soon as the user turns to the page, the slideshow will play; this is also known as "play on page load." If you select this setting, you can set a delay in the time it takes to play the slideshow.

Tap to Play/Pause: The slideshow will play when the user taps the top image or state. If you select this option, it's a good idea to give some kind of visual cue, such as an icon or text, that clearly indicates that the slideshow should be tapped to see the action, since the user otherwise just sees the static image of the first slide.

Delay: If Auto Play is selected, you can specify a delay in the time between when the user turns the page and when the slideshow starts to play. You can specify from 0 (zero) seconds to 60 seconds. It's usually a good idea to set a small delay so the page elements have time to fully load before the slideshow starts to play.

Interval: If Auto Play or Tap to Play/Pause is selected, you can specify the amount of time each slide displays. The allowable range is 0.125 seconds to 60 seconds.

Play (time): If Auto Play or Tap to Play/Pause is selected, you can specify how many times the slideshow plays. This option is not available when Loop is selected.

Loop: If Auto Play or Tap to Play/Pause is selected, selecting Loop will cause the slideshow to play continuously until the user double-taps the slideshow or turns the page. Many electronic document designers decry the loop setting as a distraction or frustration for users who don't know how to get out of it.

Stop at Last Image: If Auto Play or Tap to Play/Pause is selected, this setting will stop the slideshow at the last slide.

Cross Fade: This setting provides a transition fade to the next slide. The default time for the transition is 0.5 seconds, but you can specify any value from 0.125 seconds to 60 seconds. This applies to slideshows advanced manually or with Auto Play or Tap to Play/Pause selected.

Swipe to Change Image: This setting lets the user swipe from slide to slide.

Stop at First/Last Image: When Swipe to Change Image is selected, use this setting to specify that the slideshow stop on the first or last slide.

Hide Before Playing: If this setting is selected, the slideshow is hidden until it is triggered, either by user action or by other settings in the Folio Overlays panel.

Play in Reverse: Just like it sounds, selecting this option causes the slideshow to play backwards. It may not sound like much, but this setting is very helpful if you've created your MSO in the wrong order. Instead of having to re-order all the states, just set it to play in reverse.

Export Format in PDF Articles: If your slideshow is in an article that is built using the default PDF format in the Folio Builder (see "The Folio Builder Panel" on page 253), the options are to export the slideshow in **Bitmap** or **Vector**. Generally, it's best to use Vector for text-based slideshows, and Raster for image-based slideshows. If you're creating a folio for both SD and HD iPads or iPhones, using Vector for text-based slideshows ensures you'll get sharper text when the folio is displayed on an HD iOS device.

Controlling slideshows with buttons

Object states are used frequently in DPS apps because you can do so many different things with them. One common use of objects states is to create what is sometimes referred to as a "remote rollover."

Remote rollover usually refers to an effect on a website where the user rolls over one part of a page onscreen and a change occurs in a remote (unconnected) part of the page. On tablets, there is no rollover state, so in this case it refers to when the user taps one part of the screen and a change occurs in another part of the screen. We call this a "remote reveal." Remote reveals can be created using an object state and buttons that go to specific states in the object state.

In this example, the user taps any one of four buttons to display a different yoga pose, along with how-to instructions.

2 supported chair

Standing against a wall with your feet hip distance apart, inhale, lifting your arms parallel to the floor and keeping your wrists relaxed. Exhaling, slide your back down the wall as you step your feet forward. Keep your hips higher than your knees and your knees directly above your heels. Hold for about 30 seconds and release.

In this remote rollover, the user taps one of the numbered buttons to display a different yoga pose with instructions.

1. The first step is to create each object state. A yoga pose image is positioned next to the text frame containing its instructions, and then the two are grouped.

2. Once all four images are grouped with their instructions, the four groups are then aligned on top of each other and converted to an object state using the Object States panel.

1 tall warrior

With your feet three to four feet apart, point your right (front) foot forward and your left (back) foot slightly left. Keep your heels in line with each other and square your hips toward your right foot. Bring your arms overhead and inhale. As you exhale, bend your right leg until your knee is over your heel. Tighten the front of your left thigh. Hold for 4–10 breaths. Release. Repeat on the other side.

2 supported chair

Standing against a wall with your feet hip distance apart, inhale, lifting your arms parallel to the floor and keeping your wrists relaxed. Exhaling, slide your back down the wall as you step your feet forward. Keep your hips higher than your knees and your knees directly above your heels. Hold for about 30 seconds and release.

Each state is made up of an image and instructional text grouped together.

3. Next, the four buttons are created. Each button has a different image for the Normal and Click appearances. See Chapter 2 for information about using external graphics for button appearances.

4. For each button, the event is set to On Release or Tap and the action is set to Go To State. Below that, a list of object states appears. Select the object state and specify the State <*e.g. State 1*>. Preview your work using the Folio Overlays panel or for a quick check, the SWF Preview panel.

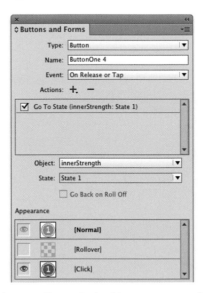

Each button is targeted to a specific state in the object state to create the remote rollover effect.

This technique offers a lot of flexibility, and with a little imagination and creativity you can produce a variety of engaging experiences for your users. You'll see this technique used in many of today's tablet publications.

Image sequences Image sequences allow you to combine many images into a continuous series that can be played automatically or stepped through by the user. It is particularly useful for creating a rotating 360° view of an object or a time-lapse series of images. Image sequencing is available for DPS only, and it uses the Folio Overlays panel rather than the File > Place command to import the images used.

There are a variety of ways to create the necessary source images. One way is to use Adobe Photoshop to export a sequence of images from the video. This can be the video of a 3D object or a movie scene.

Use Photoshop's File > Open command to open the movie in Photoshop. Then choose File > Export > Render Video. This opens the Render Video dialog. Choose **Photoshop Image Sequence** and change the settings in the dialog as needed.

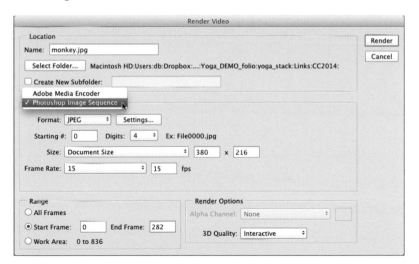

The Render Video dialog in Photoshop. You can create the assets needed for an image sequence by opening a movie file in Photoshop and exporting the frames as an image sequence.

You can also use Adobe Flash Professional or Adobe After Effects to export frames from an animation or a video. And you can use any 3D authoring application to generate images.

Images should be saved in JPEG format, or PNG if you wish to include transparency. InDesign won't compress the files in any way, so for JPEG files, use medium compression to keep your folio size down.

The files should be named with sequential ascending suffixes, such as image01.jpg, image02.jpg, image03.jpg, and so on. It's also best to make the images the same size as the display area on the tablet.

 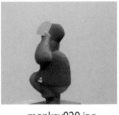 

monkey000.jpg   monkey020.jpg   monkey040.jpg

Image sequence files must be named with sequential ascending suffixes. Shown are three files from different points in a sequence.

TIP Use at least 30 to 60 images so their rotation will not be jerky. You usually don't need more than that, and using too many images will just make your file larger without a better result.

Once you've combined all your images in a folder, the next step is to create a container frame in your InDesign layout and decide on the poster image you want to display. This will be the image the user sees when the page is first displayed.

If you want the first image in the sequence to be the poster, you can draw a frame of any size, because when you load the images the frame will automatically be re-sized to fit the content. If you want some other image to be the poster, place an image into a frame that is the *exact* proportion of the images in your sequence, otherwise the image sequence will be resized unproportionally.

To include the images in your layout, select the container frame, and in the Image Sequence tab of the Folio Overlays panel, click the **Load Images** folder icon at the top. Locate the folder containing the image assets, and adjust the settings.

Use the Image Sequence controls to load your images and to specify settings such as Auto Play and Swipe to Change Image.

Image sequence overlay settings

Show First Image Initially: This setting will use the first image in the sequence as the poster and will re-size the selected frame to fit the image.

Auto Play: This will cause the image sequence to begin playing on page load.

Tap to Play/Pause: This setting will allow the user to tap the image sequence to begin playing; a second tap will pause it.

Delay: If you set the image sequence to Auto Play, this setting lets you set a delay before it starts playing. It's a good idea to set a short delay to give the page time to fully load before the image sequence starts to play.

Speed: This allows you to set the number of frames per second at which the sequence will play. It should not exceed the frame rate at which your images were sequenced.

Play: This setting lets you specify how many times you want the sequence to play.

Loop: This setting causes the sequence to loop, or play continuously, until stopped by a user action, such as a tap or a page turn.

Stop at Last Image: If Auto Play or Tap to Play/Pause is selected, this setting will stop the slideshow at the last slide.

Swipe to Change Image: This setting allows the user to swipe the image and move the images as slowly or quickly as desired, essentially allowing the user to step through the sequence.

Stop at First and Last Image: When Swipe to Change Image is selected, selecting this setting will stop the sequence at the first image and the last image. If this setting is deselected, the user can spin the image sequence continuously.

Play in Reverse: Like the setting for a slideshow, this setting will play the image sequence in reverse. This is helpful if the image sequence has been incorrectly named and you need to reverse the direction of how the image players.

Working with audio overlays

You can include both audio and video files in DPS apps. Some of the properties for audio and video are set in the Media panel, as discussed in Chapter 2, but most are set in the Folio Overlays panel.

In order to include audio files in your DPS app, use the File > Place command to position an audio file in your InDesign layout. For DPS apps, the audio file must be in the MP3 format.

Use the Media panel to set a simple poster for your video. You can also create a poster image by placing a non-interactive object (such as a transparent play button) on top of the audio object.

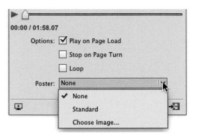

The Media panel must be used to set a poster for your audio file; all other settings can be controlled using the Folio Overlays panel.

You can use the Media panel to set the file to **Play on Page Load**, which automatically turns on the **Auto Play** option in the Audio tab of the Folio Overlays panel. But frankly, unless you want to set a single image for a poster, there is no particular reason to use the Media panel for audio. Use the Audio tab of the Folio Overlays panel instead.

If you don't use the File > Place command, you can load an audio file by drawing a container frame and using the Audio tab of the Folio Overlays panel. Click on the **URL or File** folder icon to place the audio file or to stream an audio file from an http website. Note that https (secure sites) URLs are not supported.

Controller files are also loaded in the Audio tab, and are discussed later in this section. You can set an audio file to play and pause using controller files, to automatically play when the user turns to the page, or you can create buttons that the user can tap to play, pause, or stop the audio. Button options are discussed in more detail in Chapter 2.

Normally, audio files stop playing when a user swipes to the next article. However, they continue to play as the user swipes down vertically within the same article.

Audio overlay settings

Auto Play: This setting is the same as **Play on Page Load** in the Media panel. It causes the sound to play when the user turns to that page.

Delay: If you set **Auto Play** in the Folio Overlays panel or **Play on Page Load** in the Media panel, you can set a [**delay**] before the audio plays. It's usually a good idea to set a brief delay, even 0.125 seconds, so that the audio does not start playing before the page completely loads.

Use the Folio Overlays panel to set a delay on Auto Play, which helps prevent the audio file from playing before the page is fully loaded.

Play in Background Across Folios: Use this option to play the audio file in the background while users browse from article to article. Users can pause or resume the audio clip by tapping the screen, then tapping the audio play icon that will display in the top navigation bar. This option works on the iPad or iPhone only.

Working with controller files

One of the interesting things you can do with the Folio Overlays panel is to set images to control the audio playback. You can create either a simple controller or a progressive controller, which shows the progress of the audio as it plays.

For a simple controller, you need only two files. However, they must have very specific names. Name the files with a _pause_ or _play_ suffix, such as _audio_play.png_ and _audio_pause.png_. Add these two images to an assets folder that contains no other files.

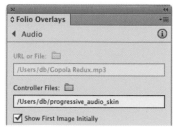

Use the Folio Overlays panel to load a series of images that will display as a progressive controller bar, showing the progress of the audio as it plays.

Next, load the images by clicking the **Controller Files** folder icon in the Audio tab of the Folio Overlays panel. Point to a folder that contains only the controller images. To use the *audio_play.png* image as the poster image, select the **Show First Image Initially** check box.

For a progressive controller, the images must be named in a very specific sequence that includes an increasing number, such as *audio01_play.png*, *audio01_pause.png*, followed by *audio02_play.png*, *audio02_pause.png*. As the audio plays, the images will be shown in a sequence that displays a visual of the audio progress. The total number of play files you use will be divided equally by the length of the audio. For example, if your audio is 30 seconds and you want the image bar to progress every second, create a total of 30 files, named *audio_play01.png* to *audio_play30.png*, with their corollary pause versions.

It's also a good idea to create the images in the exact pixel size they'll display in the app; scaling them up will cause pixelation, and scaling them down will make the file size larger than it needs to be. Use PNG or JPEG images with medium compression to best balance image quality and file size.

audio01_play.png   audio03_play.png   audio11_play.png   audio20_play.png

audio01_pause.png   audio03_pause.png   audio11_pause.png   audio20_pause.png

These images are part of a sequence that displays the progress of the audio as a controller that fills up from bottom to top as the audio plays.

Because it can take quite a bit of time to create the images for a progressive controller (unless you automate the process; see the sidebar below), it's a good idea to decide on a controller look that you want to use throughout your app publications. It can be very time-consuming to change them all with each new issue.

Using Illustrator to create audio controllers

Adobe Illustrator is the perfect application for creating the image sequence for an audio file controller. You can create objects for Start and Pause buttons and then use blends to precisely create the progress display. For example, if the audio takes five seconds to play, you create a blend with eight steps, plus the start and end objects. This creates a controller that runs for five seconds, with each step lasting half a second.

Once you've created the artwork, exporting PNG files from Illustrator is tedious. And if you need to make a small change, it's twice as tedious.

Adi Ravid has created a simple script for Illustrator, DPS Audio Player SkinMaker, that automates the process of creating those files and naming them correctly. You can download the script at *http://dl.dropbox.com/u/1719552/Scripts/Illustrator/CS3/ DPS_AudioPalyerSkinMaker.zip.* Be sure and view the sample file so you'll understand how to set up the controller objects correctly.

Working with video overlays

It's easy to include video files in DPS apps. As with audio files, choose the File > Place command to position a video file in your layout. For DPS apps, it's best to use a video file in MP4 format with H.264 encoding.

It's most efficient to use a video that is the exact proportion and size in pixels as it will appear when played. For full-screen videos, make the width the number of pixels of the device you're targeting. A full-screen video on a retina display iPad will be 1920 x 1080. A video this large can increase the overall size of your folio. A suggested guideline is to render your video with a balance of file size and quality to about 10-12 MB per minute.

After you place the video, select it and use the Media panel to set a **Poster** for your video: None, Standard, a frame from the video, or an image file. The **Loop** option is not honored in DPS, nor do the **Controller** settings in the Media panel have any effect.

Set a poster for your video in the Media panel, which is used in conjunction with the Folio Overlays panel to specify the appearance of your video.

For most settings, use the Video tab of the Folio Overlays panel. Like audio files, if you don't use the File > Place command, you can load a video file by drawing a container frame and using the Folio Overlays panel. Click on the **URL or File** folder icon to place the video file or to stream a video file from an http website. Also, like audio files, https URLs are not supported.

When a video is displayed in your app, it can be played simply by tapping. But, of course, the user has to have some way to know to do that. A video can also be set to automatically play when the user turns to the page, or you can create buttons with actions assigned that play or pause the video, as described in Chapter 2. See the next section for how to create non-interactive objects that will prompt videos to play.

Normally, video files stop playing when a user swipes to the next article. However, they continue to play as the user swipes down vertically within the same article.

Video overlay settings

Auto Play: Like audio files, when you set **Play on Page Load** in the Media panel, you also set Auto Play in the Folio Overlays panel, and vice versa. However, it's only in the Folio Overlays panel that you can set a **Delay** before the video plays. It's a good idea to set a brief delay, even 0.125 seconds, so that the video does not start playing before the page fully loads.

The Video tab of the Folio Overlays panel allows you to set a delay before your video begins to play automatically. This allows the page to load fully before the video begins.

Play Full Screen: This setting lets you specify that the video play in full-screen mode, whether via Auto Play or a tap on the screen. To return to the page after the video plays, the user taps the Done button in the upper-left corner of the screen. If this option is not selected, the video plays in the size and area it is displayed on the page.

Tap to View Controller: This setting causes a controller with pause and play controls to display when the user taps the video. This controller comes with the DPS features and does not have to be created yourself. If this option is not selected, tapping pauses the video and tapping again restarts it.

Do Not Allow Pause: This setting prohibits users from tapping the video to pause or stop it. This option is available only if Auto Play is selected and Play Full Screen is not selected.

Stop on Last Frame: This option stops the video on the last frame. It is not available when Play Full Screen is selected. The viewer has to tap the Done button to close the video.

If you want to put an icon or other visual cue on top of the video file, you don't have to create a button with an action. Simply place a non-interactive object on top of the video. When the user taps the non-interactive object, the video — which is an overlay object — will move above the icon and cover it while it is playing. When the video is done playing, it will revert to the first frame of the video, with the icon on top. This works even if the video and the icon are grouped together.

Place a visual prompt or icon on top of the video in InDesign (left) that will be visible on the video. When the user taps, the video plays in an overlay and the icon is hidden.

Creating panoramas

Panoramas let you put the user "inside" a locale and experience it as though the scene were viewed from a fixed location, looking around in all directions. For example, you could be inside a car and look around 360° or zoom in on the dashboard.

To create a panorama, you need six images that represent the six interior surfaces of a cube. If you have an existing panorama photo or image, convert it to six images. You can use Photoshop to stitch images together to create the initial panorama. Then you can convert the panorama to the required six images using a third-party utility such as PTgui at http://www.ptgui.com. The WRwave website http://www.vrwave.com provides useful information for shooting panorama photographs.

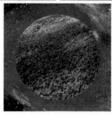

Images required to make a panorama. They show north, south, east, west, top, and bottom. Use the Folio Overlays panel to set exactly which parts of the images can be viewed.

Source files must be in JPEG or PNG format. Source files are not compressed by InDesign in any way, so to keep file sizes reasonable, use JPEG files with medium compression. The size of the panorama on the DPS page is determined by the first image, and the closer you can make the source images to their final sizes, the more efficient your final file size will be.

The six files must be named with ascending numbers, such as *pano1.jpg, pano2.jpg, pano3.jpg*, and so on. Copy all six images into their own folder, with no other files.

To import the images, click the **Load Images** folder icon in the Panorama tab of the Folio Overlays panel and point to the folder containing the images. By default, the first image in the sequence will be used as the poster. Once this image is on the page, you can resize it as you would any graphic. However, as mentioned, it's best if the image is already sized.

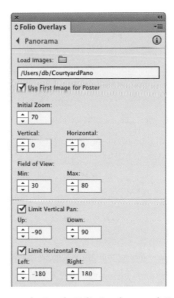

Panorama images are imported using the Folio Overlays panel. The panel also includes settings for controlling what the user sees in the panorama.

Panorama overlay settings

Use First Image for Poster: Selected by default. If you wish to use another image for the poster, choose File > Place to position it in the frame that will contain the six images.

Initial Zoom: This sets the initial zoom of the images when the user taps the panorama. Use a setting between the minimum zoom (30 percent) and the maximum zoom (80 percent).

Vertical/Horizontal: This lets you specify values that determine which area of the panorama is initially displayed. For Vertical, you can specify a value from –90 (tilted all the way up) to 90 (tilted all the way down). For

Horizontal, specify a value from −180 (rotated all the way left) to 180 (rotated all the way right). The default of 0 (zero) sets the first image to display initially.

Field of View: This setting relates to how much the user can zoom in or zoom out, not to rotation.

Limit Vertical Pan: This setting limits the vertical tilt of the panorama. If you don't want users to be able to tilt through the image until it's upside down, set it to at least −1 and 1.

Limit Horizontal Pan: This limits how far the user can view the panorama to the left and the right.

Web Content overlays

Web Content overlays allow users of your app to access all the resources of the web. Web Content overlays can be used for websites, RSS feeds, or local HTML files, including HTML5 files containing animation. However, it is important to remember that web content overlays won't work if your viewer doesn't have a web connection.

InDesign layout with the Folio Overlays panel for web content

Tablet app page before and after user taps web area

To display a web page from an external URL, type the URL in the Web Content tab of the Folio Overlays panel.

To create an overlay to a website, first draw a frame of the dimensions and location of the desired view area. If you want to display a poster before the website displays, place an image in the view area frame; if you want the website to display when the page loads, leave the view area frame empty. The user's computer must have an Internet connection in order for the web page to load.

Type the URL of the website into the panel. Remember, since your viewers will be using a tablet or a phone, you'll want to send them to the mobile version of the website (if there is one); for example, http://mobile.twitter.com/username.

If you want to display a local HTML page, draw an empty frame or a frame with a placed poster image for the viewing area. In the Web Content tab of the Folio Overlays panel, click the **URL or File** folder icon and browse to the HTML file. The HTML file should be in its own folder, along with any resources, including images or scripts, that the HTML file refers to.

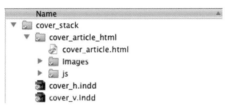

A local HTML file should be in a folder with any assets or scripts the file refers to.

You can use this feature to display things like a Google map or YouTube video widgets. Most of these websites offer code to embed for use in websites, and this code can be used in your DPS app.

Copy the code from the Google or YouTube page, paste it into an empty text file, then save the file with the extension .html. Click on the URL or File icon in the Folio Overlays panel to load the file. You'll usually want to set the Auto Play option, so the content is visible on the page.

Copy the Google maps embed code into a file with the extension .html, then load the file using the Web Content tab of the Folio Overlays panel.

TIP Some map-embed code, such as that from Bing maps (but not Google maps, at this time) can simply be pasted directly on your InDesign page. After you paste the embed code, the map will appear, and you can set its options in the Web Content tab of the Folio Overlays panel.

As shown in the table on page 223, InDesign animations are not currently supported in DPS. Animations in DPS can play only if they are converted to HTML5 files. You can start with InDesign's native animation features, discussed in Chapter 3, but then you must convert them to HTML5 files. One tool that is popular for this purpose is Ajar Production's plugin In5 http://ajarproductions.com/pages/products/in5/?ref=footer.

Alternatively, you can create the animations in Adobe's Edge software and save them to HTML5. Files are saved in Edge's OAM file format which can then be imported to your InDesign layout. Adobe Muse also creates HTML5 files that can be imported as well. Of course if you know an HTML5 genius, you can get them to write the code for you.

Once the files have been converted to HTML5, the Web Content tab is used to adjust settings for how the animation or other content appears and whether users can interact with the content.

The Web Content overlay lets you choose options for how websites or other html files will appear in an app.

Web content overlay settings

Once you've set the URL or local file that the user will view in the viewarea frame, several settings can be adjusted in the Web Content overlay:

Auto Play: This setting will cause the web page to load when the user turns to the page, without any tap necessary. You can also set a delay; it's a good idea to set a short delay so the page doesn't load before the rest of the app page appears.

Transparent Background: Select this option to preserve the transparent background in a web page. Users can see through the transparency to view the DPS content in the background. If this option is deselected, the web content background is used.

Allow User Interaction: This option lets the children play; that is, it lets the user interact with the displayed webpage, allowing them, for example, to click links and go to another page.

Scale Content to Fit: This option will cause the webpage to fit to the dimensions of the view-area frame that you created. Be sure the frame is large enough that the web page is still readable when it's inside the frame. If you do not select this option, the web page will be displayed at actual size. It will be cut off if the frame is not large enough to view the page. In most cases, users will need to scroll in both directions to view the page.

Allow Access to Entitlement Information: This option is for Professional and Enterprise customers only, and allows access to various programming APIs that are available, such as those for the Camera API or Geolocation API.

Pan & Zoom overlays

Pan & Zoom overlays allow your users to explore an image beyond what is displayed in the static view. Specifically, it makes a large image available in a small view area, allowing the user to tap the image and then pinch to zoom in or out, and move to parts of the image that are not seen in the static view.

To create an image for Pan & Zoom, make sure the image has the exact dimensions you want to use. For example, if you want users to be able to pan a 1024 x 1024 pixel image in, say, a 300 x 300-pixel view area, create a PNG or JPEG image that is 1024 x 1024-pixels in 72 dpi. You can do this using Photoshop or Illustrator: Choose File > Save for Web & Devices, then specify the dimensions.

Draw a frame that will define the dimensions of the view area, and then place the image inside the frame. The image should be larger than the view-area frame. Position the image so the view area contains the part of the image that you want your viewers to see first. Try to select a focal point or some part of the image that is interesting on its own. The image in the view area will essentially become the poster image.

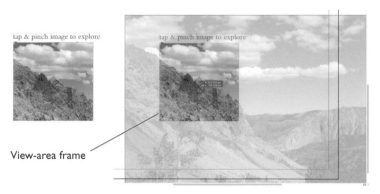

The view area (left) and the full image (right), which the user will be able to experience with Pan & Zoom enabled.

Once the image is positioned, select the image, including the view-area frame. Use the Pan & Zoom tab of the Folio Overlays panel to turn Pan & Zoom **On**.

The Pan & Zoom settings simply allow you to turn Pan & Zoom on or off for a selected image.

With Pan & Zoom, it's particularly important to let the user know that the images are not static images. Clear instructions or icons should be included on the page.

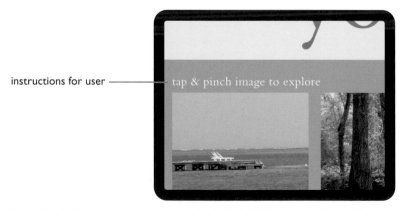

Because Pan & Zoom images present a static view initially, it's important to let users know they can interact with the images.

Once the user taps an image, the image can be scrolled or panned. The user can also pinch the image to see it reduced in the view area and visible in its entirety.

Scrollable frames

Scrollable frames are unique to tablet apps. They allow the user to view more content on the same page by scrolling that content within a fixed area. Scrollable frames can contain text, images, other overlays, or any combination of objects. Because of their flexibility, they are a powerful tool for adding interactivity to DPS apps.

Scrollable frames are created using a container frame and a content frame. The content frame is positioned in the container frame using the Edit > Paste Into command.

For example, to create a scrollable text frame, place the text you wish to scroll in its own frame on the page. Draw another frame that is the size of the area you wish to be visible.

Container frame

Content frame

Scrollable frames require both a container frame, which will be the viewing area, and a content frame, which contains the content that will scroll.

Position the text frame (content frame) where you want it to appear inside the viewing area (container frame). Select the content frame, and use Edit > Cut to move it to the clipboard. Select the container frame, and use Edit > Paste Into to insert the content frame inside the container frame. You can adjust the size of the container frame, which determines how much of the content frame will display before the text scrolls.

Any object — not just text frames — can be inserted inside a container frame. In fact, you can insert graphics which will work similarly to Pan & Zoom. (However, they will not allow the pinch and zoom control of Pan & Zoom.) You can insert multiple objects inside the viewing area as long as they are a single group. You can also include anchored objects that move with the text. You can also place a scrollable frame as one of the states in a multi-state object so when the user gets to that frame in the MSO, they then scroll through the visible text. You can use this technique to insert a button at the end of the scrollable frame that takes the user to another page or prompts any of the button actions.

Cut the content frame, select the container frame, and use Edit > Paste Into to position the content inside the container frame.

Now you're ready to select the container frame, with the content inside, and use the Scrollable Frame tab of the Folio Overlays panel to change settings for the behavior of the content.

The Scrollable Frame tab of the Folio Overlays panel with default settings.

Scrollable frame overlay settings

Scroll Direction: These settings determine the scrolling action of the enabled frames. **Auto Detect** determines the scroll direction based on the height and width of the container frame and content frame. For example, if the heights of the frames are the same but the widths are different, the content scrolls only horizontally. To make sure that the content scrolls in only one direction — even if the container frame is narrower and shorter than the content frame — choose **Horizontal** or **Vertical**. Choosing the **Horizontal & Vertical** option allows the content to scroll in both directions, assuming the content frame is larger than the container frame.

The direction options for scrollable frames.

Scroll Indicators: Select **Hide** if you don't want scroll bars displayed as the user scrolls the content.

Initial Content Position: Use this setting to determine the initial position of the content on the page. Select **Upper Left** to align the content frame to the upper-left corner of the container frame as the initial view. Select **Use Document Position** to use the location of the content frame as the initial view. If you don't want to align the content using the upper left corner of the content frame, move it over the container frame in the position desired, before you Cut the content frame into the Clipboard. This will determine its position when you paste it into the container frame.

Export Format in PDF articles: If your scrollable frame is in an article that is built using the default PDF format in the Folio Builder, the options are to export the overlay in **Bitmap** or **Vector**. Generally, it's best to use Vector for text-based frames, and Raster for image-based frames. If you're creating a folio for both SD (standard definition) and HD (high definition) iPads or iPhones, using Vector for text-based frames ensures you'll get sharper text when the folio is displayed on an HD iOS device.

The "sliding drawer" effect

Because scrollable frames can have any kind of content, you can do all sorts of fun things with them. One of our favorite tricks is to make a sliding drawer, or pull tab, effect. This lets you make tabs that users can drag out to reveal additional content. The following steps show just one example of the kinds of things that can be created using this general technique. It has the advantage, too, of allowing you to include more content in the relatively small amount of screen real estate available on tablets.

1. Create and group the objects that will make up the tab content. In this example, we have the tab graphic, some text, and an image.

The content of the tab is created, in this case, with the gray tab graphic, some text, and an image (left). The objects are positioned and grouped (right).

2. Draw the container frame. Since our tab will pull out from the right side of the container, the height of the container frame should be the same as, or a little higher than the grouped content frame. The width of the container frame should also be a little wider than the content group to allow room for the content to slide.

3. Position the content group where you want it to appear initially. In our example, we position it so the tab is just showing on the right edge of the container frame.

Content group

Container frame

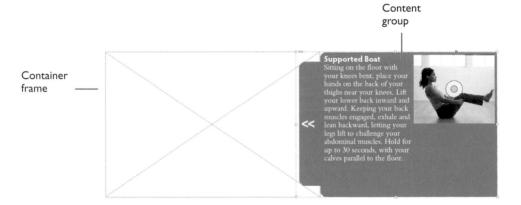

Move the content over the container frame into the position you want it to appear initially.

4. Select the content group and cut it into the Clipboard. Next, select the container frame and use Edit Paste Into to position the content group inside the container frame. If the position is not quite correct, click on the content group inside the container frame and reposition as needed.

5. Finally, using the Scrollable Frame tab of the Folio Overlays panel, set the frame to slide horizontally, and without slider control display. Since our "drawer" contains text, we're going to set the format to Vector, which will give us nice, crisp type when viewed on HD iPads.

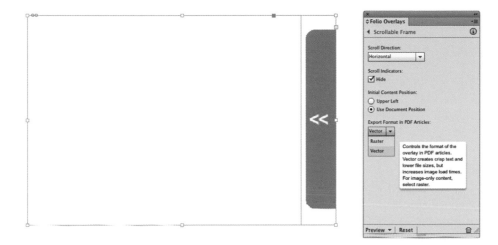

Set the "drawer" to slide horizontally, without Scroll Indicators. In order for the text to display clearly on retina iPads, choose Vector format.

6. Preview your work in the desktop Content Viewer by clicking on the Preview button at the bottom of the Folio Overlays panel .

The result, as viewed in the desktop Content Viewer, is a pull tab, or drawer, that the user taps and pulls out to reveal the content. The tab can be moved back and forth at will by the user.

The Folio Builder Panel

The Folio Builder panel in InDesign is an essential part of creating a DPS app. The purpose of the Folio Builder panel is to assemble your documents into a folio file that can be converted into an app. The panel allows you to set properties for the folio; preview your work, including the interactive components; and share your folios with others for review.

Exploring the Folio
Builder panel

The Folio Builder panel is used to create a folio file that will ultimately become either a standalone app, such as a book, or a single issue in a multi-issue app (as in a monthly magazine). Folios are made up of articles, which in turn are made up of layouts. Each folio may contain multiple articles. Each article may contain a layout that is horizontal only, vertical only, or one of each, depending on how the folio is set up.

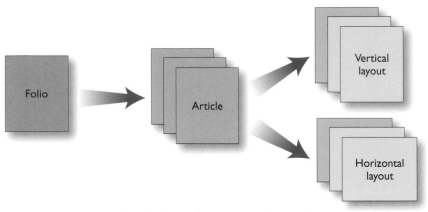

A folio consists of articles, which are made up of InDesign layout files.

The Folio Builder panel is a multi-level panel. It displays folios when you are working on folios, articles when you are working on articles, and layouts when you are working on layouts. The key to using the panel is to pay attention to the label at the top of the panel, which tells you which level is being displayed.

 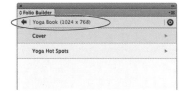 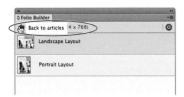

The key to using the multi-level Folio Builder panel is to keep an eye on the top of the panel and tool tips, which show you if you are viewing folios (left), articles (center), or layouts (right).

To navigate to the next level, click the arrow to the right of the folio or article, or double-click the folio or article name. To go back up from a layout or article, click the left-facing arrow at top.

When you are viewing folios and articles, the bottom of the panel will have a **Preview** button, a **New** or **Add** button, and a **Trash Can** icon to delete folios or articles. When viewing layouts, you can Add a layout only if you are missing either the horizontal or vertical version.

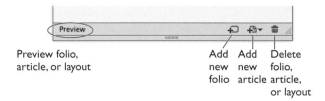

Preview folio, article, or layout
Add new folio
Add new article
Delete folio, article, or layout

The buttons at the bottom of the Folio Builder panel let you preview, add, or delete new folios and articles.

When you have a list of multiple folios, you can filter which ones are displayed. At the top of the panel, click the black triangle next to **Folios: All**. You'll see a list of the various kinds of folios that can be listed. The default setting is **In the Cloud** (that is, uploaded to the Acrobat.com web host), but there are other options that are discussed later in this chapter. Regardless of how you filter the list, you can also sort the list of folios alphabetically, by most recently modified, or by publication date.

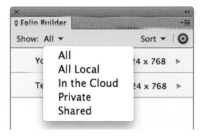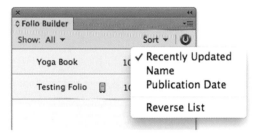

You can filter the kinds of folios that are displayed in the Folio Builder panel, and sort the filtered list.

Creating a folio

The first step to creating a folio is to open the Folio Builder panel (Window > Folio Builder) and log in with your Adobe ID. If you already have an Adobe ID you wish to use, choose **Sign In** from the panel menu; choose **Sign Up** if you don't have an Adobe ID or want to create a new one.

DPS and your Adobe ID

If you've ever registered your Adobe software, you have an Adobe ID. It's free and is your usual "identifier" to Adobe. Most people have just one Adobe ID.

However, be aware that the Adobe ID you use in the Folio Builder panel will be tied to a specific custom viewer app that is created later in the process. This means that if you have different publications, you'll want to sign in using different Adobe IDs. The folio you create may be a standalone app, such as a book, or it may be a single issue in a multi-issue app, such as a monthly magazine. Either way, the steps to create a folio are the same, but only one Adobe ID can be associated with a publication's viewer app.

Next, choose **New Folio** from the panel menu, or click the **New** button at the bottom of the Folio Builder panel to display the New Folio dialog. Here you will set various important attributes of the folio, including the **Name** of the folio. The name of the folio will be used for production purposes, and is not the name users will see in the final app.

You can also specify the **Viewer Version**. The viewer version is associated with the version of any viewer app you've previously built, or the Adobe Content Viewer on your device used to preview your work. To change the version for the folio, click on the version number in the New Folio dialog; the Viewer Version menu will display, then select the appropriate choice. You'll want to make sure that your folio is an equal version or lower than any viewer app you'll want the folio viewed in.

TIP To determine the version of the Adobe Content Viewer on your tablet device, go to any app in the Library. Tap once to display the navigation controls, then tap twice on the name of the publication at the top of the screen. The version and build number will display.

The New Folio dialog lets you define several important settings for your folio, including size, orientation, and image format.

Target Device lets you specify the device on which you'll be publishing your folio. Different devices will display dimensions, in pixels, for the folio. For example, if you choose Amazon Kindle Fire, the dimensions will change to 1024 x 600. The folio doesn't need to be exactly the same size, but the same aspect ratio is important; for example, 4:3 for iPads or 16:9 for Android tablets. If you don't see the device you want to create your folio for, simply enter custom dimensions. There is nothing special about the preset sizes. You can also set the **Orientation** of your folio to contain only horizontal, only vertical, or both horizontal and vertical articles.

The Target Device menu in the New Folio dialog lets you choose the dimensions for your folio from preset dimensions for various tablets and phones.

Default Format options let you specify the format of the flattened part of the folio. Remember that your InDesign layout is flattened to an image, with the interactive elements in an overlay. The options are JPEG, PNG, and PDF. PDF is the default selection, and it is usually the best choice for your folio format.

If you choose **JPEG**, you can also set the **Default JPEG Quality**, or compression, to Minimum, Low, Medium, High, or Maximum; the default is High, which gives good results on most devices. This setting can be changed when adding new articles to the folio. **PNG** format is required, however, for transparency effects.

But again, **PDF** folios are usually the best choice, because they hold their resolution — especially for pages with text — regardless of the device resolution. PDF folios work best for the Retina display iPads, but they can also be used for the older Standard Definition iPads as well.

Cover Preview allows you to load images for the cover that will display. For single folios, this is the cover that will display in the viewer library. Create cover images as 72-dpi JPEG or PNG files using the same pixel dimensions as the target device, such as 1024 x 768.

TIP An easy way to create a cover preview image is to simply design it in an InDesign document that is 1024 x 768 pixels, then export the page as a JPEG using the File Export command.

By default, when you create a folio it is uploaded to the Acrobat.com web host. However, if you don't need to share the folio or preview it on another workstation, you can select the **Create Offline Folio** check box. This will save the folio to your local hard drive, and is a good alternative when you want to work quickly or don't have an Internet connection. Local folios are indicated by a disk icon next to them. You can upload them later using **Upload to Folio Producer** on the panel menu.

Changing folio properties
After you create a folio, you can set additional properties for the folio using the Folio Properties dialog. You can specify the publication name that will

257

be seen by the user, as well as change the viewer version or cover image. You cannot change the orientation, default format, or image size. If you need to change one of those properties, you'll have to create a new folio.

To access the Folio Properties dialog, click the name of the folio in the Folio Builder panel. From the panel menu, choose **Properties**.

Folio properties can be accessed from the panel menu in the Folio Builder panel.

Use the Folio Properties dialog to set the **Publication Name** of the folio; this is the name that the user will see in the viewer app and is different from the working folio name in the Folio Builder panel. You can also change the **Viewer Version** number, which specifies the version of the viewer app your folio will be viewed in. Be sure the version number of the folio is equal to or lower than the version of the viewer app.

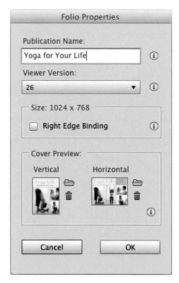

Use the Folio Properties dialog to set the name and to preview the icons that will appear in the viewer app.

The folio is represented in the viewer app library by a preview image. If you didn't load these images when you first created the folio, or you wish to change them, click the **Folder** icon next to the appropriate orientation and point to the image file. These images should be 72 dpi JPEG or PNG files and the same pixel dimensions as your folio, such as 1024 x 768. If you want to change the image, simply click the Folder icon again and select a new image. If you wish to delete the image and load a new image later, click the **Trash Can** icon to delete the current image.

To change additional folio properties for publishing a folio, such as the Folio Number or Publication Date, choose Folio Producer from the Folio Builder panel menu, and specify settings in the Folio Producer Organizer, which is discussed in the section "Folio Producer" on page 268.

Adding Articles to Folios

After you've created a folio, the next step is to add articles to the folio. Articles consist of InDesign layout files that can be loaded individually or as a group of files in a folder.

Adding a single article

Once you've created a folio, you can add the currently active InDesign document to the folio as an article. Click the folio name to go to the Articles level, then click the **Add Article** button at the bottom of the panel. This displays the New Article dialog.

New Article
Article Name:
Cover
Article Format:
Automatic
JPEG Quality:
High
Smooth Scrolling:
Off (Snap to Page)
Portrait Layout:
iPad_v
Landscape Layout:
iPad_h
Cancel   OK

The New Article dialog lets you name an article, and if you have used alternate layouts for the two orientations, it will load them automatically.

In this dialog, specify a **Name** for the article. This does not have to match the document file name and should relate to the content of the article in some way. This name is also used for creating links between articles, but it is not displayed to the end user in the viewer app. For instance, an article called "How to Train Your Cat" might be named "Cat" in the Folio Builder panel.

You can also specify the **Default Format** of the non-overlay components of the article: JPEG, PNG, or PDF. PDF is the default selection and is usually the best choice.

If your currently active InDesign document uses alternate layouts and contains both horizontal- and vertical-orientation pages, these will be automatically loaded for the **Portrait Layout** and the **Landscape Layout**. If the InDesign document is set up as a long scrolling page, you can turn on **Smooth Scrolling** for the page; the default is Off (Snap to Page).

If your InDesign file contains only one orientation, open that file or make it the currently active document file, and then create a new article. When you click OK, the file is added to the article and the orientation of the document is determined automatically. Once that file is loaded, make the file with the other orientation the active document. Then double-click the name of the article in the Folio Builder panel, which switches the panel to layout view, then click the Add button. The file will be added and the orientation automatically determined.

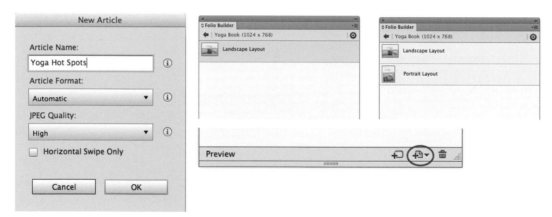

If you are creating a dual orientation folio, and have only one orientation layout per InDesign file, make one orientation active and create a new article, then make the other orientation file active and click the Add Article button.

Importing multiple articles

Instead of adding articles one by one, you can import a folder of several articles at once. The file names and organization on your hard drive must be very specific, however. Start with a folio folder that contains article folders. When you import, you'll point to the folio folder.

The folders for articles with both horizontal and vertical orientation must contain two InDesign files. One must have an _h suffix and one must have a _v suffix, such as *filename_h* and *filename_v*. If the article has a single orientation, the InDesign file within the article folder must have the correct orientation suffix.

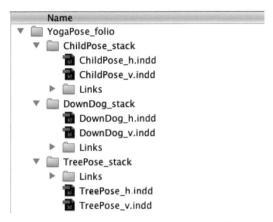

The file structure and naming conventions must be very specific in order to import articles.

To import articles, first create a folio in the Folio Builder panel. Next, choose the **Import** command from the panel menu. You can import one or more articles.

To import multiple articles into a folio, choose the Import command and target the folio folder containing the article folders.

Once InDesign has imported the article folders, the articles are listed in the Folio Builder panel. You'll still need to modify the article properties, as discussed in the next section.

The imported folders are added as articles and will appear in the articles list for the folio.

Changing article properties

As with folio properties, the information and images in the Article Properties dialog will be seen by the user in the viewer app. Article properties that can be added include information like that often seen in print publications, such as the title and the author's name (byline), along with additional information about the content.

To access the Article Properties dialog, click the name of an article in the Folio Builder panel. Next, choose **Article Properties** from the panel menu.

The Article Properties dialog is displayed by clicking an article and choosing Article Properties from the panel menu.

The **Title** of the article is displayed in Browse mode in the viewer app and also in the table of contents. The title here is different from the name of the article used in the Folio Builder panel; the article name in the Folio Builder panel is used for creating links between articles but is not displayed to the end user in the viewer app.

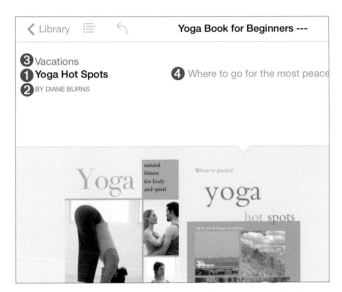

The Article Properties dialog lets you specify the title, description, byline, and kicker that will display for each article in the viewer app when in Browse mode.

The **Byline** will appear below the title in the viewer app. The byline is usually where the author's name would appear.

The **Kicker** will appear above the title in the viewer app. It will also display above the title in the table of contents. This is often used to designate the different sections in a publication, such as Departments or Features. But this is not a hard and fast rule, and you can use it for any text that makes sense in this context.

The **Description** of the article will appear above the article in the viewer app. This text could be similar to what's called a *deck* in print magazine articles — text that usually sits between the title and the body text — and further explains what the article is about.

If you're working with an article that you want to scroll as one long page, choose **Smooth Scrolling** and set the direction you want it to scroll. Choose Horizontal Orientation, Vertical Orientation or Both Directions.

If you have an article of individual pages, you can set the article to **Horizontal Swipe Only**, so that the user swipes horizontally from one page to the next. The default navigation in a DPS app is that you swipe horizontally to move from article to article, and you swipe vertically to go from page to page within an article. With this option, the user swipes through all the pages in an article horiztonally, much as you would in the pages of a print book.

The Kicker and Title text display in the table of contents in the viewer app, along with the thumbnail preview specified in the Article Properties dialog. A thumbnail image was not added to the cover, above, so a preview is automatically generated; the second article uses a custom thumbnail image.

To specify an image for the table of contents thumbnail, click the folder icon next to **Table of Contents Preview**. Select an image that is 140 x 140 pixels, in JPEG or PNG format. These images will look good on both SD and HD devices. If you don't specify an image in the Article Properties dialog, a table of contents icon is automatically generated from the first page of the article.

If your folio contains a page that is an advertisement that you don't want to appear in the table of contents, select the **Advertisement** check box. If it's some other kind of article you don't want to appear in the table of contents, select the **Hide From TOC** check box.

Previewing and Sharing Your Work

It's important with any project you're working on to be able to both preview and share your work with others, especially the client for whom you may be working.

With print publications, a PDF or printout might do the trick, but with interactive apps, the standard workflow isn't practical. Fortunately, DPS makes both previewing and sharing your work convenient.

Previewing folios and articles

It's important, of course, to be able to preview your folios, articles, and interactive layouts. But even single pages, if they contain interactive settings or elements created using the Folio Overlays panel, will not preview in the SWF Preview panel. Instead, use the Folio Overlays panel or the Folio Builder panel to access the Adobe Content Viewer.

There are two versions of the Adobe Content Viewer: a desktop application and a mobile device application. The Desktop Viewer is automatically added to your computer when you install the Folio Producer tools. The viewer for mobile devices is available for download in the Apple App Store, Google Play, and Amazon's Appstore for Android.

Preview on your computer

The desktop version of the Adobe Content Viewer provides a quick and easy way to preview folios, articles, or even individual pages in your layout, right on your computer screen.

It does have some limitations, though. You mimic finger actions with your mouse, and this isn't the same as experiencing it on a tablet. It won't really tell you, for example, if a button is too small for most fingers to tap. It's always a good idea to finally preview your work on the intended device. The desktop Content Viewer is convenient, though, for quick previews and to check if interactive elements do what they are supposed to.

To preview a folio, select it in the Folio Builder panel. At the bottom of the panel, click **Preview** to display the menu. Choose **Preview on Desktop** to display in the Desktop Viewer on your computer.

The Desktop Viewer displays the folio and all its articles. There are several shortcuts you can use to mimic viewing the folio on a mobile device. Use Cmd/Ctrl with the + and – keys to simulate pinching in and out. Obviously you can't rotate your desktop monitor or even laptop computer to change the orientation. Use Cmd/Ctrl-R to "rotate" the screen.

View	
✓ Portrait	
Landscape	⌘R
Zoom In	⌘+
Zoom Out	⌘—
Fit in Screen	⌘0
Actual Size	⌘1

The Desktop Viewer uses keyboard shortcuts to allow you to view a folio in Portrait or Landscape mode.

To view an individual article in the desktop Viewer, select the article in the Folio Builder panel and click the **Preview** button at the bottom of the panel.

You can also preview your currently open InDesign file. Choose File > Folio Preview, and the desktop Viewer will preview the file. This will preview the file even if it hasn't been added to a folio and can come in handy when you don't have an Internet connection and can't get to your folio in the cloud.

File	
New	▶
Open...	⌘O
Browse in Bridge...	⌥⌘O
Open Recent	▶
Folio Preview	
Folio Preview Settings...	

Folio Preview lets you preview your current layout file in the Desktop Viewer.

You can control the image format of the Desktop Viewer by choosing File > Folio Preview Settings and selecting the image format in which to display previews. Select **Preview Current Layout** if you want the Desktop Viewer to display only your current layout.

You can also preview the interactive content on your current page using the Folio Overlays panel. Click the interactive content on the page to access the appropriate tab of the panel, then click **Preview** at the bottom of the panel.

As we mentioned, the desktop version of the Adobe Content Viewer is a good "quick and dirty" way to preview your work, but it doesn't precisely emulate the experience your users will have when viewing your app. You should always check your work periodically by previewing it on the target device.

Preview on your device

You can also preview folios and articles on an iPad, an iPhone, or Android tablets. That way, you'll know exactly how your app will look and feel on its target device.

There are two different ways you can preview folios. In both cases, you must have the Adobe Content Viewer installed on the target device. Download the app from the appropriate store for your device.

You can preview your folios from the cloud (that is, on Acrobat.com). Simply go to the Adobe Content Viewer on your device and log in with the same Adobe ID you used to create your folios. Once you sign in, all your folios in the cloud will be available for downloading and previewing. Local folios will not be available for preview.

You can also preview your folios and articles without an Internet connection by connecting your iPad, iPhone, or Android tablet to your computer via its USB cable. To view your folio and articles, the device must be physically attached to your computer, and the Adobe Content Viewer must be open, and the device not in the sleep mode. To preview a folio, select it in the Folio Builder panel. At the bottom of the panel, click **Preview** to display the menu. Choose **Preview on** <*device name*>. The folio will appear in the Library window of the Content Viewer on your device.

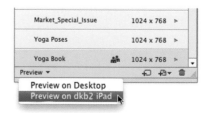

You can preview folios and articles by connecting your device to your computer, without any Internet connection required.

There are a couple of advantages to previewing on your device with a direct connection. For one, you can often preview folios and articles more quickly, as no Internet connection is involved and you don't have to wait for your articles to upload and then download. Also, you can preview local folios with a direct connection.

Keep in mind that the Adobe Content Viewer is basically a generic version of a viewer app, and its primary purpose is for testing your digital content directly on the iPad, iPhone, or Android device. The Adobe Content Viewer is updated along with the Folio Producer tools, which are updated frequently.

Sharing folios   While the ultimate goal of your tablet app is its publication to a wide audience, it's also important to be able to share your interactive content with others who are part of a smaller group, especially during the development process. Fortunately, the Folio Builder panel makes it easy to share folios and articles with other members of your workgroup or with your client.

To share a folio, select it in the Folio Builder panel and choose **Share** from the panel menu. The dialog that is displayed lets you send an email to the person, or group of people, with whom you'd like to share the folio. You can input multiple email addresses separated by commas. The default subject line reads "*<your name>* has shared a folio with you." Fill out the Message field to include a message with the email. Click the **Share** button, and an email will be sent to the addressee(s).

The Share option in the panel menu of the Folio Builder panel lets you send an email to members of your workgroup or to your client, allowing them to preview the folio.

Once you've shared a folio, the folio name will be displayed with a share icon. Hover your cursor over the folio name to display a tool tip that includes information about the folio, its owner, and how many people have shared it.

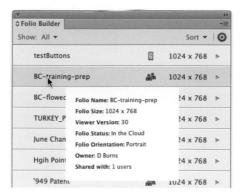

A tool tip displays information about the folio, such as that it has been shared with one person.

The person with whom you've shared the folio must log in using their Adobe ID in order to view the shared folio. In fact, you must send the email to the email address used by their ID in order for them to be able to view the shared folio. The folio will be available in the Folio Builder panel on their copy of InDesign, as well as in the library of the Adobe Content Viewer on their iPad or Android tablet.

If you want to stop sharing a folio, choose **Unshare** from the panel menu on the Folio Builder panel. A dialog displays a list of all the users sharing the folio. You can unshare with any individual member of the list or unshare the folio from the entire list.

If someone shares a folio with you, that folio will display in your Folio Builder panel and in the library of your device's Adobe Content Viewer. You'll see the folio in your Folio Builder panel list with the share icon next to it, but when you go to the articles list, the article names will be grayed out (meaning you cannot change them, but you can preview them).

TIP You cannot share local folios from the Folio Builder panel. Instead, move them to the cloud. From the panel menu on the Folio Builder, choose Upload to Folio Producer, which puts the folio in the cloud so it can be shared.

Sharing folios is the method used by advertisers to submit ads to publications. The advertiser shares the ad folio with the publication. The ad can then be added to the publication's folio in Folio Producer, the next step in the publishing process.

Folio Producer

The Folio Producer is a web-based tool that allows you to organize, edit, share, and publish the folios you've created in InDesign. It's part of the DPS Dashboard, which contains several tools and resources for publishing your app.

Because the focus of this book is on the design and creative tools in InDesign, we'll just give you a quick overview of Folio Producer to get you started exploring on your own. The Folio Producer is optional for Single Edition users, who can go from folio creation to Create App, as discussed in the next section, "What's Next: Publishing Your App to a Store" on page 271 . However, it is required for Professional and Enterprise subscribers. Single Edition users, however, may find some of its features for organizing and entering metadata convenient to use.

To access Folio Producer, choose **Folio Producer** from the panel menu on the Folio Builder or use your computer's browser to access the DPS Dashboard at http://digitalpublishing.acrobat.com. Log in with the same Adobe ID you used to create your folios in the Folio Builder panel in InDesign. Anyone with a valid Adobe ID can log in to the DPS Dashboard, but certain options are available only to Professional or Enterprise DPS subscribers.

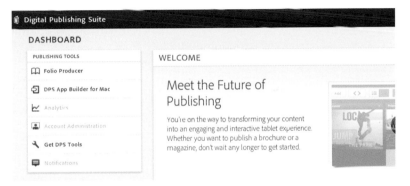

Sign in to the DPS dashboard using the same Adobe ID you used to create your folios in the Folio Builder panel in InDesign.

From the Dashboard, click **Folio Producer**. You will now be in the **Folio Producer Organizer** and will see a list of all the folios you created in the Folio Builder panel in InDesign. From this list view, you can specify various settings for the folio, such as the **Publication Name** and the **Folio Number**. Settings that are marked with an asterisk are required to publish the folio. Any changes you make here are updated and show in your Folio Builder panel in InDesign.

You can also share the folio from here by clicking the Share icon at the top of the window. Just as when sharing from the Folio Builder panel, you'll get an email you can address to invite others to share the folio.

The Folio Producer Organizer lists all the folios from your Folio Builder panel in InDesign. Changes made here are reflected in the folios in the Folio Builder panel.

If you have local folios you want to work with in Folio Producer, you must upload them. Click the name of the local folio and choose **Upload to Folio Producer** from the panel menu. The list in Folio Producer will be updated to include the local folio.

To list local folios, upload them to Folio Producer from the Folio Builder panel in InDesign.

You can use the **Folio Producer Editor** to rearrange articles, move articles to and from other folios, and change article settings. To access the Editor, click the name of a folio in the Organizer list and click the **Open** button at the top of the window.

You can work with articles in either a thumbnail view or a list view. To change the article properties, click an article and edit the information shown on the right side of the window.

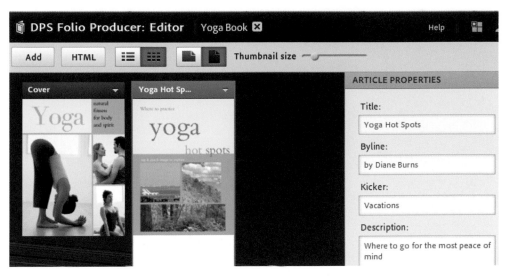

The Folio Producer Editor lets you rearrange articles or change article properties.

You can still edit your InDesign documents after you have done work on them in Folio Producer. From InDesign, click on the name of the article in the Folio Builder panel and choose **Update** from the panel menu.

Once your folio is organized the way you want it, you can publish your folio to the Adobe Distribution Server. This option is available to anyone and does not require a DPS subscription. Simply click the name of the folio in the Folio Producer Organizer window, then click **Publish**.

Think of the Folio Producer as a production tool if you're a Single Edition user, or if you're a Professional or Enterprise subscriber, a bridge between the production of your folio and the actual app development. The app development is the final step in making your app available for sale to the general public.

What's Next: Publishing Your App to a Store

The final step to selling your app to the public is to turn it into an actual device application. As we mentioned in the first chapter of this book, designers and creative professionals are expected not only to be creative and to produce documents, but also to become application developers. (Although we do know of design firms that have hired dedicated application developers to handle this phase of the app process.) Details of the steps are beyond the scope of this book, but we offer an outline of what's involved to get you started.

Once you've published your folio and exported it, the next step is to build a viewer app. For Single Edition users, the first step is to click on the folio in the Folio Builder panel and choose **Create App** from the panel menu.

Single Edition users start the process of building an app by choosing Create App from the Folio Builder panel menu.

This launches the DPS App Builder that was installed along with your DPS tools. You may be prompted to update to the most current version of the App Builder. This is a kind of wizard app that prompts you through the various steps of creating the app, including adding icons and splash screens, and incorporating the proper files necessary to submit your app. Single Edition users can only publish to the Apple App Store.

The opening screen of the DPS Builder App. Refer to the step-by-step guide published by Adobe to walk you through the multiple-step process of building your app.

Going through the steps in the DPS App Builder is a multiple step process. It is highly recommended that you download and use the step-by-step guide created by Adobe for this purpose, that you can find at: http://help.adobe.com/en_US/ppcompdoc/Step_by_step_guide_to_dps_se.pdf.

If you are a Professional or Enterprise subscriber to DPS, the steps for creating an app are different. In addition to creating iPad apps, you can create apps for other types of devices, such as the Kindle Fire. Adobe has created a detailed guide for this process which can be found at: http://help.adobe.com/en_US/ppcompdoc/Adobe_Publishing_Companion_Guide_for_iPad.pdf

If you are publishing to the iPad or iPhone, you'll also need to sign up to become an Apple Developer. The cost is $99 a year, and you can sign up at https://developer.apple.com/programs/ios/.

Amazon has its own requirements for developers for the Kindle Fire, details of which can be found at http://developer.amazon.com/. There is yet another set of guidelines for Android developers, which can be found at http://developer.android.com/.

Other Resources

As mentioned at the beginning of this chapter, the details of creating apps using the Digital Publishing Suite are quickly changing. The features of the Folio Builder panel and the Folio Producer, the details of DPS subscriptions, and the final process of app development may change frequently.

Here is a list of important resources that will supplement this book and bring you the most up-to-date information about DPS.

- Robert Bringhurst, author of the documentation for InDesign and the Digital Publishing Suite, has created a fantastic publication app for the iPad called *DPS Tips*. It's a must-have app if you want to learn more about DPS: http://itunes.apple.com/us/app/digital-publishing-suite-tips/id436199090?mt=8
- The Adobe Help files for DPS are available online: http://help.adobe.com/en_US/digitalpubsuite/home/
- The DPS Developer Center has fantastic resources, including white papers and videos: http://www.adobe.com/devnet/digitalpublishingsuite.html
- There are many excellent videos covering DPS on Adobe TV: http://tv.adobe.com/product/digital-publishing-suite/
- Adobe provides a gallery of all the publications that have created DPS apps — a great source of inspiration, and a list that is growing daily: http://dpsgallery.adobe.com/

Interactive PDFs

In This Chapter

THINK ABOUT HOW OFTEN YOU OPEN OR SEND A PDF FILE. It's such a simple idea: You create a document in one application and then convert it into a file format that can be opened by anyone using a free reader application.

As PDF technology has grown, it has been fascinating to watch how various groups use PDF files. Print houses use them as a prepress format. Editorial departments use them for marking up proofs of files. And publishers and design firms use the interactive features to create dynamic digital publications. And most forms you have downloaded to fill out are PDF documents.

PDFs have been around a long time, and they're not considered terribly sexy anymore. But we've seen some incredible interactivity included within PDF documents. One author used PDF documents with embedded video files to create a college course on movie editing. A developer created an interactive Jeopardy-style game show with categories and questions in a table. Corporations have created annual reports with movie introductions featuring the company's CEO.

PDF Workflow

The InDesign workflow for creating and viewing PDF files.

It's simple to create an interactive PDF file using InDesign. Once you create the file with its interactive elements, just choose Adobe PDF (Interactive) format in the Export dialog and set the appropriate options. (*We cover setting the options for the exporting the document, starting on page 281.*)

TIP The Adobe PDF (Print) is the format that is sent to print shops. Don't use this format if you want all the interactive features in your document.

Viewing PDF documents on Adobe readers

Interactive PDFs are a great, but as we'll discuss in the next section, the built-in PDF readers on most computers and tablet devices are limited in their ability to display them correctly.

What's even more frustrating is that your readers may not even know what program has opened the PDF document. For instance, a PDF sent as an email attachment to an iPad will be opened with the built-in iOS PDF reader, and iOS support for interactivity in PDFs is very limited. An iPad user can tap an icon and get "Open In…" options for a PDF, but the only default reader installed is iBooks, which also has very limited support for interactivity in PDFs.

TIP Only hyperlinks are supported in interactive PDFs read on an iPad using the built-in iOS PDF reader. Buttons created with InDesign objects don't even display!

However, and not surprisingly, as the creator of the PDF format, Adobe's own Acrobat Pro or Adobe Reader can bring interactive PDFs alive on computer desktops, and most computer users already have it installed. When it comes to tablets and smartphones, the free Adobe Reader is available for both iOS and Android devices, and does a pretty good job with many of InDesign's interactive features for PDF. (It's available for download at http://www.adobe.com/products/reader-mobile.html.)

The following table shows which interactive features you can use in PDF documents when viewed on computers running Adobe Acrobat Pro or Adobe Reader or on tablets and smartphones using Adobe Reader.

InDesign Interactive Feature	Supported on Computers Running Adobe Reader or Acrobat Pro	Supported on Tablets and Smartphones Running Adobe Reader
Hyperlinks	Yes	Yes
Cross-References	Yes	Yes
Table of Contents	Yes	Yes
Bookmarks	Yes	Yes
Audio and Video Files	Yes except SWF videos	No
Multi-State Objects	No	No
Buttons	Yes	Yes (limited)
Forms	Yes	Yes
Animations (*see "Adding Animations to a PDF" on page 296*)	No	No
Page Transitions (*covered on page 294*)	Yes, except for the Page Turn and Page Curl effects.	No

For the most part, Adobe Reader for tablets and smartphones supports forms and most navigational buttons. But it doesn't support multimedia events such as playing movies and sounds or showing and hiding fields. And it supports hyperlinks and buttons, but ignores some button actions, such as Go To First/Last Page and Go To Next/Previous Page.

Built-in PDF readers for computers

In 2007, PDF became an *open source* standard. This means that companies other than Adobe can create and distribute their own versions of PDF creators and readers. They just have to follow the open source standards. They do not, however, have to follow the standards exactly.

This has been a mixed blessing. It has made it possible to download free or cheap PDF applications, but it also means that not every PDF reader supports all the features that are included in interactive PDF files. *And you won't know which reader your audience is using!*

For example, Macintosh computers come with a PDF reader application called Preview. With Windows 8 and later, Microsoft bundles a built-in PDF reader called the Microsoft Windows Reader. Unless your users download the Adobe Reader program and make it the default application for PDF files, they will open your interactive PDF documents in Preview or Windows Reader.

Both Preview and Windows Reader open PDF files as "flat" documents. The images for a button, movie, or hyperlink may appear on the screen, but there will be no interactivity. The objects are still in the PDF, but they can't be used interactively. The use of non-Adobe PDF applications is the primary reason users complain about their interactive PDF documents not working correctly.

Your only solution is to firmly emphasize to those who open your PDF files that they should (*must!*) view it in Adobe Reader or Acrobat Pro. We suggest that you build in a hyperlink in your document that sends them to http://get.adobe.com/reader/ to download the Adobe Reader software. The link looks at the computer's operating system and opens the correct download page. It's free, easy to install, and is the most advanced reader for computers.

Third-party PDF readers for tablets

As we've mentioned, iOS has a built-in PDF reader, but it has really limited support for interactivity. Hyperlinks work, but that's about it. Most Android devices don't have built-in support for interactive PDFs at all.

If you want to view intereactive PDFs on a tablet or smartphone, you'll need a third-party product. Unfortunately, it's really the wild, wild west out there when it comes to finding the best one. In addition to the free Adobe Reader, there are several options, especially for iOS devices.

Another popular PDF reader for iOS devices is GoodReader. This $2.99 app was one of the first available for the iPad, and it features a rich set of features, with support for some, though not all, interactive features in PDFs http://www.goodiware.com.

One of the PDF readers with the best interactivity support we've found is PDF Expert, but its for iPhone and iPad only, and costs $9.99.This is a good option if you need to view interactive PDFs on your iPad https://itunes.apple.com/app/id743974925?.

About interactive PDFs on tablets

We love interactive PDFs, but the bottom line is we can't rely on our readers opening them in the the best third-party software in order to display them correctly. That doesn't mean that there is no use for interactive PDF presentations on tablets.

Even though you can't expect someone to download an interactive PDF from your website and read it in a specific third-party PDF reader, you can still use interactive PDFs on an iPad or other tablet in cases where you can control the reader software.

For example, each member of a sales team could be equipped with an iPad running Adobe Reader or PDF Expert, and they could demo an engaging, interactive PDF to their clients. As long as members of the sales team are in control of the demonstration, all the bells and whistles of buttons, sounds, movies, and navigation events will play perfectly. We know clients who have had great success with this approach to presenting interactive PDFs.

Fortunately, for wide distribution of interactive documents, there is an alternative to PDF files. Fixed layout ePubs are similar to PDFs, and they offer the ability to include similar interactive features, as well as animations, which can't be easily included in PDFs. We discuss this exciting alternative to interactive PDFs in Chapter 6, "Fixed Layout ePubs."

Support for annotations and forms

Most third-party PDF readers support PDF annotations, also known as comments. Comments added to a PDF in Acrobat Reader on a computer can be read in Acrobat on a tablet or smartphone, and vice-versa. This is a great way to review documents, and is also a terrific way for students to take notes in their classes.

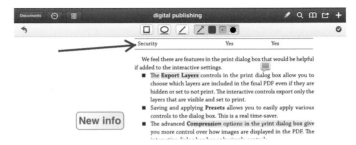

Our own book can be purchased in a PDF format, and viewed in Adobe Reader on a computer or tablet device, where students can make notes and annotate the PDF.

Perhaps it's the lucrative market for business applications, but almost every PDF reader we've seen has robust support for filling in forms. Some of the appearances may not translate perfectly, but the form itself can be filled out and sent to the originator.

PDF Export

Once you've finished your InDesign document, it's time to export it as a PDF file. To do so, choose File > Export. You then have to choose between the Adobe PDF (Print) and Adobe PDF (Interactive) formats.

Interactive or print? Why did Adobe separate the PDF export into two dialogs? Our best guess is that with only one export dialog, users would inadvertently create PDF files for print that include interactive elements such as buttons and movies. Print prepress houses complained when they got PDF files filled with elements that screwed up their prepress workflow. By creating a separate export dialog for interactive documents, InDesign avoids mixing interactive elements into a PDF designed for print.

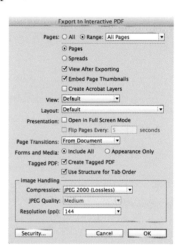

The Export Adobe PDF dialog for print (left) and the Export to Interactive PDF dialog (right). Notice that there are seven sections for the print dialog.

Here are the features and controls in each dialog.

Export Feature	Export Print Dialog	Export Interactive Dialog
Presets	Yes	No
Page Controls	Yes	Yes
View After Exporting	Yes	Yes

Export Feature	Export Print Dialog	Export Interactive Dialog
Embed Page Thumbnails	Yes	Yes
Optimize for Fast Web View	Yes	No
Create Tagged PDF	Yes	Yes
Presentation Controls	No	Yes
Create Acrobat Layers	Yes	Yes
Non-Printing Objects	Yes	No
Page Transitions	No	Yes
Export Layer Selections	Yes	No
Interactive Elements	Bookmarks and hyperlinks only	Yes, all
Compression	Full controls	Simple controls
Marks and Bleeds	Yes	No
Output	Yes	No
Advanced	Yes	No
Security	Yes	Yes

TIP If you only need hyperlinks and bookmarks in your interactive document, you can use the export print dialog. This gives you the compression options and allows you to use the saved presets.

Page controls The top section of the Export to Interactive PDF dialog controls settings related to page controls, including setting a page range, whether or not to export spreads, and layer controls.

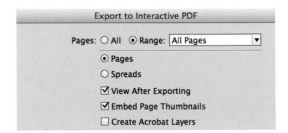

The Page controls in the Export to Interactive PDF dialog.

Specifying pages and page ranges: Most of the time you'll want to export all the pages in your document. In that case, just click the **All** selection. If you want only certain pages to print, you can designate those pages in the **Range** field of the dialog. Enter a comma to separate pages, such as 5, 7, 9. Use a hyphen to select a range of pages, such as 3–6. You can even mix hyphens and commas to select ranges and individual pages, such as 3, 5, 7–9.

Specifying pages in sections: It gets a little complicated when you have alternate layouts in the document. Each alternate layout starts a new section and then restarts the page numbering. In that case, you can have two pages with the same page number. If you enter that page number in the dialog, InDesign shows an alert that explains you need to be more specific.

To export a specific page, you can type the alternate layout name with a colon in front of the page number. For example, if you have an alternate layout called "iPad H," you would enter *iPad H:1* to export page 1 from that alternate layout. You can also type a plus sign (+) followed by the absolute page number in the document. So, for instance, if the page is the fourth actual page in the document, you would type +4 to export that page. (*See Chapter 4, "Layout Controls" for more information on working with alternate layouts.*)

When you have alternate layouts in a document, you can insert the name of the alternate layout to specify which pages should be exported.

Creating pages or spreads: You can choose to export the PDF in single pages or to maintain the spreads in the document. For interactive documents, we usually deselect the spread option and break the document into single pages. This makes it easier to view all the information on the page without having to zoom in or out on a spread.

It also solves the problem of stringing documents together using InDesign's Book panel. If you choose spreads when you create interactive PDFs, the first page of each document in the book will be a single page, with the rest of them as spreads, which can be confusing to the reader. Choosing single pages keeps all the pages as single pages.

View After Exporting: It may seem a trivial thing. But if you're going to be exporting and previewing your PDF over and over, you really want to immediately view the PDF without having to navigate to open it.

Embed Page Thumbnails: This option creates a thumbnail preview for each page being exported, or one thumbnail for each spread if the Spreads option is selected. These thumbnail images are then displayed in the PDF Pages pane as a preview of the document. The option was important in the past, when it took longer to see the previews in the Pages pane. It is not as important now, when the page thumbnails are automatically created.

Create Acrobat Layers: This converts the layers in the InDesign document into layers in the PDF file. This allows your viewers to show or hide layers using the Layers pane in Acrobat Pro or Adobe Reader.

However, instructing viewers as to where the Layers panel is and how to use it can be confusing. Fortunately, you can create buttons that will show or hide the layers in the document. Unfortunately, the Show Layers and Hide Layers actions for the PDF have to be created in Acrobat Pro.

 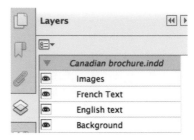

The layers in an InDesign document (*left*) can be converted into layers in a PDF document (*right*).

Setting the View controls

You can control the magnification for the PDF when it is first opened. This is very helpful if you want to ensure that the first page opens in the best magnification. Choose one of the following from the View menu:

Default: This option sets the magnification to whatever setting has been chosen on the viewer's machine. This can cause your document to open too large to be seen completely or too small to be read on the user's machine. We recommend you change it to have the document open to the setting you want.

Actual Size: Use this option to set the initial magnification to 100%.

Fit Page: This forces the width and height of the page to fit within the document window. This allows the user to see the entire PDF page at once.

Fit Width: This option makes the width of the page fill the width of the document window. This setting is helpful for documents set in the landscape orientation.

Fit Height: makes the height of the page fill the height of the document window. This setting is helpful for documents set in the portrait orientation.

Fit Visible: This setting displays the items on the page and tries to exclude whitespace in the margins. This is similar to the Fit Page setting except it zooms in a little closer on the active area of the page.

Percentage settings (25%, 50%, 75%, 100%): Use these to specify an exact zoom level for a PDF.

Setting the Layout controls

You can also control how the pages appear within the document window. Choose one of the following from the Layout menu:

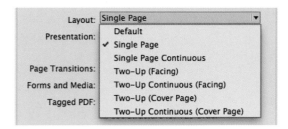

The Layout controls let you set how pages will display in a PDF when it is first opened.

Default: As with the View setting, this option sets the layout to whatever setting has been chosen on the viewer's machine.

Single Page: This option displays only one page in the document window. When you scroll up or down, the next page jumps into position.

Single Page Continuous: Choosing this option displays a single page in the document window, with the previous and next pages slightly visible. As you scroll, the previous pages disappear and new ones roll into view.

Two-Up (Facing): Use this option to set the initial display to a two-page spread in the document window. When you scroll up or down, the next spread jumps into position.

Two-Up Continuous (Facing): This option displays a continuous band of the two-page spreads in the document window. As you scroll, the previous spreads disappear and new ones appear in the display.

Two-Up (Cover Page): This option is the same as Two-Up (Facing), but sets the first page to display as a single page. This is useful for any facing-page document with a cover page in the InDesign file.

Two-Up Continuous (Cover Page): This option is the same as Two-Up Continuous (Facing), but the first page is displayed as a single page.

Presentation controls

You can set the PDF to open as a presentation.

Open in Full Screen Mode: This opens the PDF with a black background and no document window or screen controls. This allows you to use InDesign documents as presentations instead of Microsoft PowerPoint. (We're stunned when we see Adobe presentations in PowerPoint.) Press the ESC (escape) key to switch out of Full Screen mode.

Flip Pages Every x Seconds: Controls if the document will automatically change pages every certain number of seconds. This is good for kiosk presentations.

Page transitions: Use this menu to choose a specific transition, turn off transitions, or leave the ones set originally in the document. Page transitions are covered on page 294, later in this chapter.

TIP Even though you've set the Presentation controls when you export the PDF, they can be overridden in Acrobat Pro or Adobe Reader.

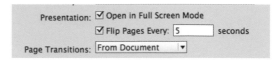

The Presentation settings for opening the PDF in Full Screen mode and for moving from page to page.

The Full Screen mode warning

It used to be that you could set a PDF to open in Full Screen mode and your viewers would be treated to a dark screen with your presentation ready to run. But then the security police made Adobe add a warning when a document tries to open in Full Screen mode. It warns that "This document is trying to put Acrobat in full screen mode, which takes over your screen..." The alert goes on, but it is doubtful your readers will ever get to the end. Scared out of their wits, they will click the No button to close the dialog and never open your PDF again.

This warning limits your use of Full Screen mode to only those people who understand the warning. It's a shame, because it used to be fun to create PDF files that automatically opened as a presentation. We don't do it anymore.

Including forms and media

You can also choose the Forms and Media controls Include All or Appearance Only.

Include All: This exports the document with all the interactive objects active.

Appearance Only: This omits exporting interactive objects but does include the object's image on the page. You may find this setting useful if you want specific images and text on the page, but want a PDF developer to create advanced interactive elements that aren't in InDesign.

Image Handling

Most of the time, your InDesign files will contain images. You need to set the controls for how they are converted in the exported document. These settings are found in the Image Handling area of the Export to Interactive PDF dialog.

The Image Handling area lets you control how images are converted in the exported PDF.

Compression

PDF files embed images within the file. This adds to the size of the file. **Compression** allows you to reduce the size of the PDF by ever-so-slightly changing the pixels within the images. There are three options in the Compression menu. The higher the compression, the smaller the final file size, but this has to be balanced with image quality.

- **JPEG (Lossy)** creates the smallest file size but can cause visible changes in images. If you choose JPEG (Lossy), you need to select an option from the JPEG Quality menu.
- **JPEG 2000 (Lossless)** compresses the images in the file without any visible changes. Older iPads may not support this format.
- **Automatic** leaves it up to InDesign to choose the best output format for images.

JPEG quality

If you have chosen the JPEG (Lossy) option, you can choose an option from the JPEG Quality menu. Your choices range from **Minimum** (smallest file size) to **Maximum** (largest file size). Choose Maximum if you want your images to look their best. Choose Minimum if you don't mind some distortion in the image and want to reduce the file size.

Resolution

There are four options in the Resolution menu — 72, 96, 144, and 300 pixels per inch (ppi) — but you can enter any number in the field. You only need to set a number higher than 96 ppi if you expect people to zoom in on your images. For instance, you might have a map that people will want to magnify. Setting a resolution of 144 ppi or 300 ppi ensures that there will still be details in the image at higher magnifications.

Setting Accessibility Controls for PDF Files

You can't assume that the information on your pages is always consumed by sighted users. You should consider the needs of sight-impaired users, who may be listening to the content of the PDF on a screen reader device, for example. These kind of capabilities are called "accessibility" features, and fortunately, the PDF format has extensive support for adding them.

You need to set the order in which the text and the descriptions of the images will be read. You also need to set the order in which the user will tab through forms and buttons on the page.

TIP You can listen to a PDF by opening it in Acrobat Pro or Adobe Reader and choosing View > Read Out Loud > Activate Read Out Loud. You can then select the commands to Read, Stop, and Pause the document. We use this to check that we've set the correct reading order of our documents.

Section 508 accessibility

Setting the correct reading and tab order with descriptions is one of the accessibility settings for electronic documents that are required by government agencies under Section 508 of the Workforce Rehabilitation Act. Many countries outside the US have similar accessibility requirements for electronic documents.

If you do work for a department of the US government—or any part of your company works with the US government—you need to make your electronic documents accessible. In addition, companies may require that their documentation for human resources and other departments be accessible under the Americans With Disabilities Act. Aside from the laws, it's only polite to create the right tab order for sight-impaired users of your PDF documents.

Applying descriptions Web page designers are familiar with the <alt> tag, which applies a description to visuals on the page. These alt tags are the text that is read aloud by screen readers. This is much more useful than listening to the drone of "image 1 JPEG, image 2 JPEG" and so on down the page. In a PDF, these are the **PDF descriptions,** or **alt text,** of the objects.

The descriptions for buttons and forms are placed in the PDF Options Description field in the Buttons and Forms panel. (*See Chapter 2, "Interactive Tools," for how to set these descriptions.*) You don't set descriptions for text frames. The text in the frame is the text that is read by the screen reader—from top to bottom.

But what about images? They have neither text nor description fields. What do you do for those objects?

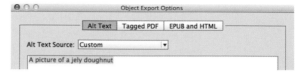

The Object Export Options dialog set to the Alt Text panel. This is where you can enter the text for descriptions of placed graphics.

Choose Object > Object Export Options to open the Object Export Options dialog. (This dialog is also used to control objects for ePub export.) Click the **Alt Text** tab of the dialog. Choose **Custom** from the **Alt Text**

Source menu and then type the description in the field. You can type as much as you want to describe the image.

Setting the reading order

Without adjustments, the reading order for a page comes from the settings in Acrobat Pro or Adobe Reader. This can cause strange text flow. So what should you do if you want your items to be read in a specific order? That's where the Articles panel comes in.

An example of the default reading order for a page.

Using the Articles panel

Use the Articles panel to drag items into the order in which you want them to be read by screen readers. Open the Articles panel (Window > Articles). The panel contains instructions for how to add items. Select the objects on the page and drag them into the panel. The New Article dialog appears. Name the article and make sure Include When Exporting is selected.

The New Article dialog appears when you add items to the Articles panel.

If you add several items to the Articles panel at once, they appear in the order in which you created them on the page. Text frames are labeled with the first few words of their contents. Graphics are labeled with their image names. Buttons and forms are named with their names in the Buttons and Forms panel (this shows you the importance of creating clear names for buttons and forms — you won't know which object is which if you've kept the generic names).

289

The order in which objects appear in the panel is almost certainly not the order in which you want listeners to hear them. To put them in the desired order, simply drag each item to the correct position.

You may not want all items to be added to the Articles panel. For instance, if you have a label that explains that the user should click a button, the button itself may have a description that contains the same information. You don't want the screen reader to speak the same information twice, so don't drag that object into the panel.

TIP You can also use the XML structure pane of the document to set the reading order of PDF files. But the Articles panel was added to InDesign specifically for those who do not want to work with XML code.

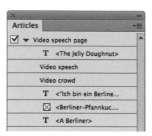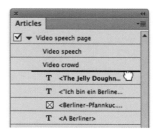

The Articles panel shows the order in which items will be read in the PDF. Drag the items to new positions to change their reading order.

Setting the tab order

Reading aloud is just one part of accessibility. You also need to set the **tab order** for buttons and forms in your document. The tab order is the order in which the buttons and forms are chosen when the user taps the Tab or Shift-Tab keys. This is important not just for sight-impaired users but also for those "power users" who want to jump quickly from object to object. This is the order that puts the focus on interactive elements such as buttons and forms using the Tab key or Shift-Tab. The tab order comes from the order in which the objects are listed in the Articles panel.

Setting the tagged PDF export options

Once you have placed the items in the Articles panel, make sure that **Use For Reading Order in Tagged PDF** is selected in the Articles panel menu.

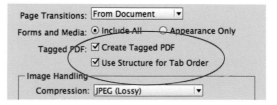

Use the Tagged PDF options in the Export to Interactive PDF dialog to set the correct reading and tab order.

This applies the order of the objects to the tab order in the PDF. When you export the document as an interactive PDF, make sure that the Create Tagged PDF check box and the Use Structure for Tab Order check box are selected.

Security

If you're going to send your precious PDF out into the world, you'll often need to control how people use the document. Can they print it? Can they edit it? Can they extract pages from it? This is when you need to set the security options. Click the **Security** button at the bottom of the Export to Interactive PDF dialog. This opens the Security dialog.

There are two parts to the Security settings: **Document Open Password** and **Permissions**. Each one is a totally separate security option.

Document open password

This is like locking the front door to your house. You are specifying that your PDF can be opened only by people who have permission to open the file. The **Document Open Password** area is the lock that keeps just anyone from opening the document. Only those with the password can open the file.

Require a password to open the document: opens the **Document Open Password** field. Type the password you want to set to open the document. You will need to type the password again to confirm you've typed it correctly.

If you're going to send the PDF to someone in an email, send the password in a separate email. It's far less likely that both emails would be hijacked by people who you don't want to open the file.

The Document Open Password area sets the security to prevent the document from being opened without a password.

TIP Make sure you write down the password or work on a copy of the file. We can't help you open the document if you forget the password.

Don't use these passwords

Information that was hacked from Yahoo! reveals the most commonly used passwords. The top three are *123456*, *password*, and *welcome*. These are pretty obvious and can be easily hacked. You should choose a password that is random, with upper- and lowercase letters as well as symbols such as #, >, &, or !. And the longer the better. An example is something such as *wgH$L8+dxew*. It's meaningless and long, and it contains a combination of letters, numbers, and symbols.

We also advise not distributing a password-protected PDF to the general public if you would lose your home, business, family, or reputation if someone were to hack into it. No security is 100 percent foolproof, and there are those who take it as a personal challenge to break into a password-protected file.

Permissions   Once people have entered your home, this area lets you nail down furniture and objects to prevent people from moving anything around or stealing things. The **Permissions** category controls what people are allowed to do once they gain access to the document.

The Permissions category controls what actions someone can take once the document has been opened.

Permissions settings are separate from the Document Open Password area. What confuses some people is that you can set the Permissions password without having a Document Open password. This is the equivalent of leaving the front door open but locking certain rooms in the house.

TIP The Permissions password can't be the same as the password that opens the document.

Once you have chosen to have a Permissions password, you have options as to what the person can do within the document.

Printing Allowed: This menu controls if or how the document can be printed. There are three choices.

Choose **None** when you don't want anyone to print the document. This option makes Print command unavailable.

Choose **Low Resolution (150 dpi)** to limit printing of the document to only low-resolution printers. This keeps people from printing your document as part of professional output. This setting is used by companies that don't want readers to take their PDF and print it for their own brochures, maps, etc.

To allow any type of printing to any device, choose **High Resolution**. Choose this when you don't care about someone printing the document, but want to set other permissions options.

Changes Allowed: This section controls what edits a user is allowed to apply to the document. There are five options for controlling what changes can be made.

Choosing **None** locks the document down, with no ability to change any items. This is the most secure setting.

Inserting, deleting, and rotating pages allows someone to add new pages to the document, delete pages, or rotate pages. It basically allows page-level changes only.

Filling in form fields and signing permits the reader to enter information in form fields and to use a digital signature to sign the document, but other changes are not allowed. This is used for contracts where you would not want someone to make changes in the prices paid or other elements of a legal document.

You can allow the reader to fill in form fields and apply a digital signature, as with the previous option, but **Commenting, filling in form fields, and signing** also allows the person to use the comment tools. This is helpful if you want someone to make notes about what's in a legal document, for example. Other changes are not allowed.

To allow any changes within the document, except deleting pages or sending pages to new documents, choose the option **Any except extracting pages**.

When you take away some features, you may want to re-enable others. If you set restrictions under Changes Allowed, the last three Permissions options let you set the changes you *do* want to allow the user to make. For example, you may want to restrict entire pages from being extracted, but you may want the user to be able to copy text from your PDF.

Enable copying of text, images, and other content: This option allows someone to highlight text or select an image and save it to another document. It also allows someone to use the Save As menu items to extract text, images, or both. Sandee turns this setting off when she sends review copies of her books to technical editors. She wants them to be able to read the book, but doesn't want them to copy it for use in their own documents.

Enable text access of screen reader devices for the visually impaired: This option is automatically selected if the enable copying option is turned on. However, when enable copying is turned off, you have the choice to turn this option on or off. Leave it on to keep your document in compliance with Section 508 (covered on page 288).

Enable plaintext metadata: This encrypts the document but allows search engines to see the contents of the file.

Page Transitions

You have the choice to add transitions or effects that control how one page changes to another. You can set these transitions as you're working in the InDesign document or in the Export to Interactive PDF dialog.

Using the Page Transitions panel

Use the Page Transitions panel (Window > Interactive > Page Transitions) to apply transitions to pages. Select the page or pages in the Pages panel and then choose the effect from the Transition menu. As you choose each transition, the effect is displayed in the preview area.

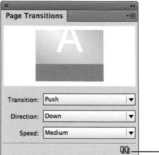

Apply to all spreads

The Page Transitions panel lets you preview and apply effects to page changes.

Some of the transitions give you additional settings for the direction of the effect: down, left, left down, left up, right, right down, right up, and up.

TIP When you add transitions to pages, an icon appears next to the page in the Pages panel.

You can also apply transitions to pages by choosing Page Attributes > Page Transitions > Choose from the Pages panel menu. This opens the Page Transitions dialog, where you can preview and apply all the transitions together. You can't, however, change the direction and speed controls of the transitions.

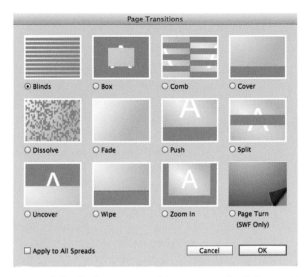

The Page Transitions dialog displays previews of the animations for all the transitions.

TIP The Page Turn transition only works in SWF files. It doesn't work in PDF documents.

Using the Export to Interactive PDF dialog

You can also use the Page Transitions menu in the Export to Interactive PDF dialog. Choose **From Document** to maintain the settings applied in the file. Choose **None** to delete any settings. Choose one of the transitions to override the settings applied in the file.

Previewing transitions on the page

You don't have to wait until your file is exported as a PDF to preview the transitions applied to pages. Open the SWF Preview panel and click the Set Preview Document Mode option. You can then click the forward and backward controls. The transitions are displayed in the preview panel as the pages change. (*For more information on using the SWF Preview panel, see Chapter 3, "Animations."*)

Use the SWF Preview panel to see the transitions applied to pages without having to export the PDF.

Adding Animations to a PDF

As mentioned previously, animations are supported only in exported SWF files or fixed layout ePubs. They don't work if the InDesign file is exported as a PDF. However, we do have a workaround that can help you display animations in PDF files. The trick is to export an animation as a SWF file, then reimport it as a movie for PDF export.

Despite the difficulties in getting SWF videos to play inside PDF files (*see the sidebar "SWF video animations in PDF files"*), many people still want animations in their PDFs. For example, picture an annual report whose front page has a brief animation that fades into the image of the company headquarters.

Single pages   You may want just a simple animation on a single page. In that case, follow these steps:

1. Start on the page that contains the animation. It's a good idea to put it on its own layer.

2. Choose File > Export, and in the Export SWF dialog, enter just that page in the Range field, or select the object(s) and choose Selection in the dialog.

TIP If you choose an animation that moves off or on the page, you must export the entire page; otherwise, you can just export the selection.

---

3. Once the SWF has been exported, go back to the original page and hide the animation elements on that layer.

4. On a new layer, place the SWF as you would any image. Use the Media panel to set the animation to Play on Page Load. You can now export the PDF with the animation on the page.

Multiple pages   You might want to include animations and the SWF-only Page Turn transition in your PDF. Export the entire PDF as a SWF with the transition applied. Then, delete all the information on the InDesign pages, leaving only a blank first page. Place the exported SWF on the page. You now have a SWF of multiple pages that contains the animations and the Page Turn.

SWF video animations in PDF files

In recent years, Adobe has "decoupled" the Flash Player from Acrobat and Adobe Reader. This means is that if a PDF has SWF content, the user may not be able to view this or any of the other Flash-only features in a PDF. An alert will display to download the latest version of the Flash Player. Most users don't want to download Flash just to play the little bit of fun in your document.

However, if you, yourself, are going to present the PDF to others, there is no reason why you can't use a SWF in your PDF file. You will be able to download the Flash Player and make sure the document plays correctly.